Ciarán Murphy is a writer and journalist from Waterford city. He graduated from Dublin City University (DCU) in 2004 with an MA in Journalism (Honours). He has written countless stories for newspapers such as *The Irish Times*, *Irish Examiner* and *Irish Independent*, along with making contributions to *Hot Press* magazine and Ireland's State broadcaster, *RTE*. His performance as a ruined developer in his own monologue, *The Lane*, won him the Adjudicator's Award at the 123 Festival of Drama in Dungarvan, Co. Waterford, in 2009. Meanwhile, his play, *All Fall Down*, appeared at the Imagine Arts Festival in the city in 2011. *What Happens on Tour...*, his first book, was launched at the Immrama Festival of Travel Writing in Lismore in June 2012.

WHAT HAPPENS ON

TOUR...

Ciarán Murphy

Sovereign Source

Dedicated to the eternal memory of little Aisling Symes

Introduction

While growing up in the early 1980s, the portrayal of Down Under on television shows such as *Skippy* [the Bush Kangaroo] and *The Sullivans*, led me to believe that it was an other-worldly place. These programmes were nothing if not educational. For example, I learned that Australians drove on the same side of the road as *us* in the Republic of Ireland, and in the UK. I discovered that the country's forces fought in World War Two. And, that marsupials were even smarter than "Lassie Dogs". Who knew? Later, of course, sickly sweet soaps such as *Neighbours* and *Home and Away* showed us that Australians didn't wear heavy duty Khaki clobber all of the time. Sorry, Mick Dundee but *NO*! And I also copped that "Petrol-Heads" and "Daaaags" were replacing retired "Strewth"-spouting former "footie" players. However, I believe Alf Steward still terrifies the Youth of Summer Bay to this very day!

I learned very little about New Zealand from television, though. Outside of those Primary School projects – you know the ones where each pupil has to "do a project" on a particular country, I had heard absolutely nothing about it. Personally, I always seemed to get the uber-exotic countries of this world during such activities. Countries such as Switzerland. Or Belgium. And Secondary School wasn't much better in this repsect. The curriculum in Geography Class tended to focus on things that really captured our imaginations. Like the formation of limestone and sedimentary rock. The countries we learned about at this stage were locations we'd probably eventually need to emigrate to, in order to improve our economic lot in life. Countries such as Zambia and Ethiopia. However, when I started becoming interested in (and playing) rugby during my teens, New Zealand made its mark through the fearsome All-Blacks. Later, the *Lord of The Rings* movies sold this unspoilt gem of a country to all of us.

Australia and New Zealand have always been popular destinations for many nationalities –particularly for the Irish and British. From Britain's brutal 19th Century penal system, resulting in thousands of convicts being shipped to Australia for a horrific life, to those emigrating for the New World in pursuit of a better life; they left here in droves. Of course in the latter part of the last Century and for the previous decade, the year out or gap year Down Under became increasingly popular. It was something I had always intended on doing myself.

Though it didn't pan out the way I expected.

I returned from a stint working abroad in late 1998, and planned on heading below for a year to suss it out. However, I subsequently ended up going to America for most of 2000. Even while living back in Ireland, it didn't happen. My friend Alan would be "doing Australia and New Zealand" [or so he wished perhaps] for three months some years ago, and while I had planned to go with him, I could barely walk due to slipped disks.

After my medical problems were solved and I finally got around to actually planning my campaign of the Antipodes – when my curiosity had reached its absolute limit – I discovered that there were few books out there to let me know what was in store for me. I wanted to find out about the infamous tours of these countries. Sure, there were *Travel* guide books on Australia and to a lesser extent, New Zealand. The *Lonely Planet* guides are worth their considerable weight in gold, and I was informed that Bill Bryson's *Down Under* was a highly entertaining read. But, these aside, what was out there was hard to sit down and read.

So, why not tie in my journey with some writing on the topic?

I planned on spending one month in Australia and another in New Zealand, though I extended the latter stay by a further three weeks. I decided that I would keep a diary of my travels. I left Ireland on September 19th 2009, and I returned eleven weeks later with a much greater knowledge of both countries, along with being a fair few dollars lighter and a few pounds heavier.

I travelled independently, and I was free to go where I wanted and write what I wished. Between spending time in various cities, I did a fifteen-day tour up the east coast of Australia. In New Zealand, I did a tour that lasted over three weeks, and partook in as many extreme adventures as I could manage. Or afford. Of course, I drank way too much! An idle boast but I drank every single night – bar three, I think – for the entire eleven weeks.

For research purposes. My next book is going to be called, *The Liver That Keeps on Living*.

What I did discover, on my travels, was an abundance of colour. There was plenty of scope to place myself in the centre of the story. To observe, participate and then report, if you will. The resulting travel log, *What Happens on Tour...*, is something of a hybrid. It looks at some extreme adventure activities, along with general facts and little digestible nuggets of historical and geographical information for the backpacker, holiday maker or armchair traveller. And it's all done in a light-hearted fashion. There is a saying among the touring group Down Under. *What happens on tour, stays on tour.*

That *was* perhaps true...until now.

And by the way, I still think that Down Under is a magical and other-worldly place.

-   Ciaran Murphy, May 2012.

Contents

1. "Paddy, Paddy!"

DAY ONE

Perhaps this wasn't such a good idea after all. It's not the fact that I had such little sleep following some hours spent in the local last night, because the feel-good factor at the start of an extended trip abroad would certainly override such trivia. Actually, wait. No, I feel okay. I think I do anyway so let's just go. The engine starts and I immediately feel queasy, however; the memory of a thousand hellish coach trips weighing down on me like the unrealistic expectations of the nation at a World Cup finals. Seriously, it has the constancy of gravity.

Ah feck it. Avanti!

I'll explain. From a Waterford perspective, the journey to Dublin has often been cited as the worst part of any trip abroad requiring the use of the coach to the airport. This, it has to be said, can largely be blamed on the roads themselves as opposed to the actual coach services. Of course, now as you're reading this, the new M9 motorway from Waterford-to-Dublin has opened. This has shaved over ninety of your earth minutes off the journey, from my home city to the Capital, and vice versa naturally.

Anyway, it's not as if there was a funnel shoved down my throat last night or anything. I could have abstained – even if it would have been faintly unpatriotic to do so. Yes, I'm a tad hungover, as last night I was at the Clubhouse – Jordan's Bar on the Quay in Ireland's oldest city. My hometown is a place steeped in history. Take Jordan's (*The American Bar*) for example. In a former life, tickets were sold here for the White Star Line company's ships (Yes, that's the Titanic crowd) heading to America via Southampton in the UK and Queenstown (now Cobh – *pron.* "Cove" – in Co. Cork). The bus will pass here, along with some other landmarks that relate to Waterford's human exports to the new world.

1

These, in particular, relate to the Antipodes.

One of Waterford's most renowned sons to travel to Australia was Thomas Francis Meagher. I'm thinking of him as the coach passes a resting restaurant, formerly known as the *Wolfe Tone Confederate Club*, on The Mall. This old building, yards away from the shiny new House of Waterford Crystal building in the Viking Triangle area of the city, is the location from where Meagher first flew Ireland's tricolour flag on March 7th 1848. Meagher was a leader of the Young Irelanders who narrowly escaped a death sentence for sedition – aged just 26 – and was instead shipped off to Van Diemen's Land. He escaped from the rock in 1852 and made his way to the US. Here, Meagher studied and practised law, worked as a journalist and editor of the *Irish News*, joined the US army at the start of the American Civil War. Abraham Lincoln elevated him to the rank of Brigadier General. Meagher led the Irish Brigade: he was Commander of the New York 69th Infantry Regiment, leading his troops into charges on the east coast such as Fredericksburg and Antietam. He became known as Meagher of The Sword.

Seconds have passed when we pass the lights at the intersection with Lombard St. There's a building on Lombard St. that is currently operating as a betting agent and has a Waterford Civic Trust plaque attached bearing William Hobson's name. Hobson was born here in 1793, which is weird because I was born in 1973. *Oi! I heard that!* Anyway, Hobnob, sorry, Hobson, became an officer in the Royal Navy and was the first appointed Governor of New Zealand, once Queen Victoria had signed a royal charter in 1840, making that country a colon. A *colony*, I meant to write the word, *colony*.

A statue of Meagher on horseback – on an island in the road here – outside the Tower Hotel has him brandishing his sword as he trundles fearlessly into the history books. The American tourists generally seem curious about this statue. Literally moments have passed when we're bouncing past Jordan's. Directly opposite the pub stands the William Vincent Wallace Plaza, named after the composer of the same name who was another one of Waterford's finest to head down under. It's fairly

2

humbling to be thinking that people who hailed from *your* own birthplace put such a considerable mark on the new world. Though, if I'm honest, I oppose Britain's colonisation of various parts of the planet. The word *colonisation* refers to *colony* by-the-way, and not *colon*. Are we clear on this now? I'm not using the word to imply that the British made an arse out of the various territories conquered and ruled on behalf of the monarchy.

I give a silent nod to both pub and monument as we pass by, while my stomach continues to remind me of last night. It's certainly unwise to have more pints than hours of sleep the night before basically, a day-and-a-half of straight travelling, which is not synomonous with journeying as the crow flies or going on a type of heterosexual package holiday. Okay? Right? Are we on the same page?

Good. I'll continue so: as often happens on these occasions, the erstwhile liquid mass was (this morning) topped up with a greasy serving of pig products in the form of a fry-up. I'm worried because we've only started the journey and the result of mixing dubious travel and alcohol can be catastrophic. Not always, but sometimes. This morning, it is war. The bottled water is acting as mediator, negotiating between both sides (*i.e.* the pig products versus the Heineken) that are busy in theatre: attempting to destroy each other in battle without counting the cost to their environment.

This aside, the frequency of the coaches and the €18 price tag for a one-way ticket to the airport and thus avoiding the hustle and bustle of inner city Dublin, makes it an obvious choice for me and for others who don't fancy driving to the capital and paying the parking fees for, in my case, eight weeks abroad. I'm risking the stomach churner today, however, because the bus goes straight to the airport. The scenery acts as a good distraction and I'm not too offended by the stretches of green that are flanking my eyes. This convenience allows me to forget that I'll be travelling mostly by coach (*Shit!*) around Australia and New Zealand over the next few weeks. I'm trying to forget that I won't be reaching my destination, Melbourne in Victoria, for about another 36 hours.

3

Throughout this three-and-a-half hour road journey to the airport, I'm recalling various other trips to Dublin by stagecoach. During one of these I got sick. That's right; I vomited all over the back seats. It all happened one dark, dreary Monday morning some years back when I was a student returning to Dublin – after a heavy weekend in Waterford – for lectures in the dark art of Journalism at Dublin City University (DCU). Of course, it wasn't my fault. Well, okay, maybe it was but I'm not necessarily proud of it. My stomach, lined with the old elixir of truth, objected to its contents under the conditions and decided to spout a Technicolour fountain from its poisoned enclave, destroying the coach's back seat, floor and its passengers' hopes of an odour-free journey. A sobering clean-up of the seats and floor with disinfectants, air spray and paper towels procured in the company's Carlow depot, served me well as a lesson in travelling with too much cargo onboard.

Or so you would think.

By the way, anyone who's offended by tales of drunkenness, tomfoolery and eejit-related eejitery, should probably stop reading now. In fact, I would insist on it if I could. Your political correctness and do-goodery are not welcome and are of no use here. This is a do-goodery free zone. In the world of this book, the only people allowed to sit on their high horses are me, Meagher of the Sword and Andy the Cowboy. Who in tarnation is Andy the Cowboy? Oh, you'll see. Ha! You won't be laughing then. Actually, I hope that you will be, eh, laughing by then. Most of you non-Irish who have never seen an episode of the 1990s comedy series, *Father Ted,* are still wondering what the word *Eejit* means, aren't you? It's Irish slang for *Idiot.* As in, "Would ya ever feck off, ya big feckin' eejit, ya?" Check the Oxford Dictionary if you wish. It's there.

"What's the weather like over there? – It's feckin' rainin' here again – No – As long as there's a bit of sunshine; this place is spittin' rain." The middle-aged woman, a peroxide blond with bright pink shoes and I guess, a heavyweight south Co. Kilkenny accent, is going to "de mid" it turns out. That's *The Mediterranean* to the rest of you. I've just learned that she's a nurse, though I didn't really want to.

4

"I don't mind as long as the sun shines, there's a bottle of wine in the fridge and Julio's out the feckin' door," she bellows into her mobile phone. Various hooded and tattooed youth got on in Carlow. Their presence has darkened the back of the coach so I can't see them but at the front, freshly perm-ed women ignore the conversational attempts offered by their silver-haired and sensibly shoe-ed husbands. I pick up my *Lonely Planet Australia* guide. I have two: one for New Zealand also. It opens at page 485. Melbourne in three days. That'll do for now. First, I must get to the airport, however.

I arrive at Dublin Airport and I'm trying to find my bearings in Arrivals. There are hundreds of people queuing for their clients, loved ones and so on and I think that I have my days wrong when I spy a large group of secondary school kids in uniform. Well, it *is* Saturday. I look up at the board; I'm supposed to go to Area 14. *Jawol*, I tell myself as I make my way to ze bunker at the bottom of Dublin Airport. The Aer Lingus check-in girl tries to move me forward to a flight at 15.50, while I'm due to fly for Heathrow at 18.00 hours or 6pm. But I'm hungry and I only have Euros and Australian dollars.

"Can't you use your Laser Card?" she asks me with what I suspect to be fake concern.

To buy a burger at the London airport?

"Actually, I'm going to take the six o'clock flight," I tell her.

Well, it suited her – her company – and not me. I can't be arsed getting Sterling pounds if it can be avoided.

The young woman turns to her neighbouring clerk.

"I've never heard screaming like that before; I wonder who it is," she tells her, obviously referring to the unified and excited screaming rolling down from arrivals above. I take the escalator two steps at a time, my journalistic training (or rather good old-fashioned nosiness) having taken charge. When I get up there the place is thronged with school kids; mainly teenage girls screaming at other school-going kids. Maybe those little shits have my bearings! They are holding up placards with slogans

5

such as "We're No 1" and "Koni won" written on them. So I ask an accompanying Teacher and she tells me that a group of the kids, The Koni Kats from St. David's Secondary School in Greystones, Co. Wicklow, won "the Formula 1 model making championship". Apparently, it's an international schools technology competition final. Oh!

That's brilliant and deadly and awesome, but all I could mumble to the poor woman is, "Oh". Is this the only praise I can lavish on these poor little creatures; these future solicitors, traffic wardens and politicians? *Oh.* I seem to be surprised that there isn't a gay boybander in sight, what with all the hormone-fuelled mania I've just witnessed.

I need a drink.

I came upstairs and ordered my double cheeseburger meal from McDonald's and now I'm heading into Skyview Bar for a pint. I get a lovely text from my pal, Ruth. She is wishing me well on my travels. I'm touched. And despite myself, by the time the barmaid hands me my Guinness, I'm wiping a couple of tears away from my eyes and, jokes about the price of the pint aside, I'm left wondering *Why?* The barmaid obviously notices but she doesn't bat an eyelid: you can tell that they see this type of thing all the time.

I've gone through departures at Heathrow and I'm drinking pints of watery Bass Ale in a bar and despite my earlier reservations, I'm using my Laser. The beers, at least the brands that I drink back home, always taste watered down here in England. I'm just ordering my fourth pint of water when I realise that my gate is due to close. I cancel the drink and run down to my gate, with the help of one of those human conveyor belt things (escalators on the flat) that always make me feel like the Bionic Man. I'm overtaking those mere mortals – less hurried or less lazy than I – who are walking on the floor at a pace rate of three steps to my one. However, this belt is particularly springy and an air hostess next to me tells me, in over-the-top seductive tones, that it feels like a water bed.

"I wouldn't know; I've never used one of them."

"Oh, you haven't lived," she says in a demure kind of way.

When I arrive, the gate hasn't even opened yet and there are scores of people waiting in a queue that only lengthens in the next forty minutes. I text my brother, Tom, and in reply he warns me to get a couple of bottles of water for when I wake up – surely bleary eyed and disorientated over India or somewhere.

DAY TWO

It's past midnight in London, and I'm stuck in a window seat about sixty rows back with two Australian gents who couldn't be more different. One of these is Indie Kid. Not the real indie kid of the *Stone Roses, Ride* or *Inspiral Carpets* variety but the modern boy band version. He is in his 20s and doesn't have much to say for himself. The other is a man in his 60s, who does. This man's name is John Donnely and he is from Queensland. He has been on holiday in the UK with a neighbour from home, who turns out to be an Englishman. Well, he knew that he was English all along, though I've just discovered it. So we read and we watch the on-board entertainments and we eat and we doze. And at one stage, presumably in the middle of some bizarre dream that I don't remember at all, I wake up and catch poor Indie Kid by the arm.

"PADDY, PADDY."

I'm surprised when I discover that I'm shouting it, and as mortified as a nun caught smoking a joint in a boozer during Lent. But thankfully he sees the funny side of it and starts laughing, though I'm sure that any further sleeping on his part will be undertaken with one eye open. I feel like that character (played by the wonderful actor Niall Buggy) from *that* classic *Father Ted* episode. Like him, I seem to "remember having a *sip* of sherry (red wine in my case)..." I draw the line, however, at claiming to actually *be* Henry Sellers, who "made the BBC". I mean, would I like to claim credit for *Eastenders* or *Cash in the* (Bloody) *Attic*? Really? In the erstwhile episode, poor Henry (twice) jumps out of the window of the parochial house on Craggy Island. However, that option is not really open to me right now. Well, let's just say that I wouldn't get a second go at it.

7

It turns out to be a relatively sleepless journey to Singapore, apart from about thirty minutes or so of forty winks. In terms of the aerial point-of-view, the Thailand coastline looks beautiful, while the Indian landscape doesn't.

I'm in the Singapore Changi International Airport and wandering towards the banks of terminals so I can avail of the free Internet access here. I amble in the direction of the food stalls and finally stop at this sushi cafe and order, well, questionable sushi rolls and a bottle of Tiger Beer. Neither of these items do I *actually* want nor finish. They're quick enough to accept my Aussie dollars at the sushi place and I'm handed Singapore dollars in change but hey, that's business, and I'm sure to spend all of it there.

So when I spot Burger King, I'm in like Flynn; chomping on my second burger, fries and cola in 24 hours. I promise myself that I'll knock this type of behaviour on the noggin. I'm in between mouthfuls when I hear the standard Aussie greeting that we all know and love from God-awful soap operas such as *Home and Away* and *Neighbours,* along with *The Young Doctors* and *A Country Practice* that went before them.

"G'DAY", he roars and I turn around immediately. It's my neighbour from Flight QF010. John tells me about his family history; how the Donnelys came from Tasmania in the 19th Century. Prior to this, the clan lived in the UK after moving there from Ireland, it transpires.

"Actually, I don't think they were convicts," he tells me, in case I was wondering. It's hard to figure out the etiquette. One wouldn't like to cause offence by calling somebody's ancestors convicts. But then again, so-called convicts were given the title and shipped to the other side of the world for, you know, stealing a loaf of bread in those times. The absurdity of it all constantly overwhelms me.

There's a bit of silence before he finally proceeds to tell me how he's a Donnely-with-one-L and how he's not to be confused with the Tyson Donnellys. I wouldn't dream of it: he's a big man and looks strong enough, even though he's "neee'ly

8

sivinty". So I don't argue. For all I know he might be trying to disown his son, Mike Tyson.

I decide to make my move and leave Donnely-with-one-L before I fall asleep. Actually, I start moving when he tells me how, last year, on a return flight from Thailand, anybody who walked past him on the way to the toilet or to stretch their legs was accosted thus: "I said, 'No one's allaaa'd to pass without tawkin' to moy for two minutes'."

"It was groyt for wimen goen' to the toilets to soy a group uf poyple tawkin' – less intimidaydin' for 'um."

Oh, that's alright then.

Dear Lord above. He sort of looks like the brilliant Aussie Actor, John Jarratt, who is of Irish lineage actually and gave us a chilling portrayal of the disturbed bushman that tortured and killed some backpackers in the excellent Aussie movie, *Wolf Creek*. Wasn't it based on real events? I seem to remember that the deranged bushman was never found by the Police.

I make my excuses and leave.

In one of the airport's smoking areas, a rooftop effort with a view and a bar, groups of weary travellers soothe their nicotine demons with cigarettes. The gluttons are chain smoking. It strikes me as a weird gathering of people and it indeed is: the common denominator here being the smoking, the jet lag, the beer (for some), and the watch-watching.

It's stupid o'clock.

I'm not drinking and I only smoke one cigarette from the carton of Camel Lights that I (stupidly) bought for over £50 Sterling at Heathrow. These would have cost me about half this price here in Singapore. My low nicotine intake here could be explained away by the fact that I've been chewing the odd tab of Nicorette Gum during my 17-hour hiatus from the filthy habit. However, it's more likely because I see it as pointless – the reason being that the air is so humid here as to render it near impossible to feel the smoke as it is drawn down to the lungs. It's like sitting in a steam room at my gym in the Tower [hotel] but without the beneficial effects.

Oops, the gate to Melbourne is opening. I rush to catch my connecting flight, half terrified that I'll meet John en route to be told some yarn such about how, for example – on some long haul flight to some destination or other, he had the excellent idea of close-lining an airhostess in order to remind her to bring him some ice for his lemonade.

Anyway, I watch a movie called *Van Diemen* as we take to the skies yet again and I suspect that one of the actors is an old school friend of mine, Keith Dunphy. It's basically about a group of prisoners detained at Her Majesty's Pleasure on the old rock now known as Tasmania – probably for stealing a loaf of bread or some other *minor* misdemeanour. The group of POMs – Prisoners of Her/His Majesty – overcome their prison guard at Macquarie Harbour and proceed to make good their escape but alas their efforts are thwarted when they are spotted and shot at by a couple of soldiers before becoming stranded when 'their' ship sails. The men scarper and are living wild on the rock: they are starving, raving and getting more and more desperate when their meagre rations run out. One by one, they begin bumping each other off in horrible ways. The descent into the madness snowballs when this foxy-locked, gobby Irishman gets it. The sods even bleed him so that the 'meat' won't get poisoned. Of course events such as these actually happened and it has been well-documented. The character that narrates the story (in the Irish language actually) is apparently a bloke by the name of Alexander Pearse who, being the last man standing as it were, is naturally the best cannibal of them all. Pearse told his story to his captors before finally being executed.

Charming stuff, welcome to Australia (small "w"). I have to admit that I'm startled when I think that Dunphy, who won a scholarship to attend the Royal Academy of Drama Arts (RADA) in London some years after leaving school, gets it in the throat with a shovel. Last thing I heard, he was touring with the Royal Shakespeare Company in the UK. And though he has secured small parts in movies such as *Children of Men*, *Inside I'm Dancing* and *The Wind That Shakes the Barley*, I'm pleasantly surprised when I think that I see him here. I always knew that Dunphy was in danger of decapitation, but from (our third year Commerce teacher) Bulldog's blackboard duster and not by a spade in the hands of a so-called mate.

While we're on the subject, the convict shipments to Australia continued over fifty years from 1803 to 1853. Along with their British counterparts, Irish people deemed criminals (including young males and females who were probably starving when they had stolen the loaf of bread, for example) were among over 65,000 shipped to Van Diemen alone. Some of these were also political prisoners – Young Irelanders from the 1798 Rebellion. As mentioned previously, among the shipped prisoners was our man, Thomas Francis Meagher.

Laurence M. Geary and Andrew J. McCarthy, in *Ireland, Australia and New Zealand – History Politics and Culture*, paint a startling and detailed picture of some of the Irish convicts who were sent to Australia. From a paper written by Richard P. Davis entitled *Irish Influence on Van Diemen's Land/Tasmania from Bushrangers to the Celtic Tiger*, I learn that earlier Irish convicts arrived via New South Wales and though the British were reluctant to "populate Van Diemen's Land with Irish people", it didn't prevent Ireland from "producing several of the colony's most celebrated bushrangers".

Some of them were more than brazen. In 1820, Matthew Brady was transported for stealing food in Lancashire.

"Three years later he escaped by boat from Macquarie Harbour (sounds familiar!), Van Diemen's Land's penal settlement for repeat offenders on the west coast...two years of dramatic bushranging ensued." Brady's gang moved north and south and "pitched battles were fought with their pursuers". According to the paper, "Brady coolly offered twenty gallons of rum for the apprehension of Lt. Governor Sir George Arthur." Apparently the rapscallion was a "courteous host" to the defenceless, female victims and to his guests at dinner. "Brady's chivalry made him a popular hero when he finally confronted the Hobart gallows."

There have also been numerous documented accounts of the Irish convicts themselves becoming constables and administrators in the prison system. In fact, under Governor Arthur Phillip's direction, prisoners could earn their ticket of leave – a parole of sorts that eventually allowed them to live where they liked and seek the kinds of work that they wanted. Did the British authorities really believe they were rehabilitating these people through hardship and basically torture on the rock that the convicts came to name Damn Demon's Land? It's all very interesting.

My mind is ruminating over the differences – at least those that I'm aware of – between Australia and New Zealand: the former is generally a dry country with a climate that approaches tropical, while the well-irrigated New Zealand has a climate reaching towards the sub-Antarctic.

(The Australian 2011 Census results have not been published yet but the population of Australia is over 22.5 million, and indigenous Australians make up about 520,000 of the population.)

Indigenous Australia refers, of course, to the Aboriginal culture (traditionally mainland, Tasmanian and some other adjacent islands' Aboriginals) along with Torres Strait Islanders. The Torres Strait Islands are located at the most northerly tip of Queensland near Papua New Guinea.

I know that Australia's history in terms of how it has treated its indigenous Aborigine in the past is shameful, while the Maori culture is largely celebrated. The countries, as we recognise them today, are relatively new and both share a love of the outdoors. The accents of both Australia and New Zealand, at least to my untrained ear, sound the same.

Data released by the *Bereau of Statistics* in 2009 revealed that 44 per cent of Australians were either born overseas or have one parent who was born overseas. Over 6.5 million migrants arrived in Australia since 1945 and 77 per cent of the population currently lives within fifty kilometres of the coast; particularly in cities such as Sydney, Melbourne, Perth, Brisbane and Adelaide. The population of the country increased by more than one million in the five years to 2006 and it is rising yet.

So with this rich and diverse international flavour, it's not surprising that in excess of 200 languages are spoken in Australian homes on a daily basis. The most common of these are Greek, Italian, Arabic, Cantonese and Mandarin.

Australasia has about one million native species of flora and fauna, while over 80 per cent of these are unique to Australia. Fraser Island in Queensland is the largest sand island on the planet and the Great Barrier Reef – there's over 2,000 kilometres of it – is the largest reef in the world. Of the world's 25 deadliest snakes, 21 live in Australia.

(Meanwhile, the Census for 2011 in New Zealand, planned for March 8th, was cancelled following the 6.3-magnitute earthquake in Christchurch in February. The Statistics New Zealand buildings were damaged in the earthquake and it was thought that the data wouldn't be reliable. The population of New Zealand at present is 4.4 million, however.)

Over 565,000 people identified (or were affiliated) with New Zealand's ethnic Maori group, according to the 2006 Census. And 643,977 people were of Maori descent. According to *Statistics New Zealand* (www.stats.govt.nz), from which the above figures were obtained, New Zealand "has one of the largest marine environments in the world" with an exclusive economic zone covering more than four million square kilometres. Total greenhouse emissions increased by 22 per cent in the 17 years up to 2007, while food prices were 12 per cent higher in October 2009 than they were two years previously. In 2008, 21 per cent of the country's adults had Bachelor's degrees, compared to eight per cent in 1990.

New Zealand is becoming increasingly popular with tourists from all over the world, including its Australian neighbours: visitors from Australia exceeded one million "in the May 2009 year".

By the way, it wasn't Dunphy in *Van Dieman*, la movie.

2. Hello New World

DAY THREE

It's after 5am, I'm at Customs in Melbourne Airport and a girl working there is ushering sheeple quickly through the gate. I'm feeling like a fleeced animal and I haven't even reached New Zealand yet.

I'm outside smoking a cigarette and looking at the yellow taxis lining up for their fares when this bloke asks me if I'm going to Southern Cross Station.

I tell him that I am.

Clearly an Australian, he asks me if I want to share a taxi because it's expensive (over $40) and I tell him that I do. The thought that he might be a mugger in search of green-horned backpackers crosses my mind briefly but I recognise him from my flight and the realisation that it would be silly of him to pay up to $2,000 Australian for a flight from Heathrow just to mug some poor unsuspecting traveller on a budget, dawns on me quickly.

So I jump onto the back seat next to him. Of course, the $2,000 price tag could be worth it if, for example, he shoved a big load of drugs into my bag at Heathrow – for them to be collected at Melbourne.

But if this were the case he'd also be unlucky because of the following:

"A'ya on tooo' (tour)?"

"Yeah, a few days here, then onto Sydney," I tell him. "Then –"

But he interrupts me.

"Yo're trav'llin' loight, moyte," he offers, spying my manbag and the duty free bag, which has my new digital camera inside.

"Oh shit; stop the taxi," I yell to the driver. "I forgot my bag."

The Aussie looks at me as if I'm an alien who has just arrived on the UFO10 from Mars as opposed to the QF010 from London via Singapore.

"It's the jet lag," I mumble in explanation, before grabbing my bags and legging it back to arrivals. We're just leaving the airport grounds and he kindly refuses my offer of a contribution towards the fare. I'm not allowed back into customs – instead, I'm directed towards baggage services one terminal up. A sprightly Melbournian type comes up, I tell him of my plight and he says he'll go into customs to sort it. Before he leaves, a woman wanders up and it turns out that the same thing has happened to her. So, we're waiting for about half-an-hour for our bags. She tells me that her name is Gormley and that she's Irish. Northern, obviously, judging from her accent. Her husband, who looks and sounds Japanese, is standing behind us. He's shaking his head and tut-tutting.

"And both of you, Irish," he keeps repeating.

And we have to take it on the chin. The baggage services chap spies my tightly-clutched plastic bag and adds, "I soy (see) ya didn' fo'git the duty froy moyte."

There's NO drink, just the camera. Cross my heart, I wouldn't lie to you.

I grab my backpack and shuffle outside again, where I buy a ticket for, and get the Skybus into, Southern Cross Station. A return ticket from the airport costs me $26). I haven't a clue where I'm going. Exciting huh? I basically just open my *Lonely Planet* at "Melbourne – Accommodation" and stick a pin (my pen) in it.

However, my internal accommodation radar rarely lets me down. And at 6.20am, I'm standing at reception in King St. Backpackers, which is on Little Bourke St., intersecting with King St. A friendly and laid back Aussie charges me $28 – the nightly dorm rate – for the use of the room up to 10am, which is kick-out time. I must present myself in three-and-a-half hours time to ascertain whether I can have a bed again for that night because I've not booked ahead. Exhausted, I clamber into my top bunk in my six-bed dorm and there are two guys in the room who are coughing and turning – presumably it's something to do with my gawky entrance. Anyway, I'm so jetlagged that I can't sleep and I'm awake when both of these unsettled bundles get up within the hour in preparation for something that is presently a distant memory. And that would be the ugly four letter word that begins in "W" and ends in "K".

At least, I assume so.

15

One of these shadows is dressed in what looks to be, in the early morning light, a weird blue boilersuit or jumpsuit. This becomes hidden by a suede jacket and is topped off with a hat – a variety of woodsman's hat or one of the many varieties that Aussies are known to wear. I imagine Michael Caine wearing one in some African Safari adventure caper. *Either this guy works in the tourist industry or he's from Perth,* I note to myself. Or perhaps he's just a German with psychological problems. Whatever, I'm glad to have the dorm to myself as I crash head first into a coma.

It's 1pm, I'm awake and almost as far away from home as I can be while remaining in civilisation. And there's nobody banging the door down. So I shower, dress and I'm down at reception by 2.30pm. And the lady at Reception refuses my offer of a further $28 for the night, because, she tells me, "You got lucky – there was a spare bed going this morning." Sweet. Ha, you see? The radar; it never lets me down.

I stop off at a café nearby for a cappuccino and a cigarette and I learn from the very handy book, *Live and Work in Australia* by Jodie McMullen Seal, that Melbourne is the "style, food and culture capital of Australia and has a hugely cosmopolitan mix of 3.4 million residents" from over 200 nationalities. Surprisingly, to me at any rate, it has the world's largest Greek community (outside of, well, Greece, funnily enough).

I'm already aware of the huge numbers of Irish, British and Europeans in general and the city's Victorian architecture, public parks and gardens, reinforces the British influence. The city incorporates a Central Business District (CBD) and, similar to Sydney; it "also has a massive" east and west divide. The east is often seen as a "more desirable" place to live, according to McMullen Seal, though "the west offers more land and bigger houses for a fraction of the cost for this is traditionally where the working class resided".

I'm on my way to Franklin St. – a hive of activity for backpackers and tourists, I'm told. I come across a courtroom (the Melbourne Magistrates Court) on William St. I have a lot of court reporting experience and I'm curious about the Australian court service. After all, this is the country that became the destination for thousands of POMs at the hands of such a brutal justice system in the 19th Century, remember.

It's basically like the District Court in Ireland and it's a slow enough day. So, like often happens back home, there are a few cops hanging about. The male ones are flirting with the female clerks and officers, while a couple of lawyers go in and out of the cells behind or below *the stage* in order to consult with their clients, torture kittens or whatever it is they *actually* do. And oh yeah, there's no judge.

Meanwhile, I scan the front page of the free sheet, *mX*, which I've picked up from one of those newspaper vending machine things on the street outside. Shannon Deery, in the splash – the main story on the front page headlined *Sounds of Silence* – tells us that "One of Melbourne's most iconic music venues, Manchester Lane, has closed in another blow to Melbourne's dwindling live music scene." What a shame.

After a while, the judge finishes his tea and toast and graces us so he can deal with some adjournments, which are further adjourned. Some bloke called Newton wants to make a bail application: he has been arrested days beforehand but his lawyer is not present. So, the hearing is put back for a few days and the judge cites it as a waste of time for everyone and urges Newton to take it up with his counsel. On his way back to the cells, Newton jokes with the Judge regarding the possibility of getting bail anyway but he gets a look in response that seems to say, *Watch it Newton, or it's not the effects of gravity but the full weight of the law that you will have to worry about.*

Of course this is all familiar terrain to me: it seems that the legal beast is as slothful down under as it is up above. The legal system in Australia is similar to Ireland in that it's based on English Common Law. Anyway, the court system here is hierarchical, with a Supreme Court that hears appeals from the lower courts. And like the US, it has federal laws. These are introduced by the Parliament of Australia and the parliaments of the states and territories.

In case you were wondering.

I've been wandering around all afternoon and this culminates in me buying an 8GB SD card for my digital camera, which will surely be enough for my adventure. I

17

finally settle in Equinox Bar on the corner of Little Lonsdale St. at Elizabeth St., eat a greasy pizza and side salad – smothered in, funnily enough, side salad – and drink a coke as I get my bearings. It costs me $16.60 and the bearings were free so it doesn't feel like a waiter has climbed up on me from behind. I have yet to book my tour up the East coast, while my New Zealand tour is already taken care of, thanks to Caroline at Travel Creations back home.

A couple of girls in the smoking area at Equinox are talking about breaking up with their boyfriends and taking a road trip to Perth. I'm sitting next to them and I want to interject – to scour their knowledge of local watering holes. I reckon a couple of girls imbibing in the early evening on a September Monday in Melbourne will have a fair idea.

Back inside the bar, I take *mX* out of my bag and it turns out that over 100 publicans in New Zealand are threatening to close their TAB (Totalisator Agency Board) outlets on Melbourne Cup day (the first Tuesday in November) in protest at "reduced returns" (a TAB can normally be found at a bar that doubles as a *bookies* if you will). Commission was apparently cut from 2.5 per cent to between 0.1 and 1 per cent for "112 of the 397 outlets with betting facilities".

"New Zealand Hospitality Association CEO Bruce Robertson said some pubs were not getting enough to pay for printer ink," according to the article. As a freelance journalist, I can certainly empathise with the last eight words quoted above.

The Kiwi couple behind me, however, don't seem too bothered. John and Jan, from Taupo Bay in the North Island, try their luck in the village sweepstake on cup day. John invites me to come visit them when I'm there. Actually, they don't. I'm promised some cheap beachside accommodation – the couple are in the property letting business. Hmmm...realtors and a journalist? All we need now are a cop, a traffic warden, a lawyer, a politician and basically Adolf Hitler and this could be the most hated table in history.

John is drinking pots of beer (285ml), which are similar enough to an Irishman's glass of beer. A Victorian schooner is 485ml, while a "pony" of beer in Victoria is a meagre 140ml and the same measure in New South Wales is known as a "five".

18

Meanwhile, a New South Welshman's schooner is 425ml, as it is in Queensland and in South Australia it's 285ml. Irishmen generally don't do glasses (or half-pints) of beer but in the main we drink pints (576ml).

With each drink, John becomes more and more opinionated and he eventually even slates the All Blacks for recently losing the Tri-Nations Cup to the Springboks (South Africa).

"They win da goymes thet don' madda' but neva' win the ones thet caaant (count)," he explains. "Thet's whoy we don' hev' the Wooo'ld Cap – out drinkin' the noights bifore metches an' foightin', the lod of 'em."

It's not that John isn't patriotic – au contraire. He is, however, bemused at the lack of silverware of late. Anyway, I have no intention of joining them in Taupo Bay for some dolphin hunting and deer watching. Well, something like that.

I need to go book my trip, but somehow, a "pint" (570ml here), has mysteriously found its way to my table.

I decide to go for another cigarette.

"Aw, I dinno: I thenk I can bead 'er (beat her)," says Marnie, one of the erstwhile Monday smoker-drinkers on the *patio*.

"I moyn (mean), a 21-yir-old thet gives hid (head), moybe. But a 16-year-old? No woyyyyy. They're probably just hengin' out togedda 'coz she's younga', ye knoy? Unliss he's emoytion'lly invulved."

This might not be the best time to intervene but what's going to happen next? It turns out that Issy and Marnie have come in for a glass of Vino Blanco after work and stayed on to, you know, keep the whole bottle company. That would never happen in Ireland. The girls are very engaging, They tell me everything I need know about Melbourne's nightlife, and we talk about the tension between the city and Sydney, Aussie rules football, Gaelic Football, the compromised rules (annual games between both countries' native games, which are quite similar), travelling and drugs. It occurs to me that most Aussies you talk to about travelling, in Australia at least; generally mean travelling within Australasia. The rest of them are in London I suppose.

Marnie tells me I should check out St. Kilda – I've been planning on doing so – and after a brief spell surfing the web, I brave the rain (I know, yeah...rain!) and make my way to Swanston St. to get a tram. So I'm waiting in the rain for the No. 16 and I get a bit wet but I don't care. In the building opposite, Corporate Suits change into their Spiderman clobber and head upstairs for the more serious business. There's only a huge and well-lit climbing wall filling the upper floors. Climbers, which can be seen through huge sheets of glass, look like ants. What a metamorphosis. It's just awesome: you've got to love the Aussies for this type of thing.

The Prince of Wales and The Espy at St. Kilda are musts, I've been assured, and it's not too long before I'm hoofing it along a path on what I assume is the main thoroughfare in St. Kilda. It's strange to see random backpackers run, then walk, then run again in short bursts towards me in the distance. I'm getting wet, then I'm not, then I am before I realise it's because some shops have awnings and some don't. There are also spaces between many of the buildings: one thing is for sure, Melbourne loves its alleyways.

Then, it appears suddenly at Fitzroy St. – The Prince of Wales. In I go, and the atmosphere is electric. Locals, heavily tattooed and wearing *wife-beater* singlet vests riding above low slung jeans, (bare) cheekily slump over pool tables in between chugging beers. At least, that's the women and I am *not* joking here. Kitschy and open plan in design, this raucous joint, with its walls smattered in posters, is heaving. St. Kilda locals, backpackers, gay couples and singles – along with their heterosexual opposite numbers – all mingle busily. The local footie team seem to be guarding the fruit (gaming) machines in the corner. A rowdy bunch and no mistake, it turns out that this boisterous group – I count at least ten of them – is celebrating, having won the local league the day previously. They haven't stopped partying yet. And who would blame them when there are $2 pots (jugs are $8) of Boags Beer on offer. As far as Aussie (*Tazzie*) piss goes, it's quite drinkable. I befriend St. Kilda locals, Paul and Ingrid, and we start chewing the fat. Speaking of which, Paul has a beef with Sydney.

"Thu' very uptoight," he explains. "Araaaa'n here, ye heve Aaart, beaudiful scoynery (scenery), a laid beck and intelligent way of loife – people aaa' liberal heee'e.

"The buildings an' pubs heee'e aaa' beaudiful and the beach is jus' down the royd (road)," he continues. "Everythin' ya' wan', eh?"

Paul is a life-long Geelong supporter and Ingrid follows local team, St. Kilda. I mean to ask him why he's a supporter of everything St. Kilda but their football team. Then I forget to. It's five days before both these teams will meet in the AFL (Australian Football League) final. All eyes are on the screen: voting for the Brownlow Medal is afoot. The medal is a posthumous award for footie players of exemplary character and skill awarded by the League's umpires in a ceremony not dissimilar the Oscars in scale. Gary Ablett, a Geelong player like his dad of the same name was before him, wins out in the end much to Paul's delight.

"Good on ya, Ablo," he shouts – his fist clenched and punching the air.

Meanwhile, the local footie stars are getting more and more animated with every beer, as are Sue, her flamboyantly gay nephew, Brett, and his beau, Colin. All three start pushing each other – it gets messy and turns into arse-slapping and finally, face-hitting but it seems good natured and the bouncers don't look overly concerned. Attention-seeking idiots.

In fact, the bouncers are busy keeping an eye on the footie players who are now gathered around a girl who's gyrating her pelvis in various directions towards all of them. She's wearing six-inch heels, the team's jersey and little else. Her legs have been Tangoed (a term used when objects are daubed in the colour orange in an old UK advertisement for soft drink, Tango) and her peroxide blond hair is OTT. She dons a coat just to take it off again and then bends over to give all and sundry a bird's eye view.

I'm wearing my Asic trainers – the type whose instep are basically covered in a soft mesh material. And in her eagerness to get at Paul's glasses, she only goes and spikes me with her bloody heel. Ouch!

Paul nods towards the St. Kilda Killers.

"Be careful of those goooys Ciaran – they're alwa's gettin' throywn outta heee' – just make sure yo' not the royzin."

He starts laughing and I'm left thinking that it's some private joke about me being a piece of dried fruit. Until I realise that he meant, "Reason".

"They'll prob'ly all have a go off ha' (her) laid-aaah (later)...haha," he adds.

Groups of (mostly) gay punters swarm the section of path that is the smoking area outside. A fight ensues. It's between a huge, stocky bloke in a baseball hat and wearing the type of jacket that was held, in no insignificant measure, in disdain by my friends and I back in the day when we were still singing the praises of Nirvana and the like. The day in question would have dawned and set in the early-to-mid 1990s, when Ravers put their hands in the air like they just didn't care as long as Technotronic, 2 Unlimited or some other such nonsense was pumping through any given speaker. Sadly, a resurgence of this crap occurred back home in some circles in the past year or so, though I'm guessing this is lost on the huge bouncer involved in the tangle with the drunk.

Anyway, the bouncer in the bright yellow lagging jacket grabs the much smaller guy and starts swatting him with the baseball hat, is easily fending off the wimp's blows, and the scene is feckin' hilarious.

When we can finally see that the bouncer is a woman, the scenario is funnier still.

Inside, meanwhile, the place has cleared out, apart from a few regular drinkers. I say my goodbyes to Paul and Ingrid and head next door, on the same premises mind. Gay bars anywhere are definitely not my scene but the drag show, I'm told, is hilarious. And it is. I get drinking with a few bi-sexual and lesbian women – so they told me – who are a good laugh. After a while, I leave and go to The Espy, nearby. However, on the way, I take a corner and see Brett and Colin doing things to each other that no unsuspecting heterosexual male should *ever* have to see *any* number of men do – unless he wants to. Er, I don't. However, one of the girls, Marnie, who directed me to the area, obviously felt that I couldn't live without this experience.

Brett and Colin seem to think it humorous in the extreme. I turn away and move on.

At The Espy, a solo musician whose name I don't get is playing. There are only about twenty people here, probably because it's lashing down outside. He really is quite good. I go and get the last tram into the city and jump off at Flinders St., merrily persuading myself that I know the way back to the King St. hostel. I don't though and end up having to get a taxi (it's raining) – but only after I pay a visit to a Hungry Jacks outlet for my third burger, a massive thing, in about as many days. I'm jetlagged and tanked up, after all, so counting is out. I climb into my top bunk at about 4am and adjust to the musty smell, the snores, the air conditioning and other sounds of the room. And seconds, later my conscious mind is enveloped in a blanket of nothingness.

DAY FOUR

I'm woken at 6am by my neighbours again: I hear whispers in Aussie accents. There seems to be more light today, at least in the room, and I can see that the men are small in stature and that they're sporting moes, or goatees as I would call them. They're clearly getting a head start for Movember – when Aussie, Kiwi and even some Irish guys, me included, will sport the beards or handlebar-like moustaches for men's charities, health awareness or just for fun.

The pair look Mexican or something. The taller one is wearing jeans and a tee-shirt today and is sans sheepskin jacket but he keeps the hat. I'm betting, with my hungover and still jetlagged brain, that he's a cowboy on tour or, perhaps, an Indian who's working in construction for a bit. Or maybe he's a pirate – *Even pirates have to clock in at 7am these days*, I tell myself.

I wake up following a few hours sleep, when I hear my name being called out over a tannoy. I'm thirstier than an Irish father after childbirth. Thirsty work, I'm told. I lash back a half-litre bottle of water and go to reception: it's 10.13 in the am. I must pay for tonight or lose my bed. I pay and then look through some brochures for a tour of the Great Ocean Road for tomorrow. I go online and then trundle back upstairs to the 75th floor.

A guy on the bottom bunk in the dorm tells me: "If you want you cen esk fur another bottom bunk if these are free." He's pointing at the other bunks that the Mexican pirates are staying in, further down the room. His accent is French. "They haven't left," I tell him. "Besides, I'm grand where I am." He's rude and he smells and now he's looking at me as if he doesn't understand, which probably makes him hate me even more.

But I don't care.

Take a shower you smelly fuck, I tell him, but only in my head.

I take my own advice and shower before I leave the hostel for Bourke Mall.

I stop here at the mall for something to eat, before leaving with a takeaway hot chocolate. And it's a beautiful day. After all the rain yesterday, Melbourne once again looks awesome in the early afternoon sunshine. I take in Ethiad Stadium and go up the Bourke St. pedestrian bridge and onto Spencer St. I need to get to the Peter Pan office at Elizabeth St. near the junction with Franklin, to pay for my tour up the East coast. I go North along Spencer St. and then head East on Latrobe St.; walking past the Flagstaff Gardens, my senses soaking up the atmosphere. A sunny day with some clouds in the sky means that walking in a light jacket is comfortable, even when going at a good trot, because there's a slight intermittent East wind a-blowing in my face. A light sheen of perspiration on my body at least tells me that I'm sweating out some of the remnants of last night's booze. The sun is shining through the budding branches of the park's trees and the grassy hills of Flagstaff act as a haven in the busy Central Business District (CBD). Meanwhile, the pretty flowerbeds are an excellent distraction from the busy city traffic. Spring hath indeed arriveth.

I go so far as to tell myself that Melbourne's CBD is a much prettier, friendlier and more accessible – and of course, cleaner – version of Manhattan. Well, part of Manhattan anyway. It's much more laid back but the streets are grid-locked in pretty much the same way Manhattan in New York is. But it is of course much more laid back, more akin to Baltimore, Maryland, where I lived for most of 2000. I'm working off my Italian BMT and Coke from Subway at Bourke Mall, as I continue across

Latrobe until Queen St., head north here and reach Franklin, then go East to hit Elizabeth. I hit the street mind, not my mother or sister of the same name.

The saleswoman I'm destined to deal with is chewing gum – that's not her name, it's what she's doing. Anyway, I can just about see a mop of greasy brown hair, because she's sitting so low down in the seat. She goes through the offers and I'm shown the brochure for the Adventure Tours Australia option. Although owned by the Oz Experience Company, this is not one of the hop on-hop off buses. Basically, I will have two weeks to get up to Cairns from Sydney, after spending a few days there. This is the only option for me really: my flight to New Zealand on October 13th, dictates this.

Anyway, clearly lying through her teeth or 'mistaken', she tells me that there are only two places left on the bus and that if I don't book it as soon as, I might not get to board. The thrash-talk part of the pitch comes next.

"You goys will be out paaaa'dy-ing every noight," she says.

"Et fiiii'st, the girls will be reluctan'...but by the toime yu' get to Caaa'ins, yu'll just be loike, 'Hey, yu wanna come back to mu rooym?' And the giii'ls will just go beck and fack you."

Seriously, this is how she talks to me. I'm not surprised at her little sales pitch: if you had seen the group of Irish blokes that came in just as I was leaving, you wouldn't have been either. The profile of these was early-to-mid twenties; drunk, wide eyed, sharp of tongue, loud and boisterous – as they probably should be at that age. However, I won't be offended if she thinks I fit the age bracket.

I tell her that I'll come back, likely tomorrow, after I've looked at other options and have had time to digest all of the information. She looks away, suddenly, I suspect, disinterested in my existence and just says, "Olright". However, she says it in a way that silently adds something along the lines of, *You stupid dickhead...this is your only option...don't say I didn't warn you.* In my head I've just cured her of her Australian accent .

I leave her to it.

A few hours have passed and I'm back at Peter Feckin' Pan. I'm disappointed to learn that they can't accept my Bank of Ireland Laser card. And I don't possess a diseased credit card. The ANZ bank outlet nearby is not of much help to me and I've already withdrawn the maximum daily quota allowed (about $350). I need to pay $3,010 (about €1,850) for my tour. There are times when being a nameless and faceless tourist is a pain in the arse. I know what you're thinking but it's Tuesday and I leave for Sydney early Thursday and the accumulating withdrawals will not be enough to pay for the trip. Plus, I don't have internet banking either because I don't trust it so I can't transfer funds from my savings account. The BOI helpline invites me to leave a message so I must now call my sister to see if I can lump the price of the trip onto her credit card and pay her in cash upon my return.

Grrrr...I've used my Laser all over Europe and I hate doing this. Perhaps I should have really researched all this before I came over but I stupidly took a friend's advice: namely, that I could use the card here. I dread to think of what bank charges I'll be faced with, upon my arrival home.

So today, I've learned that Australia hates Laser, and that a friendly conversation with a hot Sheila at a bookstore doesn't necessarily lead to a hot date with her. I also discovered that it's unwise to go for a poo in a toilet at a bar without checking first to see if there's paper of the bum-wiping sort present.

I get $350 from an ATM, again shuddering at the thought of the bank charges. And I hate having to enlist the help of my older sister Lorraine, but needs must. I cancel a diving trip in Cairns that I've booked with Peter Pan and I plan to sort that activity out when I finally get there. Anyway, I finally get through to Lorraine and she's cool with it all, God bless her cotton socks. Forking out $450 in cash, I debit her credit for $2,200 (I have already paid the rest).

It's time to get on with enjoying the trip.

I'm looking for The Workshop, a bar over a bookstore on Elizabeth St. I take a detour up Latrobe St. and I find some lively outdoor gem: I pay $27 for a two-course meal, opting for the pumpkin and potato soup, followed by a T-bone steak. A glass of crisp, fruity and musty Pinot Gris washes it down nicely. I would normally go for red but it is not written. On the pedestrianised street outside, where I'm dining, a drummer/percussionist – who looks to be of Latino origin – has set up an impressive array of percussion instruments. There are bongos, Congo drums, snares, toms and hi-hats. The drums and a speaker are hooked up to a mixing desk. The music has a decent range in terms of style but his contribution to hits such as Bob Marley's *Buffalo Soldier* and Ray Charles's *Hey Hey* is, at best, an exercise in mimicry and at worst, pointlessness. The diners don't seem to mind, however, so neither do I. I've just had gorgeous soup, a very nice steak, a tasty glass of wine and a cappuccino; the service has been excellent, friendly and professional and I've just paid $37, which is less than €25. It's great value. The waiter is getting a tip. Melbourne can be OTT with its beer prices sometimes, but I'm extremely happy with this. As far as I'm aware, Max Brenner's is a chocolate bar of some description, but the wallet that the bill came in had "Max Brenner" splashed across the front. So there you go.

Before I left the Small Dog, a friend of mine, a cultured doctor type who's the type of foodie that loves eating it but couldn't normally be arsed cooking it, seemed more excited about the food I would get to consume on my travels rather than the places I would get to see or activities that I would get to indulge in. She had a point; the variety of food on offer here in Melbourne lends me to believe that it's an extreme activity.

Well, exotic at any rate.

The array of restaurants on offer is dizzying. It's clear that Melbourne's close proximity to the shore, the influx of immigrants from continental Europe and of course Asia, have added something special to the British and Irish influence on the cuisine. The range of fish and vegetables on offer is very impressive.

Don't get me wrong: the Aussie still loves his/her meat pies, as do most of us; though they can keep the Witchetty grubs that the POMs are made to eat on the British reality programme known as *I'm a Celeb...*

It's 9pm and I'm in the Workshop on Elizabeth St. At the entrance on A.Beckett St., drinkers are faced with a steel door, exposed brick, blue walls splashed with graffiti and on the landing, the walls are covered with carefully selected wallpaper: mean aliens that do not look unlike invaders of the spaced out variety march across it. It's art deco, laid back and lofty – like my kid of woman. A couch backs onto the large warehouse windows and it's flanked to its left by a large steel workbench. Think more butcher's table than engineer's though. To the right of the couch is a wooden bench. Partitions protrude in angles and the place is bathed in red light that's beaming out from the candleholders on the tables.

A couple – they look Argentinean or Chilean to me – are deep in conversation. He's consoling his girlfriend, who could be a recent ex by the look of things. Meanwhile, groups of Aussie-accented youth congregate around tables reverently. They talk animatedly but the religion here is Chill. On Elizabeth, below, groups of oriental women charm the oxygen from the air. The scene is stunning. I'm sipping on a Monteith – Kiwi for beer – Golden Ale which has cost me $7.50 and that's not cheap. The only other draught is Monteith Cider.

The smoking area nearby is all wooden pews with bare naked wooden joists for a ceiling. There's much cigarette rolling afoot among this congregation, who are of Bohemian cut. A weird timber-framed arch that's not arch-shaped as such but more rectangular, splits the area, while the gentle hum of a tram seeps in through the opened windows. Stragglers slumber up A. Beckett St. to the bar's entrance, as Tom Waits croons from inside the speakers. It must be hot in there.

The tattoo-flashing, beanie and hoodie-wearing audience seems comfortable in its natural habitat. A girl speaks to her "best friend" for over an hour on her mobile phone, only coming up for air twice – to stroll across and ask me for a cigarette, actually. But that's okay. Students, I assume, sip slowly from beers poured out of jugs while outside, the lone rider of a carriage leans back as his wax jacket and broad brimmed hat add an air of authenticity to his part in the Play on Elizabeth St. The streets are calm and the promise of summer is in the air. It's an eclectic vibe. I keep to myself tonight amongst this self-consciously cool set, and lay back with them.

28

It's a quiet one tonight because tomorrow at 7.25am I'll be whisked away to the Great Ocean Road for some "spectaculaaa' soights", as Ericka in King St Backpackers has earlier told me.

But for now, this is the CBD in laid back Melbourne on a balmy Tuesday spring evening in late September.

DAY FIVE

I drag myself out of bed after my 'restful' four-hour sleep. It's only restful in that I'm laying on a bed in the dark with my eyes closed for a handful of hours. And although I'm mildly hungover and still jetlagged, I don't really care because today I'm doing the Great Ocean Road tour with the awesome and eco-certified Bunyip Tours company.

Having been picked up at Little Bourke St., at the front door of my hostel which looks like it's actually on the side of the building, I'm whisked away to their offices downtown. Here, travellers and tourists choose from between trips to the road or the set of Aussie soap opera, *Neighbours* – where I'm told certain actors might "perv on" and try to steal your girlfriend, daughter or whatever. Penguin Island is another tour option that takes in the ocean road.

Time-wise, I've been worried that I wouldn't get to taste much of Victoria (the province and not a girl) outside of Melbourne. But this digestible bite, I hope, will fill the gap. The tour takes over twelve hours in total and there's a picnic lunch consisting of bread, ham, cheese, tomato, cucumber, lettuce, grated carrot and – enter sound of needle scratching record – tomato feckin' ketchup. The trip costs me €115, which is good enough value.

There are about twenty of us onboard and the demographic is: An English mother with her daughter; Richard, an English chap in his 20's who is my tour buddy for today; an Aussie couple, Warren and Hilary (heavy set folk in their late 60s or early 70s I guess); a German couple; a German girl, Marie, who's travelling alone, and a clearly-gay New York couple in their 40s sporting wedding rings, Michael and Bill (I think they may be married to each other).

The remainder are of Oriental in origin. I hate using the word as a blanket term but at times I honestly can't tell the difference between the nationalities. I estimate that most of them are Japanese and Chinese, however.

And then there's me; the lone Irishman.

Our driver/guide is Anthony, an intelligent Aussie who and a gent who is a mine of information regarding the area's history, climate, geography, topography, animals, marine life and so on. So we're making our way out of Melbourne towards Torquay, where the Great Ocean Road officially begins. On both sides, Eucalyptus trees (Aussie's national tree) and stretches of green separate the road from the suburban houses. Squeaky clean *Neighbours*, the erstwhile TV show, is probably based on these suburbs and for all I know or care it could even be filmed there. One thing I do know is that people actually live in the houses where it *is* made. You're right, we NEVER see them. So are they invisible people? I hear you ask. No, no, of course not; they are miniature people – kind of like Rick Moranis and Co in 1980s kids' flick, *Honey, I shrunk the Kids*. And let me tell you, they are *not* happy little bunnies.

I look over my right shoulder and watch the buildings that dominate the cool and cosmopolitan Melbourne city skyline, disappear.

A short while later, all that can be seen are trees, hills and fields – dotted with cows and goats that laze about the place. Some of the hills appear to be separated by seams, reminding me of earthquake activity, ice age action and Furry Murray's First Year geography class. When we reach Bells Beach – our first stop on the road – the green scene on our left (off the south coast obviously) has disappeared and is replaced with a sheet of aquamarine blue. The sea glistens and darkens in patches, as it flirts with the fluffy balls of cotton that hover above. "Mooo'e (more) th'n 750 ships have crashed on the shipwreck coyst (coast)," Anthony tells us. The longest running surfing competition in the world, the Rip Curl Pro Surf and Music Festival, is held here. And by the way, *Point Break,* starring Keanu Reeves and Patrick Swayze, wasn't really filmed here.

Occasionally, I play a little game of Master of Puppets with the German guy behind me. Every so often, I go, "Wow", or draw in some air sharply and quickly. As

30

soon as I do, he's straight in there with the camera. *Click, Click, Click.* The Japanese girl sitting up front, who's in charge of the music and does a decent job with it, seems to be competing with him. Anthony informs us that Airey's Inlet is unlike other towns on this beautiful coast because it was designed as a resort, and not as a whaling town. On we go, snaking our way west around the southern coast, surrounded by huge craggy cliffs to our right, while a barely-visible Van Diemen, Tasmania, with its reddish hue, lines the horizon across the Bass Strait to our left.

To our backs, the erstwhile hotchpotch, consisting of each sheer and zigzagging section of cliff making up the coastline, seems to be trying to outshine each other, as in turn they appear and then disappear with abandon.

And I'm having the time of my life.

We're on the approach into Lorne and I become jealous of the town's residents when Anthony describes the swimming race from the "pier to pub" race. Not adverse to the occasional distance sea-swim myself during the summer months back home, I'm green when I learn that up to 4,000 swimmers every January get to partake in the swim – a 1.2 kilometre splash through the Loutit Bay that finishes at the Lorne Hotel – for a few pots or schooners or whatever you're having yourself. It doesn't get much better that that: not for me anyway. In 1998, the race entered the Guinness Book of Records for the world's largest open water swim. I do a 1.3 kilometre swim myself back home in Tramore, Co. Waterford, though my club would be lucky to get 100 swimmers. But this is Australia: the "largest swim" part refers to the numbers of swimmers – 3,071 took the plunge here in Lorne in 1998.

I could live here, I tell myself, as I notice over a dozen surfers bobbing up and down in the flashing surf, which seems to be picking up as it makes its way inwards. I'm on the pier side, framing a Kookaburra who's resting haughtily on the branch of a tree with the beach and the surfers in the background. The camera doesn't do this scene justice, however.

Another highlight of this magnificent seascape trawl includes The Twelve Apostles, the most popular rock formation in Victoria. Actually, it turns out that there are only

31

eight Miocene or "less recent" rocks, which means they are only between ten and twenty million years old. A little birdie tells me that a few of these tried to follow Jesus Christ but could not walk on water and sank into the drink below. The truth remains, though, that there never were twelve of them and the reference to a dozen of the sandy coloured rocks was literally coined for tourism purposes. There were nine actually, and one fell in July 2005. These massive jutting stacks are separated from the eroding limestone cliffs by the enticing aqua blanket of water. Nearby, tourists swarm like bees around the Port Campbell National Park visitor information centre and helicopters whisk the buzzing plenty away for short and speedy runs around the apostles for about $70. Others crowd the viewing platform, snapping Mathew, Mark, Luke and so on. We brave the unforgiving, seemingly gale force winds sweeping up to us from hundreds of feet below. The surf laps the coast ferociously today, and the helicopters battle boldly with the wind.

I meet Stella again, a ditzy New Yorker of Chinese lineage, or at least that's what she tells me. Well, she doesn't tell me about the ditzy bit, but it became apparent from our first meeting earlier that day. She's on another tour but I met her earlier at some location or other, where we took pictures of Lorikeets, Koala Bears and some other shit. Here, she slipped down a short embankment and would have ended up on her backside in a mucky puddle had I not grabbed her by the arm. We were jockeying for position to get snaps of a snoozing Koala when she lost her footing. She thanked me, told me that she was okay and I left her to it, as she absent-mindedly tried to stabilise. However, she fell again and landed on her rounded posterior. Speaking of which, I sooo would.

"That's what happens when you take a city girl out of the city," she remarks now, cheerily enough it has to be said. Amen. Not that *I* can talk about being clumsy.

Other gems along the road include Apollo Bay and Mait's Rest, taking in a gentle rainforest walking trial in the Great Otway National Park. Described by Anthony as "a temperate rainforest", it is dotted with impressive Mountain Ash trees that are second only in height to the Californian Redwood, we learn. We skip Anthony's favourite stop, Loch Ard (for now) and head a few hundred metres to view "London

Bridge", a huge natural archway lodged off the shore from Pont Hesse. London Bridge was once a double arched formation linked to the land but it collapsed into the sea in 1990.

Here, I join Michael and Bill, as the former tells the latter that that he can't believe he is here. Bill tells him to wait until his wife finds out that he is. They laugh. I'm not ear-wigging as such but perhaps listening so I'm not sure if the joke is meant for my ears but I laugh anyway. For a moment I suspect that it's *for* my benefit.

We double back and on to the final spot on the tour – Loch Ard Gorge. The Gorge is named after the clipper, *Loch Ard* which ran aground – after a three-month voyage – on Muttonbird Island in June, 1878. The ship had been travelling from England to Melbourne when tragedy struck. There were about fifty passengers on board and only two of these survived. The memorials at the site maintain that ship's apprentice, Tom Pearce, was washed up onto land during the tragedy, while he then swam out to rescue Eva Carmichael, from Ireland, after hearing her shouting in the water. Then, he raised the alarm.

Apparently, they never met again, with Eva returning to Ireland and Tom becoming a ship's Captain.

I tell Anthony, if he's interested, that the Gaelic words Loch Ard means "high lake" when translated into English. He nods enthusiastically, telling me that this is the name of the location in Scotland where the sunken ship was built.

Essex boy Richard, along with Munich Marie and mé féin (*myself* in the Irish or Gaelic language) make our way up to some distant viewing platform and then down to one about midway along this particular trail. Richard and mine's gaze rests on a lone figure in a red jacket – near the cave's walls hundreds of metres below. This person appears to be fixing bait to a fishing rod. We don't comment on this but Richard suggests taking the steps down to the beach. The three of us head down and mess about for a while, take pictures, that kind of thing. The figure in the cave seems to be standing perfectly still, with right hand raised aloft: it kind of looks like a priest during the communion part of the Catholic Mass when he lifts the bread and everyone lowers their heads. We approach and as we get closer we notice it's a woman. We're facing her back and now she's lowering her hand to her forehead, towards her right shoulder and back on up to the exposed cave wall above. The woman appears to be in a trance. Aaaah, of course, that'll be because she's drawing ancient healing energy from the cave, fair play to her.

We can't resist posing for pictures; making ridiculous shapes with her stuck firmly in the frame (in the background).

3. A Red Mist

DAY SIX

I'm up and at them again this morning and I'm a bit tired but fresh enough as I didn't go out last night – apart from a curious pint at La Di Da Bar across the road on King St. It wasn't up to much: I noted that it was tacky and had pretensions above its station. And get this: a pint of Asahi Beer costed a staggering $14, according to the barmaid, which just compounds how shit the place actually was. I ordered a pint of Boags for, like, $8.

Back in the billet, a new French guy has moved in, but this guy is as sound as Milford (*Sound, The,* in New Zealand's South Island), unlike the smelly and intense one who has been sleeping on the bottom deck for twenty hours out of twenty four, for the past few days – seemingly, without showering. Perhaps he's depressed and maybe I should be more understanding. But if I wasn't loving it here I would be leaving it.

I have breakfast with the new French guy, and a *hilarious* girl who calls herself Kimzee, joins us. She's from Adelaide and she wants "to goooy backpacking in Nooo'th Amarica and Mexicoy next yeee'" and came to Melbourne to see what it's, er, like, when one is backpacking alone.

Well Kimzee, if you're from Adelaide and you come to a backpackers' hostel in Melbourne for a couple of nights...it's NOTHING like that.

Of course those words never actually left my lips.

Why couldn't this pair been here three days before now? It always seems that you meet the nicer ones, including the hotter girls who actually like you in return, just before you must leave a particular place. That's my story and I'm sticking with it.

So I went down to Southern Cross Station, took the Skybus back to the Airport, and headed straight to the Qantas desk to check my bag for the flight to Sydney.

In my tiredness I slip the attendant the receipt for my camera. "Could you tell me where I can get a tax refund on this?" I ask him. He looks at the receipt and then stares up into my face, his expression probably expressing that I am, in fact, *a mad Irish bastard*. Don't say it. Pointing at the tax and duty free logo on the top of the receipt, he goes: "This was boughd in dudy froy."

"Eh, I gave you the wrong slip," I reply quickly, taking the receipt from him and stumbling off.

Now you can say that I'm mad.

I'm herded through the gate with the other lambs to the slaughter that is Qantas Domestic. I'm pulled aside by a busty, big-haired beauty of a woman who tells me that I've been "singled out for a seeea'ch". She jokes with me as her hands run lightly up and down my limbs, along with her Cocainey-probey-sticky-yokeymabob thingy-you'd-see-on-that-Border Patrolly-programme-thingymajig.

She's checking for explosives. Or cocaine. Yeah drugs, that'd be it. Well she can sod off and buy her own!

I tell her that she has five hours to get her hands off me and not a minute longer. She's laughing. She sticks her detector into my manbag and she doesn't find any semtex or whatever the kids are using these days. I'm free to go so when I pass through and look back, a businessman is being pulled aside. I can't hear but I suspect that he's getting the same parley.

After sipping on a cappuccino I move on to my gate where two young Aussies explain that their 11am flight to Sydney has been cancelled.

It's 10.45 and my flight is due to depart at 11.30. But the gate hasn't opened yet so I go check my emails. I get carried away on the social networking website that needs little by way of introduction, Facebook.com. As most employers (there's still the odd one about the place) would tell you, Facebook tends to eat into productivity...speaking of which, 11.15 has somehow crept up on me.

I rush back to the gate but thankfully it hasn't opened yet. This Aussie banker is standing there with his wife and he's defending Melbourne's food and drink prices, like a big Australian eejit. Generally, I found the former to be reasonable but not the latter. We talk for what seems like an eternity and the wife can barely get a word in. Actually, she looks bored to tears. Wait. He's got a beard. Are bankers allowed to have beards? I think not! I'm afraid to look down at his feet in case he's wearing sandals. That would be just too much to take in. Everything would go swimmy like in some dodgy movie from the '60s and I'd have to sit down with The Weakness. I look behind his back but he's not sneakily waving about a copy of *The Guardian*, and he hasn't stroked his hairy chin once so, we might just get away with it. My actual understanding of the Universe, as I know, it remains intact. But, what, in the name of Jesus and all the Blessed Saints, is a banker doing queuing up with the rest of the peasants? If this were Ireland, he'd have taken a private jet, bought by the bank with 'borrowed' funds that didn't exist but it wouldn't matter because it would all be paid back by the taxpayer in the form of a bailout, of course, only so the poor bank could remain in business and loan us our own money and charge us extortionate interest rates for the privilege. And, we peasants would be stuffed down in the cargo hold with the caged chimps and the Fowl – no doubt left to our worries about catching Blue Fever or whatever.

So this bloke, The Banker as he's known, tells me about the red dust that's blown in from the desert and is choking Sydney, as if I hadn't heard. I was always more of a fan of *Purple Haze* rather than the red variety. Actually some friends and I have just been posting online messages to each other on Facebook regarding the mysterious mist.

I drift off in my head – kind of like JD (Dr. John Dorian) does in US comedy series, *Scrubs*, and I'm secretly hoping that the red dust, sand or whatever, will still be there when I arrive. I'm imagining orange skies and nightmarish, B-movie scenes upon my arrival. I'm dreaming of soldiers taking to the streets with megaphones and instilling Marshall Law. I'm imagining flight shutdowns, quarantines and even monsters that lunge angrily from giant red billowy clouds as people scatter – screaming with terror. Meanwhile, plucky newspaper men with notebooks, pencils and flashbulb cameras, all sporting those trilby hats with press tags on them and with rolled up sleeves, loosened tie and with cigarettes hanging from the side of their lips, ignore official warnings in their attempts to get the scoop of a lifetime. In fact, I now silently demand seeing a red sandy mass in Sydney. And if I don't, there'll be a choking red mist rising from an Irish GIANT.

I only come out of my waking dream when the mere utterance of the noun "Ireland" bounces off my inner ear. He's telling me now about a trip to the Small Dog with some friends of his back in 1987. He went to Co. Wicklow and apparently, his good self and the posse took a "wrong tuuu'n" down a side street in some garrison town or other and were greeted by an angry mob of Vikings, over ten centuries after the band of scamps (largely rapists and pillagers of some degree, I suspect) actually arrived there from Denmark and Sweden. Ah yes, the 'oul ancestors: what are they like eh? I could be wrong but sure, the Vikings can't sue: one can only defame a reputation that another has. And I've never heard of anyone taking legal action for themselves from Valhalla anyway.

Running into a group of Vikings on small streets in rural villages: these types of things still do happen in Ireland, I'm afraid. Thank God.

The man, we'll call him John because I don't get his name, warns me about Qantas Domestic, who formerly operated as TAA (Trans-Australia Airlines). He warns me of delays and even tells me that the pilot will blame this on "technicol problems".

So we board and I take the wrong seat.

I move when I'm informed of this by an old dear and I take the seat behind, the one I'm due to die in – or so I would believe just hours later. Sing along now boys and girls: "The wheels on the 747 don't move 'til 1.20pm; 1.20pm, 1.20pm; the wheels on the 747 do not move until 1.20pm; we'll be here all feckin' day long."

And that is it exactly: we're waiting for one hour and fifty minutes after the flight was scheduled to depart. To my right, but one seat, is a businessman whose head is stuck in *The Financial Times* or some other recessionary Bible throughout the flight. Meanwhile, to my left across the aisle, a young and right-on mother breastfeeds her rather large baby discreetly and efficiently. Hang on, I wasn't giving her marks out of ten. I'm just saying. The flight is unremarkable in every other way except that the male stewards do *not* sound feminine to my ear in the slightest. *Come on, I hear you say. Not one?* None that I come into contact with at any rate. All of them appear manly or macho but hey, this is Oz.

I expect a friendly punch in the arm as I'm woken with a bag of refreshments including a bottle of water, some chocolate, a muffin and some dried fruit. "Wakey, wakey moyte – have somethin ' fo' ya spooo't (sport)," says the punch-less mass. Oh my God, the turbulence...we are all going to *actually* die. Why is he smiling? I could slap his blond, curly-framed head. I'm good on airplanes but I don't do well with air around planes.

The pilot, about twenty minutes before landing, apologises for the erstwhile delay in take off. But get this. He cites technical difficulties AND, he also slyly sticks the boot of blame into the ribs of the passengers. I mean some, passengers, understandably pissed off with waiting for the plane to take off, decided to not bother taking the flight or else thought they would fare better by, oh I don't know, walking or something.

Imagine, if you will, Businessman/woman (A) waiting on Tarmac – s/he is going to meet client or, worse still, prospective client at Sydney. A gets so pissed off, or is so late as to render the trip now pointless; gets off plane. Meanwhile, pilot (B), by way of explanation, remarks: "This [passengers getting off plane, with luggage] changes the paperwork."

The audacity of it. I mean, perhaps the red dust or whatever was a contributing factor but even referring to the fact that passengers had to resort to getting off, without bowing down to kiss the customers' feet in apology? Seriously? Not on. The service and efficiency on my international Qantas flight(s) from Heathrow to Melbourne via Singapore; my first actually, was top class. But this offering from the domestic company is just not good enough.

Anyhow, my will beats the turbulence and the plane stays in the air until it's time to land and I'm a bit put out that nobody has thanked me to be honest. But the landing is bumpier than a pregnant leper with chronic acne wrapped in a lumpy mattress on a bunk bed with three wheels that's rolling down some chipped granite stairs in a Polish hostel.

There are lots of "Ooooohs" and "Aaaaahs". I'm surprised at hearing these, however. I expected to hear "shit"(s) and "fack me"(s).

STREWTH! OH MA FACKIN' GAAAWD, WUR ALL GANNA DIE; GET ME AAAWF AH THIS FACKIN' BUCKETA SHET.

That kind of thing. However, no: "Ooh"(s) and "Aah"(s) are the order of the afternoon.

I make my way to the train down below the airport in Sydney and a very helpful young man working there points me towards my platform. I spend the time checking out possibly the Yummiest Mummy I have ever laid eyes on and the trains come by very often so I'm not waiting long at all. And then I board the speeding snake, in the belly of the bustling beast. A man, his son and an elderly woman are the only ones on my carriage. The father and son talk about camping and so on. The boy is one of those kids with shoulder length hair and both of them are wearing clothes that are made from woven wheat or some nonsense. So, you won't need me to tell you that dad is one of those weird and trendy hippy-esque men (small *m*) who probably won't let his son play rugby because of its aggressive ways.

That's the woy ta goooy son: one plain, one puuu'l (pearl). Can you imagine it? Maybe that's the *camp-ing* they're speaking of. This isn't the Aussie male I envisaged. Then again, I am surmising and this is Sydney so I guess anything goes.

I get off at the Central Railway Station and then I'm on Pitt St., trying (and then I try some more) to get accommodation in the city. But I fail miserably, at first anyway. I probably should have booked ahead but I didn't – I wanted to see if I could wing it. The answer is *Yes,* I could get somewhere to lay my weary head but with some difficulty. The folks at Wake Up hostel say, *No.* A girl working there a bit too cheerily tells me that I do not have a reservation and therefore, cannot stay here. What a strange way to be told to more-or-less, you know, *Fuck Off!* It reminds me of the way I was dealt with at the ANZ bank on Elizabeth St in Melbourne.

40

Next.

After a few more "No"(s) later, I find a place, which is basically someone's spare room on Pitt St. But it's a dive so I sneakily tell the bloke there that I must find an ATM before I can book it and I'm knackered so I leave my bags there with him.

In the meantime, I get a dorm at Westend Backpackers up the same street. Another dorm. So I go back to the aforementioned shithole and tell the guy that I'm sorry but that I'll not be taking the room. I take my bag and I leave. It's not the cleanest but considering that it has all the amenities that a person who packs their back for travelling needs, and costs $31 per night, I think it's the lesser of two evils. At this stage in the evening it's a bit late for sightseeing and the like. I take my camera with me, even though the light has gone out of the late September sky. I drop my bags and check emails and Facebook, before going on the hunt for food. I'm astounded by the sheer volume of Asian restaurants about the place, it of course not dawning on me that I could be in the heart of Chinatown. In spite of this, I find a bar on Elizabeth St. that does food and I eat a rank flathead fish, which is hidden somewhere beneath the huge slab of heart-stopping batter.

I text my friend Gerry: he's from Waterford and lives in Sydney with his newly-wedded wife Laura, who's also from home. I tell him to text me back if he can meet me at Shark Bar on Liverpool St. at 7pm. They can't meet me over the next few days because they're going on a wine trip to the Hunter Valley wine region. But there's nothing back from him so I don't go. (Later, I will find out that he turned up at the bar and joked with my cousin Liam, in a text, about how he "felt very unloved" when there was a no-show.)

I get a taxi to King's Cross, where I've been assured it's all happening. The taxi driver drops me off and I feel as though I've been had, or otherwise seriously misunderstood. Naughty women of the evening advertising their wares try in vain to get me to part with my cash in return for some physical love but that's not my bag. I pass the numerous sex shops and peep shows, finally ending up in some bar, mostly out of curiosity it has to be said. This bar, whose name I do not even get, to my astonishment has a group of women and men (miniscule *m*) sknitting in its windows. What is sknitting? It is a word I have christened the awful combination involving participants *sitting* in a circle on bean bags and *knitting* at the same time, of course. And they are using giant knitting needles. For feck sakes, this is inappropriate behaviour in the extreme. It is for men at any rate, the big eejits.

But I'm in the bar now so I stay for a bottle of Heineken. Then I leave to face the hookers and the sleaze. I walk on by and turn a corner and see queues of people outside some clubs. Aha, this looks interesting. There's a long line of skinny-jeaned, baseball-cap wearing and hooded hipster youth standing outside a club. The sign says World Bar (I will later find out that there is a sister club of the same name in Queenstown, New Zealand). Most of these have carefully messed up hair and wear big-tongued trainers that I wore in the 1980s, of course at that time without any self conscious notions of retro and the like in my head.

I feel my age but I don't care.

Everyone, and I mean EVERYONE, is carded on the way in. Secretly, I'm delighted. At my age...are you kidding me? I don't have any age-proving ID on my person purely out of habit but, chancing my arm, I show him my press card which does not have my date of birth on it and to be honest, I'm sure he let me in just for the hell of it. I hardly look twenty one. Ha. Along with my fellow clubgoers, I've secured a voucher for a drink on the way in. Cocktails are served in teapots, though you'll be thrown out for drinking from the spout, apparently. Well, according to their mission statement or whatever on the accompanying cards.

I get fed up here after a couple of beers so I leave. Next door is Candy's Apartment, which is not a sweet shop or an abode but another club. Strangely, the bouncer here tells me that I've had enough and I've only had three bloody drinks (well, not *bloody* as such, I'm not a vampire). I'm taken aside by a stocky US jock who is as high as a maximum security prison wall (I guess that he's on ecstasy) and he's giving it loads because the bouncers won't let him in. He thinks that he's got an Ally. I look down. He's wearing shorts. WHOA! Left in? He shouldn't be left out wearing those. The beers at the club and a pint of ale with dinner are all I've had to drink all night. Honest. I challenge the bouncer politely but he is not for turning. So I go to some joint across the road. It looks like a hotel and there are a lot of steps leading up to a smart veranda but hey, I need the exercise.

Here, there are many stick insect beauties with male gay accessories in tow. I get talking to two Pauls, rough-looking beefcake cousins who both clearly have broken noses. They ask me where I'm from and I tell them and Paul Number One says he loves my accent. "We'eee Croyatian and the Oirish we'e fi'st ova' the woooll," points out Paul number two, clearly referring to the Serbian-Croatian conflict in the 1990s where Irish UN troops would have been deployed. Paul speaks through a thick-ish Aussie accent, however.

I nod in acknowledgment, in between sips of my Crown Beer. I don't want to break his bubble by telling him that the Irish soldiers were told that a pub lay over *that* wall.

When I ask the Pauls about the Melbourne-Sydney tension, Paul Number Two claims that it's Melbourne that has a problem with Sydney. But I'm not buying it. The other Paul says "it's bicoz wheneva we goy theee'e, the womin stoym (steam) roight into ass (*us*, as opposed to *arse*)". I believe you Pauls, honestly I do. There's a rivalry between the two cities that runs deep though and it's no coincidence that the Australian Capital Territory (ACT) is the country's capital. The Federal Government couldn't decide which of Australia's most popular cities to designate its Capital so it made the ACT its main cheese instead.

A friend of the Pauls, Tom, comes along with a girl called Fleur who tells me she is "half French" (her mother is from there it turns out). I tease her unmercifully about her Gallic roots, asking her to translate ridiculous phrases such as, "My eyebrows are creeping across my forehead like giant caterpillars" and so on. She is faux-mad, laughing and loving it. I tell them about being refused from Candy's Apartment and Paul number two assures me that the bouncer was more than likely intimidated by me because I was "bigga than hem (him)", which I told him I was but only when I was asked.

The gang include me in their next round of drinks but are leaving when I try to buy one back. They invite me to a party but I decline, choosing to have one more in World Bar. Here, I get talking to some weird Aussie girl who claims to be Irish by blood, even though she doesn't know where her parents hailed from. I am wearing a blond wig. I erase the shots from my camera. Le Mullet, it is not a good look for moi.

In the end this crazy chick invites me back to her place but before I can even reply, she asks me if I'm going to pay the $90 taxi fare.

"TAXI!!!"

I'm on my way back to my hostel, sans crazy chick. Except I don't go there – not straight away at any rate. I go to the bar in The Chamberlin Hotel, at the end of the block near my current abode on Pitt St. The place is across the road from The Capitol, a theatre on Campbell St. that intersects with Pitt St. So of course the place is full of stage hands, actors, writers and the like. I get talking to some of these, mainly to one chap who's a writer but works at the Sydney Opera House by day as Chief Playwright Bum Wiper.

When I eventually get back to the hostel, just yards away, I'm met with a Maori guy on the desk who brings me coffee. He's a very friendly chap and it turns out that his name is Alan and he has lived in England with his English wife for some years. And he plans to return there soon, he tells me, without me asking. Actually, he tells me loads of stuff about himself without prompt, presumably because he's bored, and because he is *actually* speaking to somebody who seems to believe all of his lies. I log onto Facebook and drunkenly message some friends and so on. This is not a good move but I don't have anything on my mind, probably because I drowned most of my brain cells with booze, so the only thing I'll need to worry about in the morning is misspellings and poor punctuation. It takes me ages to type. The problem lies in the fact that I write for my bacon and I'm always self editing, as I'm trained to do. But the next morning, laughable typos, sack-able punctuation errors and sickening syntax will surely be my lot. The buttons keep moving: either that or it's my Giant fingers, with their clumsy, zombie-esque clunking stabs at the keys. I imagine reading some

44

Frankenstin-ish commentary on my status update such as *In sSYDnay...derunky ands ABOU To KILL THem aaaaLllll!* Of course I'm joking about the last part. I don't plan to kill *all* of them.

I need to get my head down so I take the lift (Oirish for elevator) up to my door on the gazillioneth floor and fall into it but not before I wake up everyone in the room, I'm sure. I think I'm being considerate by not turning on the light but being filled to the brim with beers at five-ish in the am in a dark, unfamiliar and small space can only mean one thing – carnage. However, the Dutch lads don't seem to wake from their slumber at all because they're in a Drincoma, which is Latin for being comatose-ically challenged from alcohol, is it not? Anyway, the alcoholic fumes emanating from my pie hole have probably put them deeper under.

I start worrying about what's holding the building up so now I know that I've had enough to drink.

So much for the Dutchies' idle boasts about getting lucky at the Greenwood Hotel.

DAY SEVEN

I wake up after 10am and the Dutch lads will be getting brain stem cell tests by the medics soon if they don't wake up. The sun is shining in the window next to my bed and the Hangover from Hell hasn't had time to surface yet so I take the opportunity to get the Down-Low on New South Wales. According to my *Lonely Planet Australia*, the seemingly self-styled Bible of the Backpacker, NSW is divided into four regions. These are, and I quote: "The coastal strip; the Great Dividing Range, about 100km [kilometres] from the coast; the Blue Mountains west of Sydney; and the Snowy Mountains in the south."

West of the Great Diving Range is farming country, which are dry western plains that cover two-thirds of the state. The plains fade into the barren outback in the far west, it goes on. And temperatures here can to soar to above 40°C. The main rivers are the Murray and the Darling and these "meander westward across the plains". Generally speaking, the further north ones goes, the hotter one will get and it gets drier to the west. And the Snowy Mountains, get, eh, snowy in the winter. Aha. I'm

45

surprised to learn that while temperatures can rise to 40°C (as I've already mentioned), the "average summer maximum is fifteen degrees lower. Temperatures rarely drop below 10°C at night. Thank Heavens for that.

The hangover must've taken a while to reach me on the nosebleed floor. I'm now as sick as a large hospital full of lottery winners who have just lost their winning tickets. So this is what the morning after a big night out in Sydney feels like. But, as soon as, I'm up and I go out to get something to eat, while my two Dutch roomies are still out for the count.

Back at the room, the lads are coming around slowly. I take a shower and then we're all talking about our various experiences in the city during the night – "Wheres in de fuck did you go last night you Irish prick?" – when there is a loud rap on the door. It's the English chap at reception with the awful peroxide dyed hair with dark roots and he's covered in what I suspect to be fake tan because it's streaky.

I'll deal with these little Dutch shitheads later!

There's a sign on my door telling me that I must clear the room. It's after 1pm and I was supposed to vacate at 10am. I suspect that he has put it there earlier.

"Is there a girl here called Ciaran Murphy?" asks the Bimbo.

Is this guy taking the piss or what?

"No," I tell him bluntly.

"But there is a bloke here of that name," I go on, standing aside to let him in.

I still have a towel wrapped around my waist so he surely has to believe me. Or does he? He steps into the door frame and has the grace to look embarrassed after his gaffe. Basically, my current bed is booked for tonight it emerges, as are the other empty ones in the room – so I must go to reception to book another in some other room should I wish to stay.

When he leaves I dress quickly and go down to reception. I book another bed for tonight, along with a ferry tour around Sydney Harbour for that afternoon (it costs

$25). It's 1.30pm and I must wait until 2pm to check in again, I suspect it's a punishment in his little world.

Whatever, Dickhead.

The hangover's worsening so I get a can of Pepsi from the vending machine on the first floor and I pound it – trying to shock my system into compliance with sugar, caffeine colouring agents, carbonated water, and more sugar. It helps a little but the horrible little bastard has called in reinforcements, the Waves of Tiredness.

I want to take the Cook Cruises tour at 2.30pm – there's one at 4.30pm also – but I'm delayed by the 2pm check-in. The Wham fan (from my room earlier) at reception tells me that it'll take about twenty minutes on foot but it turns out to be the biggest lie in the history of untruths, ever. Well, apart from lies such as *Elvis is Dead* and that *Freddie Star Ate My Hamster*. Twenty minutes my arse; it takes more like forty five. I'm on the way, taking snaps of the weird monorail and of the Sydney (AMP) Tower on Market St., and all the wonderful architecture at the financial district leading down to Circular Quay. It somehow lifts my heart to see about eighty excited schoolchildren queuing there. Although the cynic in me is rising and before I can catch it the thought that it's good to see them this way before *Life* gets its hooks into them, rises into consciousness. Watching them take their seats is this woman who's currently living in Malawi and is on holidays with her daughter who lives in Brisbane. Maj, a well-groomed, effeminate and affluent-looking Danish bloke of possibly Indian lineage who looks like he has had much Work done on his eyes, is also standing around at the back of the ferry with us.

We introduce ourselves to one another and, as we're all in the (watch this) Same Boat as it were, we decide to help each other out by taking pictures of us individually with the Sydney Opera House in the background – before saying goodbye and never seeing one another again. But the mother, I don't get her name, tells us that her battery is running on empty. I know how she feels. She has bought an old school type of Panasonic camera and she only purchased the thing because she thought it was the original model. Strewth! Ironically, the woman bought it because she thought it was easy to use but it's proving the opposite for her. And because of the battery, the new

47

model that looks like the old one – in this instance at least – doesn't function as well as the actual old one, which looks like the new digital one that doesn't work here today, would.

Right?

I offer to put her SD card into my camera for a bit so she can take her pictures with my machine. And she's like: "Oooow, I need to get special angles with the light for my painting." I'm thinking, *Arse*, but she's rattling on as the ferry starts and I switch off.

Still, the offer stands.

She's in my ear about "The Irish" now: she is telling me about how her grandparents came down to the southern hemisphere; about how they came here at the turn of the 20th Century. Her grandmother went to Queensland at that time, while her grandfather went to South Africa in order for them to see which location would be suitable for their family to live in and it's an interesting enough yarn. However, the Anglo-Boer War broke out (1899-1902) while her granddad was there and he had to "go to war" for King and country, as people dutifully volunteered in those days (and still do I guess). How unfortunate. The family, including her mother it turns out, moved to South Africa in wait for daddy to return to them. And when Johnny came marching home, well, to his new home anyway; he decided that he would buy land in Rhodesia (Zimbabwe). One would assume at a knock-down price having served Britain in the war.

Clearly a landed Gent, he had previously owned Loftus Stable (in Castlemorris, Co. Wexford), she tells me. This is not to be confused with the ghoulish Loftus Hall on the Hook Peninsula, built by the fourth Marquis of Ely in about 1870 on the ruins of the 14th Century Redmond Hall. It's near enough to the Hook Head Lighthouse and is an extremely haunted place. From an early age, most children down my way were terrified by indulgent adults and know-it-all peers in relation to Loftus Hall. The story, loosely told, is that a traveller in times olden stopped at the hotel during a thunder and lightning storm (naturally) and joined in a card game. One player dropped a card and upon bending down to pick it up, saw the man-beast's cloven hoof.

48

Well, the Devil or whatever, just shot up through the roof and the hotel had to close down because any attempts to fix the roof always proved fruitless.

In fact, the details of the story are sketchy because something keeps going wrong when I try to do the research. The computer freezes, the cursor keeps floating around the screen and attempts to click on any links related to same are pointless as it always gets re-directed. Anyway, us Irish are a superstitious bunch so I'd better Dún mo bhéal, meaning I'd better, *Shut my mouth.*

I find myself looking downwards for hoofs but I'm sure this woman is more of a Witch, as opposed to Old Nick. The eccentric African rattles on as we take in the opera house, Sydney Harbour Bridge, Shark Island, Manly and so on. And now I'm feeling really weak. Perhaps the battery in her super-sensitive camera was drained by her inane yapping. The tour is good and the weather is beautiful, it has to be said. I snap out of my daydream when the recorded monologue that has been prattling on over the PA system tells us that some house or other on the harbour has been sold for $19 million. Everyone is looking at some building with a giant glass pyramid on top of it. I'm tempted to tell our African Queen to buy the thing if she's as rich as she is subtly trying to tell us that she is. That would surely shut her up.

Apparently Mark Twain described Sydney Harbour as "the darling of Sydney and the wonder of the world". The tour narrative tells us about its history but I'm too engrossed to pay attention, take notes and enjoy the sights all at the same time.

According to *Live&Work in Australia* – from which I've learned of the Twain quote above – Captain James Cook sailed into Botany Bay, just south of Sydney, in the *Endeavour* in 1770. In May 1787 the first fleet of 1,044 people – 759 of which were convicts and 191 were women – set sail from Portsmouth and "arrived in Australia eight months later". So unimpressed were they with the windy and barren Botany Bay that they moved north and arrived at Port Jackson some six days later.

It wasn't all plain sailing, if you will, and crops failed here while the badly needed supply ships "failed to arrive". The colony did survive though and eventually, under the watchful gaze of the "Father of Australia" Governor Lachlan Macquarie who replaced Captain Arthur Phillip, progress was made. In the meantime, free settlers had

49

also began arriving and from 1831 to 1850 "more than 200,000 Government-assisted migrants streamed into the colony to begin a new life as far away as possible from the urban nightmare of Victorian Britain". And then during the 1850s a gold rush brought a fresh influx of settlers and this continued until the end of the 19th Century. By 1925, the area around Sydney had a population greater than one million people, according to McMullen Seal.

Sydney's CBD hosts a plethora of international businesses' (Australian) headquarters in the city. Darling Harbour contains the Sydney Aquarium, Chinese Gardens, the National Maritime Museum and it's all linked to the CBD by monorail.

I take back my SD card and capture some snaps of my own on the way back in. And when the ferry docks, we go our separate ways. My way is to the very swish Cruise Bar directly opposite the opera house. I'm worried that Maj, who I think is half-expecting me to invite him with me, is going to follow. He's a nice-enough guy but he doesn't really talk so it's all a bit weird in that there'd be no point in having a beer. But thankfully he doesn't follow. It's not that he doesn't want to. It's because he can't. I look back and stifle a laugh as I see him struggling to break free from the ropes that I've used to tightly bind him to a fence.

The guests from the reception of a wedding at Cruise Bar revel with well heeled financial whizz-kids, whose tanned, smiling and relaxed faces do not give any indication that Australia is in financial meltdown. Because unlike the rest of the world, it's not. At least not to the same degree.

Ah, denial...isn't it wonderful?

Although, there still does appear to be, there must be, both casual and professional work on offer here in NSW. Especially in the financial sector. However, anyone looking for work here in Australia must have a Tax File Number (TFN), which can be obtained from all Centrelink or tax offices and can take up to six weeks to be issued from the date of application. However, applicants with valid visas can apply online – even before entering the country. McMullen Seal states that both Queensland and ACT show growth and optimism in terms of the financial and professional and IT sectors, while Victoria show "continued growth in the government and social infrastructure sector, followed by the consumer, IT and telecommunications sectors". Meanwhile, Western Australia "shows the largest employee growth spread over the three sectors of industry, consumer services, and government and social infrastructure".

Of course, it being Friday evening, the bar is bustling. The Opera House opposite is bathed in a cloak of pale lavender and the eyes (windows) of the numerous hotels and banks encircling the harbour seem to spy jealously at us from above. I stay here for four beers and catch up on some journaling, all the while watching *them* come and go as various hues of natural blue descend on the harbour. I'm drinking Amber Ale, which, at $7.30 per schooner, is not cheap but for a bar like this in a location such as the harbour, it's probably about right. I can't really see much of the harbour now, compared to earlier on the cruise when we had little shade from the low sun shining on the broad harbour.

According to my *Lonely Planet* guide, the gateway to Sydney Harbour is made up of North Head and South Head. "Watson's Bay nestles on South Head's harbour side, fostering a salty cottage atmosphere" – whatever that means. However, the harbour beaches are "generally sheltered, calm coves with little of the frenzied foam of the ocean beaches". On the south shore is Camp Cove, which is apparently "a photogenic swimming beach where Arthur Phillip first landed" and Shark Bay. Meanwhile, the guide recommends checking out Manly Cove, Reef Beach, Clontarf Beach, Chinaman's Beach (which I suspect would surely be renamed by now if it were situated in most other countries worth visiting) and Balmoral Beach. The Sydney Harbour National Park "protects scattered pockets of harbour side bush land with magical walking tracks, lookouts, Aboriginal engravings and historic sites". Five harbour islands are also part of the park and these are namely Clark Island off Darling Point; Shark Island off Rose Bay; Rodd Island in Iron Cove, Goat Island and "the small fortified Fort Denison off Mrs Macquarie's Point".

51

And unfortunately, I didn't have the time to explore them. In fact, I don't have enough time to check out any of the city's beaches or its suburbs. Not Bondi, Coogee, Watson's, not Manly – nor have I visited Mosman. I've been told on numerous occasions that Bondi is, amongst other things, "a kip" and "a shithole" and that I can expect to see lots of Irish GAA jersey-wearing youth walking about the place, drunk. I didn't sign up for that so they're welcome to it, though on my next visit down here I'll surely pay a visit. Of course I'll probably be wearing my Waterford Hurling jersey; wouldn't like to see my county under-represented now, would I?

I'll have to make sure I bring a slab of Dutch Gold as well. Somebody must fly the flag, after all.

The Opera House was designed by Maj's fellow countryman, Danish architect Jørn Utzon, and according to *Lonely Planet*, was inspired by snails, orange segments, palm fronds and Mayan temples. It's been "poetically linked to a 'nun's scrum' (I don't even want to know what that is) and the sexual congress of turtles" no less. It's "architecturally orgasmic from any angle" (only if you insist) and the 67-metre high roof includes 27,230 tonnes of Swedish tiles or 1,056,000 of them if you prefer. The Opera House comprises "four main auditoriums for dance, concerts and theatre events, plus the left-of-centre Studio for emerging artists". And get this; it takes a staggering 2,400 events annually – costing $40 million – to keep the 10,500 pipes piping. I genuinely don't get all the overtly sexual references though. It must be the weather; I imagine that it's lambing season down here all the frickin' time!

The Sydney Harbour Bridge, known as The Old Coat Hanger by locals, links the CBD with the North Sydney business district. It's a bridge that's used, so you can expect to see people climbing it, rollerblading on it and sailing under it. It cost $20 million to complete in 1932 and it took the city sixty years to pay it off. Apparently, the best way to do the bridge is on foot, using the staircases from both shores and the BridgeClimb can cost up to $300 so that means I have Buckley's chance (none!) of doing it.

Apparently Crocodile Dundee himself, Paul Hogan, used to work on the bridge as a rigger.

I'm tired so I get a taxi back up Pitt St. and jump out a couple of blocks away from my hostel because I want to get something to eat. I wander down Chinatown and feel like a Giant amongst men, and women. It seems that every swish towering apartment building on Pitt St., George's St. and around has spewed out its residents tonight. I suspect that most of this youngish group are being funded from afar by mother and father.

I order spare ribs, steamed rice and a coke at this outdoor restaurant – one of countless that's separated by a couple of feet of natural walkway. It comes to $20 – and that's not the cheapest.

I pop into Maloney's Hotel on my way back to the hostel. I'm stopped by the door staff on the way in, however. A small but squat bouncer allows me in but not until he runs his hand-held metal detector up and down my arms and legs. It's the first time this has happened to me here since leaving the airport in Melbourne. I order a pint of Golden Ale and sit outside at a table, smoking a cigarette. Six police officers with a sniffer dog rush in the door and, my curiosity getting the better of me, I follow immediately. The dog is sniffing at all the bags there but they don't seem to find anything of interest. They better not come near my bag because the smell – of week-old, unrefrigerated, bacteria infested pork sausages and rashers (bacon) that I've smuggled over from Ireland – will lead to me getting arrested.

Okay, relax, Border(line) Patrollers, it's all a big feckin' joke.

I take my *Sydney Morning Herald* out of the bag and learn that "the cost of lost productivity was estimated in the millions yesterday" because of "Wednesday's freak dust storm". In Sydney, over 100 street sweepers were sent out with twenty tipper trucks to help with the clean up, it emerges. Water Minister, Phil Costa, in the article says that "dust can cause respiratory problems and health implications for people with Asthma and breathing difficulties". Emergency services received 890 calls for help – most of these dealing with the 323 trees blown over in the storm, with another 105 trees threatening property.

Interesting, it may be. But it's not as interesting as my pit on Pitt St.

DAY EIGHT

Saturday, and some crazy tour guide has appeared in the Oz Experience office on George's St. and I'm tired so I don't know if I can trust what I'm seeing or not. It's 7.30am, and he's clad in green shorts and fleece with brown boots. He (unselfconsciously) shouts out through a pair of huge, jutting false teeth that seem to have burst out through his lips. *Too many teeth* – easily big enough to allow him to eat an apple through a tennis racket or a nun's arse through a hedge – I note. Astonishingly, the choppers are greenish in colour; it seems like an awful lot of trouble to go to in order to ensure colour co-ordination with his uniform. He's got dark, greasy tufts of coarse hair sticking out from under his baseball cap. And, he's very crazy. It's a surreal experience.

It turns out that this Nut is to be our tour guide, of course. When we are about to leave he leans into the bus and tells us that his name is Knackers (apparently, all of the guides get nicknames to protect their real identities). Suddenly, he whips out the teeth and removes his baseball cap to reveal hair that is similar in colour but is better kept. The giggling, staring and nudging erupt into laughter.

Our day-long trip to the Blue Mountains has begun.

Funnily enough, the word "Knackers" – at home in Ireland – is used as a derogatory (plural) term for members of the Travelling community and it is also used as a colloquial slang term for what some people might call "Scumbags". But to be more precise, the word "Knacker" actually refers a horse that's about to be destroyed or put down. The similarity with the horse ends, however, as soon as Knackers removes his teeth. He seems like a decent chap and he's good at what he does, keeping us informed regarding what's what along the way. I could be wrong but I suspect that here, the word Knackers refers to testicles, probably banging together. Ouch, the thought alone.

The red dust has reappeared overnight it seems and various people, mainly Asians, can be seen walking and cycling about the place sporting face masks. I suffer a low grade of manageable Asthma and I'm also a bit of a smoker (I know, I know!) but personally, I think it a gross overreaction because the only thing of note really is a thin red film on the passing cars. Also, when heading down George's St. earlier that morning I noticed a reddish fog on the horizon but sure that could have been from my drink-induced red eye.

Anyway, Knackers takes us in around the Olympic Village and he boasts pompously of his country's athletic prowess much to the annoyance of an English bloke who good-naturedly heckles him.

Whatever Knackers, just take us up the fucking mountain.

It turns out that today is the 50th Anniversary of the Blue Mountains (well, the anniversary of it being a national park or something) National Park. I bet he says this to all the tourists. Our first stop, after breakfasting at various pies shops, cafes and fruit shops at the base there, is designed to afford us the opportunity to take pictures of Kangaroos. And they are cute in fairness but I get bored so I start winding up some of the girls from the bus.

There's a gaggle of Dutch girls in our group and no matter what section of walk we arrive at, they're late. The laughter they bring is endearing at first, and then it becomes annoying. I have not a clue about the Dutch language but they laugh at everything. I mean, EVERYTHING!

They don't seem to be smokers but I'd love some of those magic cookies obviously hidden in their bags. They would want to keep their wits about them; it's not been two months since a 19-year-old British backpacker by the name of Jamie Neale went missing and was lucky to survive for eleven days in appalling conditions in the harsh Blue Mountains bushland. The story goes that Jamie checked into a Katoomba youth hostel in the mountains on July 2nd and was last seen the following morning in an area known as Ruined Castle (the Aussies are not very imaginative when it comes to place and animal names).

A huge search ensued for Jamie's whereabouts thereafter.

Jamie's dad, Richard Cass, came to the rescue. Well, he came to Sydney to help look for his son and later found himself assuring the media that his son's

disappearance was not a mere publicity stunt. According to an article by Adam Walters and Tim Vollmer in the *Daily Telegraph* dated July 15th, Mr Cass "said Jamie had survived by eating seeds, leaves and berries as he moved through the inhospitable terrain, sleeping rough under logs and trees". The Telegraph is a reputed British broadsheet but the quotes are classic tabloid fodder.

In an interview from the story, Mr Cass said: "...'He put us through so much – I always knew he was tough – he could have walked to the South Pole and back in his underpants – I said to his mother, *Give up, he's dead, they would have found him by now otherwise*'..."

To the South Pole in an underpants and back? Memo to self: there's a book in that.

Mr Cass continued: "...'He has cost your country millions, he has practically broken the heart of his mother and grandmother, and me, of course'..."

But he was found days later.

And now, here's the science bit. In a piece written by Holly Byrnes, which appeared on the *news.com.au* website ("news website of the year", apparently) on the same date, July 25th 2009; it's claimed that "now Jamie Neale has been abandoned by his father, who has rushed home to London to be the first to sell his son's amazing tale of survival to the British Press". This apparently happened not twenty four hours after his recently hypothermic and exhausted son was released from hospital. It's "understood" that the dad was basically miffed when he could not get his hands on a fifty per cent share of "Neale's deal with Channel 9's *60 Minutes* programme".

"Neale had refused his father's plea to split the $100,000 he was paid for the story, while honouring his pledge to donate proceeds from the deal to the emergency services that helped him."

In a related story on the site, Jamie said that the deal included a proviso for $100,000 of local advertising to inform the public about a "safety beacons scheme" for the emergency services concerned and that this was "one of the major reasons I agreed to do the interview" with Channel 9.

56

Knackers hands out these wigs and gets us to re-enact an Aboriginal Creation story about the Three Sisters – three rock formations that stand at over 900 metres in height and dominate the Jamison Valley below. The story goes (roughly) as follows. Three sisters named Meehni, Wimlah and Gunnedoo are members of the Katoomba tribe within the Gundungurra Nation. Their dad was this awesome witch doctor and the girls were warned not to go to the sprawling Jamison Valley because this horrible Bunyip lived there. Of course, the girls' curiosity got the better of them and they peered down into the abyss, dislodging some rocks and awakening said Bunyip. He got mad and climbed up to eat the poor girls but luckily, dad was on-hand with his magic stick and turned the girls into pillars of rock. And then the Bunyip became madder still, turning on dad who promptly changed himself into a lyrebird and flew away. However, he lost his magic wand in the heel of the hunt and therefore, both he and his daughters remained in their altered states. Rumour has it that if you pop down into the valley and listen carefully, you might see a lyrebird searching frantically for his magic stick.

Of course I've been picked to play one of the sisters and the audience is made to sit; cross-legged, open-mouthed and wide-of-eye, as Knackers tells the story through his false teeth. Hmmm, the wig is bloody hot and, it's a blond mullet. I suspect that I look like John Farnham. The others just stare at me as if I'm mad when I start searching frantically for the magic stick that will return me once again to a Man of Stone.

Alright, alright, it's not that funny!

It seems to me that we can learn much about the Aboriginal way of life; the psyche and so on, through their Art – through their storytelling and painting. A bit of a dig around later and I learn – from John Gunther's excellent book, *Inside Australia and New Zealand*, which was completed and revised by William Forbis – that "Art seems to have come so naturally to the Aborigines that they had no need to invent a word for it, though they have words for the individual acts of painting, carving, singing and dancing". He says that most Aboriginal men can paint, carve and incise, while of course some are better than others. The motivation for such work is not purely the

57

artistic yearnings of the artist, but the need to communicate, he says. "It teaches the laws of the tribe, explains creation, endows weapons with visible potency, keeps alive religious beliefs." Objects both sacred and secret including "churungas, oval-shaped slabs of painted wood or stone contain such powerful symbolic messages among their abstract dots, meanders, spirals and animal tracks that in some tribes women who catch a glimpse of them are put to death".

Arguments and of course the facts related to Aboriginal Art are expanded upon in *Aboriginal Culture Today*, edited by Anna Rutherford. For example, in an editorial by J.V.S. and M. Ruth Megaw entitled, *The Dreamers Awake: Contemporary Australian Aboriginal Art*, paintings are generally a "formalised mapping of a particular geographical location associated with a specific mythological happening or individual". The word used for paintings, *tjukurrpa*, "denotes at one and the same time 'story' and the Dreamtime". It goes on to say that the rights to the stories depends on gender, descents, age, initiation and status. "Only those with rights in them may reproduce them or, as is sometimes the case, authorise their reproduction by others."

Prior to the arrival of Europeans, Aboriginal Art told a story of a complicated network of social relationships, according to the editorial by Messers Megaw. It was ceremonial in nature, and related to connections with land and mythological origins, while it was not made for outsiders and had no monetary value.

According to whom you believe, Aboriginals, Indigenous Australians – humans – arrived in Australia between 40,000 and 60,000 years ago. Some estimates go back to 125,000 years ago.

The Blue Mountains is a beautiful, peaceful place. We spend our time posing for pictures and the like and then we're taken up to a tourist centre at the top on "the steepest train in the world", as Knackers keeps telling us. I'm first in the gift shop, which is unusual. Today will be no different; apart from the purchase of a few postcards, these places never make much money out of me. Oh, I also buy a cappuccino. I am disappointed at not getting a slice of Blue Mountain Birthday cake with it though – if there is such as thing. I wouldn't be surprised if it was eucalyptus flavoured, the miserable bastards.

On the way back to Sydney, Knackers asks me to pick out a movie from a stack of DVDs he hands me in a leather pouch. I opt for *Liar Liar* starring Jim Carey. But I don't enjoy it as much as I did when I saw it all those years before. On that occasion, I was in my mother's house with my friend, Leonard. It was a Sunday evening and of course, we had been to the pub. My sister, Liz, came down from upstairs because she couldn't sleep with all the laughing coming from down below.

I put my lack of enthusiasm down to the fact that Jim Carey has starred in better movies since then, my favourite being the rather hilarious *Me, Myself and Irene*.

I buy a hooded top that is on sale for $40 in a Mall back on Pitt St. And when I go back to the hostel I take my bags from storage and go to another room...again! However, this room, on the 17th floor, is a bombsite I tells ya; a bombsite. Can you even use analogies like this anymore? I mean, could I be arrested for using that word to describe a messy room? Really? I know some folk are hyper-vigilant in terms of political correctness and get uptight about such things. However, there tends to be a bit too much pussy-footing around people like that these days so...feck 'em! Eh, I do come from Ireland you know? We've had to deal with more brutal terrorism than most, for longer than most. I know what I mean and I don't mean, and so will lots of people I'd wager. And that will have to do I'm afraid.

Anyway, rant over. Back to Sydney.

Some girl, Kate from the UK, comes into the room. I'm standing there, pre-shower, in just a towel and she doesn't bat an eyelid. You get used to this kind of thing when you are staying in dorms with strangers. She tells me, a bit too unselfconsciously really, that she's "living" in the room and I bite my lip before I can ask her if she is sharing the room with a nest of rats. Her clothes are scattered everywhere and the bathroom door is broken. Inside, the shower is dirty. Shortly before this a Japanese dude, Jay, came into the room. He's fresh off the plane and is as clearly as apprehensive about his year out in Aussie as a Groom waiting at an altar. I made an effort to talk to him despite his broken English but Kate just blanked him, which is kind of rude if you ask me. He got into bed fully clothed and despite Kate's natter and the fluorescent lights that give everything an ugly, stark look, he passed out immediately. Or he at least pretended to. A French couple are sitting on the bottom of one of three bunk beds there, playing cards and whispering from behind a sarong and a towel they have erected as a partial screen.

Kate has a quick shower and change of clothes before leaving again, and I can't help but noticing her low cut top revealing the faded rose on her curved breast. And if mine ear doth not deceive me I'm sure 'It', meaning the conjoining of bodies here, hath more-or-less been offered to me on a plate for later on. Now, there's no Halo over my head or anything but there's nothing of interest to me in this room and that's the truth.

An Austrian girl, Noelle, enters. She turns out to be a Ski-Instructor who has been working in Victoria, and is intent on enjoying her last few days in the country before returning home again. I ask my roomies if they would like to join me for a drink.

"Vhere?" Noelle asks me immediately.

"Just across the road in Maloney's Hotel," I answer.

I explain that I'm going down to the lobby to use the internet and that I'll be there for about twenty minutes. I leave the room and I don't know how she does it but I swear to you that Noelle is sitting at a computer in the lobby before I get there. I don't remember seeing her in the lift and an Olympic sprinter couldn't have got down the stairs in the time concerned. Maybe she took the black slope! It is almost midnight. And she's trying to Skype her mother or something but the computers crash. Alan, at reception, tells her that he will give her more time on her Global Gossip card when the computers are reset.

So by the time she's done my erstwhile Dutch dorm mates have arrived in the lobby and ask me to go out with them. However, their night out is sure to be a wild one and the want for a drink is nearly gone off of me. Also, I have to be up at 6am for my tour to Cairns, so I decline. An English girl with them, Zoe, tells me she loves my accent. I realise that I probably sound like a right Ham bone here – this is where you go, *No, no...not at all* – but this is how the events are transpiring.

The bouncer at Maloney's thinks that I may have had enough to drink because my face is red. At an Irish bar? Has he actually ever met an Irish person who's drinking every day, in a sunny clime? I wonder. Anyway, that's crap. If I had enough, I'd hardly be wanting more now, would I? Hmmm. He lets me in eventually, and by the time we're actually drinking it's almost one o'clock. Noelle has three schooners to my four pints and she's well on. There's the clichéd blues rock band, an old woman sitting there talking to herself and the bored bar staff. The place is straight out of a Tom Waits song, the night's last chance saloon. I'm tempted to ask the band if they know anything from Waits's albums, *Closing Time* or *The Heart of Saturday Night*.

We go back and then I go online again. Noelle is waiting nearby. She slumbers off and when I go back to the room, she has crashed out.

That'll be the lack of oxygen at this altitude.

4. Surf's up...apparently

DAY NINE

It's too hot to sleep and I wake tired, and thirstier than an undiagnosed Diabetic. I perch myself on the edge of the top bunk and wonder how I'm going to get down. Alas, Kate below has returned. I carefully place my foot on the edge of her bed to buffer my journey downwards. In one quick manoeuvre I'm down and in one piece much to my surprise. Almost every inch of floor is covered in clothes at this stage and I woozily try to pick my way around the upturned plugs that Kate has strategically placed as a trap. I'm smothering numerous yelps in swallows as I plonk my feet on the plug pins from the hair straighteners and other implements of torture. Afraid that I'll wake someone, I manage – with much trepidation – to get dressed and make my way out of the door.

I bid Alan at Reception farewell, and I notice that he's still wearing his baseball hat back-to-front, the poor chap. And for the second day in a row I'm padding my way down Pitt St. to the Oz Experience office. I'm in desperate need of sustenance. I'm not a fan of Sydney, from the few bits that I've seen – Melbourne being more my speed. However, I'm wondering what the draw is for so many. *Live&Work in Australia* quotes the Australian Bureau of Statistics (ABS) predicting that by 2051, "Sydney will have a population of 5.6 million", which, if accurate, would make New South Wales the most densely populated state in Australia. A "current ABS study concluded that there were 4,000 people jammed into every square kilometre". This isn't just co-incidental, obviously, nor is it simply just related to the nightlife, the beach and the suburbs. The Sydney workforce – with its prosperous economy – "enjoys the highest median household income" ($46, 463) of any of the country's cities.

I secure a cappuccino and hot sausage roll from this 24/7 type effort across the road from the Oz Experience office. The tour guide is checking off our names as we embark and when I answer "Ciaran Murphy" solemnly, he says: "No proizes fu' guessing where yo're frum then mate."

Jesus, banter...do I have to?

The Adventure Tours Australia bus, which is owned by the Oz Experience company, is basically like one of those you would see in an airport that shunts people from aircraft to terminal. And I'm pissed off because of the lie I was told at the Peter Pan Adventure Tours office in Melbourne about it being (almost) sold out.

Our guide, Beaver (don't ask), later tells me that this is commonplace and that he will report the matter to his boss who will not, he assure me, be one bit happy. (Yeah, right!). On board is a Canadian woman, Lynne, who's travelling alone; Marianne and Patricia, a mother and daughter from Switzerland; Lee and Hannah (travelling separately) from England and German friends, Anya and Alexandra.

And there's me, the moodiest Irishman in New South Wales this morning, I'd wager. Eight people out of about twenty one that I was promised are on this bus. Maybe all the others pulled out when the saw the bus, which actually belongs in an airport, ferrying fat, pale tourists from aircraft to terminals. I must be on the wrong bus. Where's the Adonis Express? We even have a trailer for our bags. Not what I was expecting. Hannah and Lee are talking excitedly and loudly about this, that and the other. About nothing really. Two guys were supposed to turn up but they are a No-Show. Beaver takes us around the block rather than wait for them outside the office. Then he gets a phone call telling him that the pair thought the bus was leaving at 10am or something. Erm, okay then. Did these people not think to, oh, I don't know, check their tickets or something.

This pair, it turns out, will take an overnight bus in the evening and meet us in Byron Bay in a couple of days. Beaver makes us listen to some awful Aussie folk music as we leave Sydney on a bright and clear Sunday morning, conditions alien to my poor, sleep-depraved, alcohol-soaked brain. Eucalyptus trees, interspersed by sections of rock face, dominate my peripheral vision and I am mindlessly lost in it.

"Are you I-rash – do you speak with an I-rash accent?" asks Hannah blandly. "Na, I don't" I snap immediately. "What do you think?" I'm surprised at my own reaction.

Strewth, I'm wondering. *Has the spirit of Alf Stewart* – the grumpy old sod from Aussie soap opera *Home and Away* – *actually invaded my body?* I'm being a temperamental git. But I don't finish there. Beaver, Lee and Hannah are having a loud conversation at the front of the bus and the rest of us are chilling and basically trying to get some sleep or pretending to be asleep already. The music has changed to heavy rock now and because the trio are talking, Beaver has turned up the volume. I'm getting frustrated: the talking I can just about tolerate but not this. I ask Beaver to turn it down and he fiddles around with the volume but it's just as loud.

I can stands no more.

I jump out of my seat and walk up towards the front.

"Listen, I don't want to get off on the wrong foot with you but half the bus is asleep and I asked you to turn it down," I tell him. "Aw, coaaa'se (course) moyte – I caaan' (can't) hear it properly frum up he'eee'," he replies.

I sit and I calm down. When we stop at a roadside cafe for breakfast somewhere between Sydney and Maitland and we're getting off the bus, I shake Beaver's hand and I say, "No hard feelings mate." He's gracious about it and tells me to let him know if "these thengs hippen" or else he won't know about them.

We get talking and it turns out that Beaver, 37, is a real asset to the company. A character and a free spirit, he's been working with Oz Experience for two years. We stop in Kempsey, a forgettable place, for lunch and afterwards on the bus north I sit next to him at the front while most of the others are asleep. I sip from a can of Victoria Bitter (VB for short) – one of eight I've bought at lunchtime – as he tells me that he's still in love with his ex-girlfriend who works in Airlie Beach. He says that she wants to get back together but that he won't have it; mainly *he* says, because she's got a five-year-old son and he doesn't want the youngster to get used to his presence as Beaver will be on the road most of the time.

Beaver tells me that he has slept with over 300 women (Aha!) in his years and that he lives life according to his rules. "I don' let staff get to moy (me)," he explains. I can't help but think that 300 conveniently sounds like a nice round number. With a scorecard like that, it's little wonder that he doesn't want a relationship then.

"Mos' people aaa' conditioned ta get married, heve kids, stay in the same job foreva' and make maney for the Gavamint (Government)...that's not for moooi."

We stop off in Coff's Harbour and cop the first of the "big staff" we'll see. So here I am, taking photographs of a Giant Banana in Russell Crowe's back yard. Well, close enough to it at any rate. It's very strange but we'll get used to seeing Giant prawns, apples and the like. Apparently, Gladiator himself invests a lot of money in sports facilities at "Coff's Ha'baaa'", fair play to him. "The Gavamint won' do it," says Beaver. "So this is wheee' Russell gows out, gets inta foights an' throws his phone at payple," he jokes. "Bu-cha' hef to toyke the good with the baaad."

We arrive at Arrawara Beach and tonight we are staying at Mojo Surf School, for lessons at the *Spot X* surf camp or whatever it's called in the morning. It's stunning here and very quiet, little wonder that holiday homes and caravans fill up the area next to the beautiful beach really.

The surf lolls gently against the shore and well-to-do Aussies say their hellos as they let you pass first on the jetty leading down to the beach. The surf camp itself comprises drop-out surfers and backpackers who work for their board (pun intended), access to surf equipment and the best surf spots. I cringe because some of them have obviously understood Alex Garland's wonderful but worn out work of fiction, *The Beach*, to be the Bible itself and want to follow it to the letter. There's plenty of dreadlocks, boardies (surfing shorts) and *tatts* – that's tattoos, sorry to disappoint – on the go.

We get settled in and then eat from a buffet comprising chilli, pizza, salads, pasta and so on.and it's all good. Our group sits around a table in the outside dining area as the light leaves the sky, the cackle of the nearby campfire fades and the temperature drops. The workers do the wash up and other chores before drifting off to a communal area to play pool and watch a movie. Apart from our chats and laughs about everything from sport, politics and horror movies to computers and music, there is silence.

At the end of night, it's just Beaver and yours truly. We have only had three tins of VB each and I'm listening to his tales of life on tour – pretending to be more impressed than I actually am. Then, tiredness besets us and it's time to crash. I pull up my hood and wander around looking for my billet in the dark, as the cold evening air wraps itself around my bare legs, my hands, my face. I don't want to wake Hannah and Lee as I stumble into the dorm that I'm sharing with them. So I carefully remove the cymbals from my knees, the kazoo from my mouth and the bass drum from my back. It's a long and narrow room, a sort of comfortable prefab. In the darkness, I stumble straight into a table – it's just about crotch high so it's *O* to the motherfucking *U-C-H*. I brush my teeth and fall into bed, exhausted.

And it's not even 9pm.

DAY TEN

I get up about six-ish and have a breakfast of one large sausage and you're only allowed one. There's also beans, some hard boiled eggs and fruit. Shortly afterwards, we head into a shed for the first part of our surf lesson. Our Instructor, Paul, is a weather beaten local who tells us that he has been surfing since he was six. He's middle aged, and looks easily over fifty yet he dresses like he's twenty two. Today he's wearing trainers, tee shirt, a hoodie and Gstar jeans. *Like, radical duuuuude.* He's an affable chap and kind of, off-the-wall.

Paul mumbles along for the next thirty minutes or so and kind of speaks in metaphor, albeit in earthy tones so it all makes sense. His assistant today is Ben, a British ex-pat with grungy peroxide hair who is in his early twenties I guess. Last night Ben told Beaver that his grazed face was metered out by a pavement after one too many beers.

"Weee' yu lovin' someone yu shouldn' hev been lovin'?" Paul asks him on his arrival this morning. But Ben's party line is rolled out again. Ben looks strange today

– his face is smothered in a dramatic oily beige substance. It kind of looks like Germolene ointment, as layered on by a four-year-old girl with a trowel who's insisting on making Daddy look beautiful. When I ask him, he tells me that it is "zinc, because we (meaning the instructors) will be standing around in the surf most of the time". *Wise choice so,* I note, *if he doesn't want to add Elephantitous of the face, or at least skin cancer, to his list of facial woes.* With the warpaint, he looks like a Terrahawk from that 1960s puppet animation show.

So after a brief lesson on the fine white sand, Paul lets us loose on the Arrawara waves. They're gentle enough at first but then the wind picks up and it's carnage. However, it's devastation of the extremely fun variety. At first, I can get to my knees but alas, no further: the last time I went surfing; exactly three years ago in Tramore in Co. Waterford with my friend Ruth and some others, I couldn't even do that. I had, some months prior to this, underwent keyhole surgery in London for two slipped disks in my lumbar vertebrae. At that time I was still in recovery, which basically consisted of physiotherapeutic exercises and swimming. Today, however, my back is as good as it will probably get, which is pretty damn good. (*Touch wood* – taps forehead!).

As a matter of fact I was supposed to 'Do' Australia and New Zealand three years ago with my friend Alan but couldn't, my back being so bad that I could barely walk. I've never experienced pain like it, although anyone reading this that has given birth is allowed to metaphorically throw a freshly filled nappy at me...now.

Go!

I'm here all week!

Funnily enough, I really don't get up properly on the surfboard until Paul stands behind me in the surf. What is funny (and by this I mean "peculiar" or "weird") about it is that he earlier told us that he can get everyone standing, once he is behind them. And he does, at least with me. It's not like he does anything special; he just pushes the back of the board and shouts words of encouragement. Without doubt, some of his class – and all of his experience – in the activity, sport or whatever, just rubs off.

Anyway, standing up is not the big problem now. Remaining on the board for just a matter of seconds so I can claim to have surfed even a small bit, is. Crash! Down I come, time and time again. It's in stark contrast to what Paul had told us earlier on the beach. He told me, along with some others as we practised the transitory move from lying to standing, that I'm a "natural surfer". Others were "goofies", it emerged. However, I must come clean here and explain to those of you not down with the kids enough to know that the "natural surfer" tagline belies the fact that I naturally stand with my left foot to the fore of the board, while goofies put their right foot forward.

We're crashing about in the water like plastic soft drinks bottles that are bobbing up and down in the wake of a liner. I feel like a two-year-old being dragged to the naughty step by a firm parent following some misdemeanour, such is the chance of my forcing the surf's course to bend to my will. Some of them (albeit the younger, smaller and leaner ones) get to grips with the waves after a while. After some time we leave the waves reluctantly – some more so than others it has to be said – and we drag our boards across the fine, white, scorching, hot sand to the sheds. I try to be macho and put one of the girl's boards under one arm and my own under the other. But I have to drop them on two occasions during the walk to the storage shed, a few hundred metres away.

We shower and get our bags from a common room. Except when I look for my digital camera in my backpack, I can't find it. I panic, and brief paranoid scenarios rush through my head. But surely nobody here would steal it? It doesn't feel right. I scour my bags and then the dorm I had slept in, which has since been cleaned. There is neither sign of the camera nor the box it came in (the USB cable, recharger etc are in this box). Beaver calls management and he is not happy about it, while I am naturally so inclined.

"It would be unusual fo' someone not usin' the room ta come in heee'," the manager tells me. "But not impossible," I snap in reply to her, with too much haste really.

I feel like a right idiot when I find the camera in a little zip pocket in the bag (and rightly so I hear you say), while Beaver finds the box in the trailer. This must have fallen out during manoeuvres. I feel terrible. I came just short of blaming someone for taking it. And then I do a cowardly thing. "Quick, lets leg it," I tell Beaver.

"Hang on, I've forgotten my towel," I yell at Beaver from my seat near the back of the bus. He stops and I run into the showering/changing area there, where I left my towel and Speedos (the, er, cool modern ones), hanging on the volleyball net, soaking up the hot morning rays. I run back and take my seat again. Embarrassed, I keep looking out of the window because I know that he will be trying to make eye contact through his rear view mirror. But when I think it's safe and look up to the front a couple of minutes later, he's staring, still shaking his head and smiling. He's like some hotshot sniper in a war movie: he knows that he has me. "Blaaady Oirish," he says. And in this instance, he's right. I sink into my seat and keep my head down for some time.

We arrive at Byron Bay in the mid-afternoon. And it's here that we meet Bobby and Tony, the two twenty-something Londoners who missed our departure from Sydney two days previously. It turns out that the chaps have been travelling in Borneo, Hong Kong and Thailand.

Hannah, Lee, myself and German girl, Daniele are bunked up in a dorm. There's a common area including a bathroom, with a communal sitting and dining area. And in the other room are the likely London lads, who explain how they managed to miss the bus. It turns out that they were out boozing and ended up at a party with some Swedish girls (I think) and got blindsided by love. Or more likely, lust. Or perhaps mace. When they got back to their hostel after 6am, they decided to have forty winks, which apparently turned into 4,000 or so flutters of their eyelid during their REM sleep – or rather, just one big wink that took over three hours to complete.

Outside, the place is full of hippies, well-to-do drop outs and a whole array of tourists. I go looking for some tee shirts, shorts and flip flops (I can't bear to ask to see the female store assistant's *thongs*, in case the whole of Aussie is trying to catch me out – I imagine over twenty two million people laughing in unison when I ask for them.). But I do get a pair of Havianas for $14, one of the more popular brands used in the country. And that's a good bargain, although it's one of the few I can seem to

69

find in Byron Bay. Tee shirts for over $80 are not uncommon, while shorts are even more expensive. I told Beaver that I would wait until I got here to buy the relevant apparel, ignoring his advice like a stubborn goat. I thought that I'd be better off buying the clobber in trendy Byron and while the stuff here is cool, it's hotly priced.

On the beach at dusk, shortly after 6pm, a guy in his 20s is meditating. It looks like a cross between Tai Chi and some God Awful free dance or whatever they call it.

Nearby, his hippy mates (one would assume) play bongos and juggle fire. I don't get it – I really don't. Each to his or her own I suppose.

As planned, we meet at a place Beaver has called "Rails" (The Railway Friendly Bar), a chilled and unpretentious spot. It's 6.30pm. After dinner, a few drinks and laughs with Beaver and Co., we make our way down to Cheeky Monkeys – a cheesy meat market that does exactly what it says on the tin. We laugh at the ridiculous party games, which largely involve British tourists. The contestants always seem to end up with no clothes on and even when the guys win, the clever girls seem to escape from removing all their clothes. These chaps don't, however, and it looks like tonight's players are relishing it; covering their valuables with Large Sombrero hats (front and back).

Curiously, groups of – mainly girls it has to be said – play Jenga, an oldskool game involving wooden bricks. Players must take turns to add brick on top of brick to make a tower, while the loser is the one who knocks the lot over. Meanwhile, girls dance on tables and seating to incessant house music and techno. For some time, I forget that I am in the Antipodes and instead am transported to some eighteen-to-thirties cheesefest in Ibiza or Ayia napa. At one stage, when I go outside for a cigarette and I'm told to leave my drink inside with a thick Aussie accent, I remember where it is we are.

We all go break up into different groups and at one stage I end up arm wrestling this chubby (Yes, that's right: *Chubby!*) Canadian girl at the bar. The stake is a drink and although I win, I don't get the drink.

Hannah and I end up looking for a kebab. It's about 1.30am. We're told that the "kebab house" up the road is open and we can make out a red-light sign a few hundred metres away, but it's closed when we get there. We mosey across the road to some late night pizza joint.

Suddenly, Hannah wanders inside.

Or at least she tries to. "Thunk": she hits a glass panel. "Oh", she goes.

There are two large dudes with afros outside and I later find out that they are Samoans. Well, they seem stunned for a second but when they see that she's okay, they just start bursting their arses laughing. Everyone does. The place is closed, the guy working there tells me. "You don't say!" I reply.

We're on our way back to our abode when we're stopped by a guy – who I suspect is psychologically impaired to some degree. "Theee's a bak'ry up the roooyd," he tells us, over and over. But despite his awesome sales pitch, we decline. We're already half-baked. So it's back to the hostel and to bed.

The others are due to get up at some unspeakable hour to take shots of the sunrise over Byron Bay, known as *Cawanbah* by the Aboriginal people who came here to seek out a partner, swap stories or to ply their wares. We're close to eight hundred kilometres due north of Sydney and on the most easterly point of Oz. Well, those who head to Cape Byron in the morning will be. However, I decide that I'm going to be too tired for such shenanigans so before bed I give Hannah my camera to take some pictures for me. And hence, Helper Monkey is born. From here on in, she will cater to my every whim: think of a servant crossed with an assistant and you are almost there. Just joking girls, relax.

I am kind of joking but do relax.

DAY ELEVEN

Today we're leaving Byron for Rainbow Beach, where Beaver previously lived and worked for two years. Lee of the Beer, Hannah Helper Monkey and I pack up quickly rush down from our dorm to reception; hung over after lager, shots and of course, the dreaded goon. Shudder.

It's annoying here, at Byron (Bay) Backpackers, to be told that one must pay a $30 deposit: $20 for the key and $10 for the sheets. The tall and spectacled manager on reception is talking to a worker. "So yew jus' coll me and Oi'll come daaa'n and pud it in fo' ya mate," he tells the younger man. I'm waiting. And then I'm still waiting. It's the guy who slagged me off for being Irish not twenty hours previously.

Moments later, he turns around.

Check.

"Ye know, I hate walking into a room just as the older bloke tells the younger one that he'll put it in for him when he's called." He knows he's been had. *Check Mate.* He's good enough about it though. "Haha, fair play to ya Ciaran." So I drop the sheets in the basket there and he hands me the $10. But I forget the key and his look changes to shock, then suspicion.

"And the key?"

"Oh, sorry," I reply. I hand it to him and he looks extremely relieved, as he slips me a $20 note. Jesus, this place is seriously weird.

It really is time to leave.

We're on our way to Brisbane where we will pick up the "pre-honeymooners". Beaver reads from his manuscript: "What da fack aaa' pre-honeymoonaaa's? What da fack does that mean? Sex a week bifooo'e the wedding or somethin'?"

We stop somewhere in Surfer's Paradise to go zorbing, which is basically rolling down a big feckin' green hill in a big feckin' plastic inflatable ball. It costs us $33 and it hardly lasts that many seconds, so I'm looking at the guy running the show and I'm septic. No, I'm not: I'm a sceptic – wondering if Paul McCartney, Bono or *An Taoiseach,* the Irish Prime Minister himself, earns more than one dollar per second. Tony and I both decide to do the water-based zorb, if you will. There's another version on offer where the zorber is strapped into the inner bubble, which is housed in the centre of the bigger, outer bubble. I'm looking at Tony as if he's mad when he signs the disclaimer that I suspect absolves the operator of all responsibility, should we continue rolling out over the end of the complex, ramp up over the fence and float off towards infinity or beyond.

"This doesn't diminish his responsibility," explains Tony, who's a recently-qualified lawyer.

The guy in the stall is nodding in the affirmative.

"It just means you've been made aware of the risks," he goes on.

I'm not entirely convinced but I nod anyway. We change into our shorts and we're driven up to the top of the perfectly-kept hill on a driveway to the side. We're helped into the inner bubble, which has a good bit of water swilling around inside. Presumably, it's there to stop friction. The next thing I know we're rolling down the hill at what seems like an unstoppable pace and it's hard to see because water keeps getting splashed into my eyes and there are arms and legs everywhere. I'm kind of worried that I'll flatten poor little Tony and all I know is that I can't stop laughing. I'm surprised at how much. We're still laughing uncontrollably when the ball stops and the hatch is opened up. Our erstwhile driver is holding the thing steady and the water pours out onto the ground. It's a strange sensation, getting out of the ball. I'm imagining that it's kind of like being born.

And oh, the trip was worth every cent.

We stop and pick up Sarah and David in Brissy, and I avail of an opportunity to take probably the longest piss that has ever been recorded in the southern hemisphere. And once again I forget to check which way the water actually gets washed down the toilet. I'm sorry but it later turns out that any toilet or sink I try in the southern hemisphere actually goes down straight – not in a circular motion like it does in the movies. The pre-honeymooners are tall, very quiet and sombre-looking people. They don't talk much – neither to us nor to each other. At least for now. But I'm sure they'll get into the swing of things.

I'm laid out across *my* three seats, three seats up from the back. I'm sleeping, then I'm not, and then I am again, then...you get the picture. We stop in some God awful place or other for diesel. I'm bare of foot and the rough tarmac at the filling station is hurting my feet nearly as much as the heat is.

I come back out with an ice cream.

"Fuck me, there are some scary, scary truckers in there," I tell Bobby.

Scary indeed. I'm a big bloke but I would not get into a truck with this lot on a lonesome highway at night (or day) in Queensland or anywhere. Some of these look like the kinds you would see in a 1970s movie set in Butt Fuck America. There are guys hitting seven feet tall, weighing about 150 kilos with their hair slicked back. Others wear ancient baseball caps or those kinds of hats that mailmen wear in the US. Otherwise, they have mullet hairstyles, denim jackets and ketchup-stained wife-beaters from varying bygone eras. All seem to be covered in oily tans. And they're probably the nicest chaps in Aussie for all I know but hey, I live in my imagination for long periods. It's good for the writing anyway, is it not? Don't answer that.

We pass through Gympie (by name and by nature, you can just tell) and thankfully it doesn't take too long. Lonely Planet described it as a "peaceful little town", though Beaver tells us that at one stage Gympie was the murder Capital of Queensland. He said that he once had a passenger onboard who was a relative of the Mayor of the unfortunately named former gold mining town, which has a population of about 11,000 and is about eighty kilometres northwest of Noosa Head when one veers slightly away from the Fraser Coast. Basically, this busybody reported him to the first citizen for saying that the town belonged in a *Murder She Wrote* episode or whatever. Anyhow, the Mayor apparently then wrote a stinging letter of complaint to Beaver's boss at the Oz Experience. Apparently the town was trying to change its image. I can understand their point but if that was their aim, why didn't they just, oh, I don't know, STOP MURDERING PEOPLE!

Actually, while on the subject, crime patterns differ throughout the states and territories, according to McMullen Seal in *Live&Work in Australia*, which was published in 2008. In terms of actual territories, the Northern Territory, presumably for that year or those preceding, had the highest per capita rate of homicide and sexual assaults while it had the lowest rate of armed robberies. "Western Australia has the highest number of motor vehicle thefts and burglaries, but its rate of murder and attempted murder are at, or below, the national average". New South Wales had the highest number of armed robberies, mainly because it has the largest heroin-dependent population in Oz.

And the highest rate of kidnapping goes to Canberra, while the highest incidence of blackmail and robbery was recorded in South Australia.

We check into our Rainbow Beach hostel: we're staying at Fraser's Hostel. This is how Byron Bay might look without development, though I'm told this is changing and a major resort has been earmarked for the beachfront.

The bar at the hostel, however, closes at 10.30pm so we go get some beers and bring them to our room. Someone has also acquired some hash (aka cannabis resin). Lee is slagging me about my hat, telling me that it makes me look scary. So I feel it necessary to get at him about his hair band, "Alice band" or whatever in the name of God it's called. He's also wearing a lemon sleeveless hooded top of some description. Myself and Beaver slag off Lee for probably the seventy fourth time for looking like performer, H, from the outfit, *Steps*. Or is that *S Club 7*? I'd actually douse myself with petrol and beg for a light, as I hung precariously from our balcony with a wrestler jumping up and down on my fingers, were I to know the answer – let alone care if I was right or wrong about the answer – to that question. We go on to tell him that he is actually H, hiding out in Aussie to get away from the limelight because of a failed return to the pop world. We also call him a bitter old queen – but he takes it all in his stride and the teasing is in jest.

As I've said, the fun-times, like the coveted alcohol, have spilled over into our room and out onto our balcony. Until, at one stage, Bobby says, "Ye know the way England owns Ireland?"

Time stands still.

One, two, three – my blood is up.

I tell him about The Irish Question, beginning with, "WHAT DO YOU MEAN, 'YE KNOW THE WAY ENGLAND OWNS IRELAND?'?" Tony has gone AWOL

75

at this stage and Hannah and Lee seem to be sympathising with Bobby's argument. I take a deep breath.

Bobby is a nice bloke – they all are actually. However, he is ill informed about the history his country shares with mine. I tell them about the Northern Ireland peace process, about Unionists, Catholics, and so on. I talk to them about self governance and I go back and I wax lyrical about the history: about the War of Independence; about politicians/rebels Michael Collins and Arthur Griffiths, about Éamon DeValera, who became Ireland's first Taoiseach (Prime Minister), after Collins and Griffiths signed the Anglo-Irish Treaty with British Prime Minister Lloyd George. It was ratified by Dáil Éireann in 1922, effectively signing away the six counties in the north of Ireland to British rule. Shutting up now.

Anyway, there's no real harm done. We move on and continue with the craic. But they've seen a flash of Irish passion, as expressed through debate, and there is a healthy respect between us now.

I can't sleep because Tony has crashed out and he's snoring so hard that I half expect to see Bobby – like a possessed demon on the bunk above him – bouncing in the air with every exhalation emanating from his best mate below. Also, I feel as if Tony could be possessed. He seems to be speaking in some devilish tongue. Well, either that or a recording of Scooby Doo on acid at the wrong speed, but backwards. In my exasperation, I go over and try to wake Tony but to no avail. I shake him vigorously this time but still, there is nothing. He's small enough in stature but a dead, drunken weight is just that and my attempts to turn him onto his side prove fruitless. This guy could sleep anywhere. There is much ceiling-watching after this.

DAY TWELVE

We get on the bus for Fraser Island and Kevin, a chunky Aussie easily in his 60s, is our driver, while Damo is our flamboyant tour guide. Damo has turned 23 today and early on, he invites us to toast him in the bar at our island hostel later that night. It's a

76

short bus ride from Rainbow to the ferry but before boarding we must pay an €18 Government tax at a nearby filling station. Here, we stock up on water, crisps (not chips) and pies. Lee, Tony, Bobby and I rush into the pie shop next door and I join the lads in trying out a breakfast pie. This consists of the obligatory pastry with a fried egg, bacon and some class of sausage – basically, baked into the top of it. It sounds disgusting and should but we're hungover so it goes down a treat.

We take the ferry across to Fraser and after a short drive we arrive at this building in some vast complex or other for "mornin' tay".

How quaint!

To my untrained eye, Fraser Island actually looks very similar to New Zealand in terms of its shape (if you can imagine the latter's north and south islands fusing together!). After numerous glasses of orange juice, coffee and tea – not to mention the fruit and muffins that are in plentiful supply – we're off further up the beach for a five-kilometre round trip that, we're assured, will be worth the effort. We're wildly hung over and in our flip flops and short trousers, feel very vulnerable, what with the snakes and all. Kevin warns us of these and the dingos before we leave.

Apparently, the "thiii'd (third) piii'son" is in most danger from the snakes. The reptiles, sensing our presence through vibration alone, will be alerted at the first step and will then be up and hissing at the second. Walker number three, which in my experience is actually an unlucky number, will be pierced with venomous fangs. And the last person is in danger from the lovely dingos, which are prone to sneaking up from behind, we're told. I've left the babies at home (he jokes, I don't have any – that I know of, "ba dum tss!") so I suspect that the dingos will steal my flip flops from under my feet, and not my offspring.

The sun is belting down, the sand scorches our feet and did I mention that we're hungover? We're traipsing through some class of rainforest and when we emerge we're met with a vast expanse of sand. Our feet are black from it, thanks to its mineral composition. We appear to have stepped into a painting: dramatic dunes are flanked with vegetation and the aqua blue sea sparkles on our horizon – seemingly getting over its shyness at last and peeking at us from behind the massive, undulating

77

sand dunes; like a child might peer from behind its parent's legs. We trek through the hot masses that make up the Hammerstone Sandblow and most of us are quiet now, busily snapping the endless sandy hills that appear and then vanish from our view. According to our Fraser Island factsheet, supplied by the good folk at Kingfisher Bay Resort tours, the dunes have the "longest and most complete age sequence" of coastal dunes in the world. While most of the sand that makes up Fraser Island has come from the far south east of Australia, "some of it has travelled for thousands of Kilometres and millions of years from Antarctica", while this "journey" started before Australia and Antarctica split from each other.

Fraser was first sighted by Captain Cook in 1770 as he made his way up the east coast. Cook must have been suffering from a lack of inspiration when he named the island "Great Sandy Peninsula", believing it to be connected to the huge mainland land mass. However, in 1799, Matthew Flinders, exploring parts of Hervey Bay in *The Norfolk*, discovered that Fraser was indeed an island. And then in 1836 Captain James Fraser on his brig, *Stirling Castle*, "was wrecked" (I know how he felt) north of Fraser, at Swain's Reef. Some of the survivors scrambled into a raft and drifted south to Fraser Island. And perhaps remarkably, Captain Fraser's wife, Eliza, was the only survivor and apparently that's thanks to the Aboriginal people living there. However, the Europeans did not name the island after Captain Fraser's wife, but her perished husband.

Finally we arrive at Lake Wabby, which is surrounded by sand on one side and eucalyptus forest on the other. It is heavenly. Apparently, the lake is in danger from the huge dune because the sand is slowly choking it. Those dunes are just psychopaths, aren't they? Children's voices breeze down to the lake as we plonk ourselves down on the incline sweeping down to it. I take off my boardies (calm down, my speedos are underneath) and I run down to the water. I dive in, as do the boys and some of the girls. The water is still and very warm compared to the cold water off Ireland's south east coast that I'm used to. I swim about two-thirds of the way across and then back again. The boys, Lee Tony and Bobby, take off their shorts and put them on their heads while traversing. I finally get back out again and sit down on my towel next to Hannah Helper Monkey. The boys are taking turns in linking hands and flipping the third over so that the flipee does a back flip. They call in the big guns so there I end up holding a foot in my interlocked hands and flipping the relevant others. However, when it's my turn to be flipped, it doesn't work for some weird and unexplainable reason. Until they call in a third pair of hands, that is. *And a crane*, cried the Wit. Helper Monkey and Trisha join us and we spend our time thus until it is time to trek back to the four-wheel drive. We're taken back to the complex for a buffet lunch and I end sitting at the table with the women. I'm having trouble opening the weird (miniature) mustard container. It consists of a double container of the tangy yellow mush in hard plastic and Trisha shows me how to do it. But when I try, I end up with mustard all over my white *Australia* wife-beater tee shirt. Of course her mother Marianne, who has very little English, starts bursting out laughing at me because I am destroyed with the stuff and all the others, about eight of them, join in. The mean females tease me in a way that only a gaggle of chicks can. I am vastly outnumbered and I go down in a ball of flames, a blazing hot flush filling my cheeks.

In the afternoon, we are heading to McKenzie Lake and it's a short trek down to the water from our drop-off point, thanking His God-ness. We're met with an enticing gorgeous body of water, which is circled by white sandy beach and again, eucalypt vegetation. The Sphinx-like lakes are based on a layer of humus impregnated sand or "coffee rock", which was formed by accumulating organic matter and sand cementing together into an impenetrable seal. The fine sand acts as a filter, leaving the water as clear as perhaps a John Rocha Waterford Crystal champagne flute.

Or whatever.

Following some swimming and girl-flipping in the water, I play some touch footie with the boys before taking to the water again for underwater image taking (Bobby and Lee have waterproof cameras) and tomfoolery with our driver Kevin, some German girls and an English girl, Keisha, who are all on our Fraser Island tour for the two days.

We go for a two-kilometre trek through a section of rainforest. It's a walk through a trail yet still I feel trainers would be more appropriate footwear for what we are doing. However, the scenery is awesome. Then, we're ferried back to the hostel and we are assigned our dorms. Lee and I share with Jeremy, a career backpacker (or should that read, "slackslacker") from Iowa in the US who is pissed off that "most Americans haven't a fucking clue whur my home Stade is man". He's impressed that I do. So impressed that he seems to want to be my NBF – that's New Best Friend to the less popular amongst you. Aah lighten up; I'm just pulling your collective leg. And now I'm imagining a Giant version of myself pulling a leg the width of Ireland and the length of Norway. "HEEEEAVE-AAAH"!

Yes, my mind sometimes scares me too.

Lee crashes out almost immediately and I'm sipping a can of Castlemaine XXXX, mainly because I'm stuck talking to Jeremy, who talks in that monotone and nasal type of American college accent. Driven to the drink, that's what I am. I've offered him one but he declines; presumably because, were he to drink, he would need to stop talking for seconds at a time. The plain lager is almost as boring as the man himself. The more Jeremy gives out – about this and that –, the more I nod off. I can't sleep because even when I do nod off and wake up about a minute later, he's still talking. This guy must not have had a conversation in months.

Finally, I tell him that I need a shower, which I do, so he actually leaves. After dinner, I return to my room, re-emerge shortly after 9pm and make my way to the bar.

I'm an awful bitch.

A pint of Toohey's New and five Jäger-bombs for the kids, please?

(A Jäger bomb is basically a shot of Jägermeister mixed with Red Bull or whatever energy drink takes your fancy, I would imagine – and depending on whom you talk to, cola!)

I'm charged €54 and to be honest, I feel robbed, mugged and conned. You get the picture. We go to the beer garden and there's me, Bobby, Tony, Birthday boy Damo, Trisha, Helper Monkey and the two German girls, Catriona and Marguerite. Kevin joins us for a while.

After some ridiculous drinking games, along with actual drinking, Damo suggests going to the beach across the road for some "skinny deppin'". On the way through the bar, we sing along to *Kids* by Robbie Williams and Australia's own Kylie (Minogue). The German girls and I wait on the beach because we don't want to go in the water. So we keep an eye on the gang's clothes so the dingos won't eat them or whatever.

We walk back to the hostel in the pale moonlight and are met by some Aussies, drinking near the entrance to the beach, and there is a bit of good natured banter between them and a few of the lads. Metal bars make an electric grid at the entrance to stop the dingos from leaving the beach I imagine. The low buzz of the charge lets us know that the circuit is waiting to fry the wet dippers. Tony and I are in front and shouting back to the others to take care and be sure to use the gate at the side. Our feet sink into the cold and soft sand, in stark contrast to its temperature in six or seven hour's time, at dawn. We see a lone dingo following us cautiously.

We head up to Tony and Bobby's room for more drinking and messing. We start playing games including one that involves bouncing a coin onto the table. The aim is to land the coin into a cup full of goon and when a player succeeds, they can nominate a drinker. There's Tony and Bobby, Trisha and Helper Monkey, Catriona, Lee, Damo and myself.

We also play Fives (where each player puts out an opened hand and when the previous winner shouts out a number in derivates of five, the players must remove or indeed leave their hand out. Whoever has guessed the correct total number of fingers, such as five, ten or fifteen, is out, while the last one remaining must drink). We also play, I Have Never. This involves starting a sentence with these words and following them with others such as, "...cheated on a partner" or "...told someone I loved them just to have my wicked way with them" and so on. And I barely have to take a drink, would you believe? No, you wouldn't? Ha, sod you so! Tony and Bobby have made impromptu hats from the cardboard boxes that hold the foil packets of the corrosive substance inside. Damo's over-the-top flamboyancy has us doubled up.

We're on the balcony and there's a lot of noise. An Aussie who looks like a big, mean scary biker (though I don't see a bike) shouts up at us from below, telling us that he will report us if we don't quieten. We move inside but alas, we don't quieten, though we think we do. Another guy, a member of management we think, knocks at the door and tells Tony that we need to quieten "or everyone'll be throoown out onta da roooyd (road)".

On my suggestion, Damo, who has only been working with his company for two weeks, hides under a duvet on the top bunk, lest the Nosey Parker storm into the dorm. Helper Monkey has the cigarettes so I'm asking her for "tabs", as she calls them. She objects to my calling her Helper Monkey, probably because the boys have joined in, now calling her "Monkey" for short. I warn her that insubordination of such a nature will be going on her permanent record and that if she keeps it up, there will be extra duties and chores for her by the break of day.

This quietens her, momentarily.

Tony pulls out the Holy Bible from a drawer – there's one in every room – and we go straight to the scriptures at the back, blasphemously quoting with much fire and brimstone. Maybe it's the deep Co. Kerry accent that I put on, but the lads think it hilarious when I read from the great book. After a while, we get worried about being thrown out, or at least getting struck down by lightening, so we call it a day.

DAY THIRTEEN

We're on the second day of our Fraser Island tour and of course it's beautiful. We go to the Maheno Wreck, a luxury cruise ship that was built in Scotland in 1905 and sailed between Sydney and Auckland. The cruiser set a record for the fastest crossing – at two days and twenty one hours – of the Tasman two years later, so says the Fraser factsheet. During World War I she was tasked as a hospital ship in Europe and around before later being put out to pasture as a cruiser. However, on July 8th 1935, as she was being towed to Japan to be scrapped, she was washed ashore by a cyclone to her current beachfront grave. And if that wasn't enough, the poor wreck was used as target practice by Air Force bombers.

We paddle around in the shaded parts, taking turns posing for pictures in between our strolls in the shallow water. Various four wheel drives, jeeps and buses, mandatory on Fraser, dot the horizon. The white sand stretches for miles on both flanks. Above us is an expanse of deep blue sky and in front of us, whales splash around in the middle distance and we can sometimes see them. After we get on the bus again this wild looking, devil-may-care pilot in his 20s hops on-board. Three of the girls – the German girls – are sucked in by his sales pitch, which promises "aaawesome" views of the beach and the wreck from above, for $70 I think. This seems reasonable enough and we meet them at another point further down the beach about thirty minutes later. We go on to the Champagne Pools and I can't wear my flip flops because they are cutting me deep in between my big and second toes on both feet (apparently it takes time to break them in). Instead, I carry them, preferring the effects of the searing heat, coming up from the timber on the long walk down the decking provided, to the chaffing from my footwear.

I stroll in between the bank of pools, formerly used by the Aboriginals to catch the ill-fated fish tossed into them by the raging surf. Some brave souls go swimming in the anarchic surf beyond the rocks but I don't because I'm enjoying the pools, and it may sound wimp-ish but I don't fancy sitting in wet board shorts for the next while on the bus, only to get them wet somewhere else. So, I just wander around, soaking up the sun and taking snaps. I ask an Aussie male, relaxing in a shaded pool wearing one of those UV-reflecting tops and a Fair Dinkum (which actually means "very fair" or "true") Hat as I have taken to calling them, if I can take his picture. Lifting up his can of beer, which is firmly housed in one of those weird foam coolers the Aussies simply love, he smiles and duly obliges. To me, it sums up what Australia is largely about: sun, sea, beer, being friendly, active and then of course, chilling the fuck out, outdoors.

Tony does go swimming and later tells me that other swimmers there told him to get out "bicoz the'e was a shaaa'k and a stingroooy" spotted in the very same surf. Apparently, our driver Kevin saw them through binoculars from the viewing platform above and spread the word. Although I also heard that the shark could have actually been a dolphin. The idiot. But I'm serious about the sun block kids...and the stingray. However, none of this seemed to bother the Fit Family that I have been watching who have swam around the rocks and back – a distance of about two kilometres – with very little effort. Silver-haired-yet-lean and athletic dad who would put most thirty-year-olds to shame, leads two boys and a girl in the impressive swim. Believe me, these waters are not for the faint hearted. And I mean that both literally and figuratively.

We leave for Indian Head, named so by Captain Cook who saw Aboriginals peering at him from his offshore ship on the approach. Fraser was a permanent spot for the Butchulla, whose name for the island was K'Gari (*proun.Gurrie*) which, strangely enough, translates as "Paradise". With six clans, the indigenous Butchulla would rise from about 700 to about 2,000 in winter when other tribes would come to enjoy large quantities of fish.

Of course Cook's first encounters in "New Holland" with the "Indian" were, putting it mildly, tentative. I find the details of this in *An Account Of The Voyages Undertaken By The Order Of His Majesty, For Making Discoveries In The Southern Hemisphere (Vol. IV)* by John Hawkesworth, John Byron, James Cook. In his Log from April 27th 1770, offshore some "leagues" north of Cape George, Cook says that The Endeavour's crew "saw several of the natives walking briskly along the shore, four of whom carried a small canoe upon their shoulders: we flattered ourselves that they were going to put her into the water, and come off to the ship, but finding ourselves disappointed, I determined to go ashore in the yawl, with as many as I could carry".

Captain Cook and a party rowed into shore.

"The Indians sat down upon the rocks, and seemed to wait for our landing; but to our great regret, when we came within about a quarter of a mile, they ran away into the woods: we determined to go ashore, and endeavour to procure an interview, but in this we were again disappointed, for we found so great a surf beating upon every part of the beach, that landing with our little boat was altogether impractical." He noted that their canoes, "upon a near view", seemed "very much to resemble those of the smaller sort at New Zealand".

However, when further north slightly the following day, April 28th, "as the pinnace proceeded along the shore", one of the Aboriginals had invited them ashore.

All of them were armed with long pikes, and a wooden weapon shaped somewhat like a cimeter. "The Indians who had not followed the boat, seeing the ship approach, used many threatening gestures, and brandished their weapons; particularly two [Aboriginals], who made a very singular appearance, for their faces seemed to have been dusted with a white powder, and their bodies painted with streaks of the same colour". Cook certainly loved his commas, didn't he?

He went on to say that white streaks painted around their chests and backs seemed to look like the crossbelts worn by the British soldiers, while they also wore white painted hoops around "their legs and thighs like broad garters". Eventually that evening, steps were taken to land onshore but "two of the men came down to dispute our landing, and the rest ran away". Each had a lance that was "about ten feet long" and a "short stick" that appeared as if it were a "machine to assist" in managing to throw the lance. The Aboriginals shouted at the party, brandishing their weapons and seemed "resolved to defend their coast to the utmost, though they were but two and we were forty". Cook made efforts to convince them that he meant no harm but the natives quickly opposed the Brits putting their boat into the water. Cook says that he fired a musquet between the pair, a "youth about nineteen or twenty, and the other a man of middle age". A "stone" was thrown back, "to which I ordered a musquet to be fired with small shot, which struck the eldest upon the legs, and he immediately ran".

Cook and Co. landed, but the men came back and threw lances at them. A shot was fired, a lance was returned and the rest is History.

The game of hide and seek continued. On May 19th, when Endeavour was four miles from the shore in a depth of seventeen fathoms (102 feet), the ship "passed a black bluff head, or point of land, upon which a great number of natives were assembled, and which therefore I called Indian Head". Near Indian Head the crew saw more Aboriginals, along with "fires by night and smoke by day".

I'm blown away by Indian Head – I suspect that the most cynical and worldly viewer would be. I've actually planned on sitting this one out but thank God I didn't. After a ten-minute climb up the rocky terrain in flip flops, the reward is a breath-taking view.

Hundreds of feet below there's a giant, almost perfectly still blanket of piercing azure blue. It looks like the sky has been flipped onto its head. Thousands of tourists take turns in being speechless and, apart from the low mumbles of the humble, there's almost total silence. Large orangey beige sections of curved rockface can be seen on both sides in the distance. Vast stretches of white (on Seventy-Five Mile Beach) are sandwiched in between the green-topped cliffs and the sea – for miles on both sides. Beneath the water's surface, a dark shadow gathers near the shore and suddenly, scores of breaks appear on the surface. And the shoal of fish has moved. Men fishing onboard a yacht, who are not Fishermen as such, follow keenly. I strain my eyes to see dolphins' fins surface before diving again, resulting in an immense feeding frenzy.

The beauty of nature at work.

I just know that there's a great Aboriginal Creation story about this place. We easily spend an hour up here before going back down for a picnic lunch consisting of sandwiches, orange juice and apples. We move on to Eli Creek, where we break up into separate groups. I end up sunbathing with Trisha, her mother Marianne and Monkey. I lash on the sunblock liberally. But I get bored. I'm all about chilling in the sun but I don't have the patience for sunbathing as such. I paddle up the cold water creek, dodging the masses, finally stopping when I see a group of the overhanging branch of a tree. A snake is lazily coiled up on top of it. Fraser has seventy species of reptiles with nineteen different types of snake. It also boasts of over 350 recorded species of birds. There are forty eight or so mammals in total, while the most renowned is surely the dingo.

Back in our Fraser hostel on Rainbow Island, I eat a rather disgusting beef meal that has been included in our package. Of course, the plan here is to keep el dopey tourist in the bar, drinking watery beer. One or two of our crew gets given out to by this fat, nasty Fat Ignorant Barman for bringing in a couple of cans to have with dinner. (He's an English man but every country has its own particular bland of FIB.) Fair enough but the Oz Experience shower need to lay off this kind of antagonistic bullshit! The guides basically get everything free – in a good deal of the bars and restaurants that they take us to – and that's part of the play. Largely, they're on commission for various activities and so on. But backpackers are people not sheeple (I've been waiting for ages now to work that madey-uppey word in again) and more consideration needs to be given as to a) where the tours go b) how long they stay there amd why c) why there's this *veil of secrecy* as to how the whole thing really operates behind the scenes. The word "tourist" does not actually equate to "idiot", though at times the relevant locals would be forgiven for thinking it. Though being a nameless and faceless visitor has its plus points, I'm sure.

Anyway, the FIB is doing his whole, let's-show-off-to-the-stupid-regulars-at-the-bar routine and he's taking the piss out of me because I'm drinking Fosters and I tell him to shut up and just pour and "What would an Englishman know about beer?" anyway and it's good craic. He's doing his "I'm your friend really" bullshit I'm playing along with him. Until, after a few pints in, I hand him a $50 note for a beer and a glass of red wine.

And the creep gives me the change of a $20 note.

However, when I pull him on it he denies it and shows me that there's no $50 in the cash register. I suspect he has hidden it somewhere else but I have no proof. Then the really drunken regular standing next to me, who could barely see a fly landing on his nose, pipes up.

"Yih; I'm preddy shore ya gave 'im twenny dollahs mate."

Ah, for fuck sake; is this shit really happening here? I suspect a con. So there's to and fro with the *What Actually Happened(s)* and I'm getting annoyed now, though I know I'll come off as the aggressive drunken Paddy if I make a scene. So, I decide to play it cute and to take my pound of flesh in another way.

And that's all I'm saying about that.

I meet a really cool Aussie bloke and his American girlfriend in the smoking area at the bar here over both nights. I don't get their names but when I first spoke with her she tried to catch me out with some yarn about "drop bears". It's a pretty poor tale about these bears that will drop on you from a height in the outback and tear you a new one but I can see the gag coming from a mile off. Sorry love, I'm Irish...we've been telling people stories such as these when the only American that existed was the country's native *Indian*. The real American.

Nice people though.

I also meet Kenny, an Aboriginal gentleman who has apparently worked as a tour guide for many years. And get this...it turns out that he knows Lord Waterford from back home. So Kenny takes a number out of his wallet and gets onto the payphone. This guy could be just a barfly but I don't know, you couldn't write this stuff. Evidentially, you can. However, you couldn't make it up, as they'd say back home. *His* "Peter Waterford" (I later find out) is a farmer/businessman who's apparently been having awful problems with his pears on his sprawling holding on Lorne Station near Lightning Ridge, also in NSW. According to the *Sydney Morning Herald* on September 27th, Peter's "awaiting the arrival of the cochineal bug from Mexico to save his 4,000-hectare Lightning spread from alien invasion". "For 20 years he has tried burning, slashing, and spraying the Hudson Pear, which injures humans and livestock, and wrecks boots and tyres with its copious barbed spikes".

Ouch. Lord Waterford in – funnily enough, Waterford back home, is a director of the Curraghmore demesne in Portlaw. In 2008, Coillte agreed a €3.75 million-deal with him to end a long-running legal battle between them over the preservation of the historic demesne walls on the 2,000-acre family estate. "Coillte", by-the-way, is Ireland's biggest forestry company and the Irish word means "Woods" in the English language.

We have a few beers tonight but it's a much quieter one and we're all in bed asleep by midnight, worn out after two days on our own paradise island. Tomorrow we'll go inland to explore a bit of rural Australia, to see what beauty will be gifted to us by this diverse, mysterious and unique country.

5. Mystique...the Gay Dolphin

DAY FOURTEEN

I wake at 4.15am and with arms folded in behind my head, I'm staring at the wooden planks holding up the mattress on the top bunk. It's not that I'm not tired, because it's quite the contrary. However, I'm as awake as a hungry newborn with a soiled nappy at 4am on a freezing Tuesday in January. And I will be for the next few hours, my body surely adjusting to the many changes of schedule imposed on it over the past fortnight. Sorry, my body *trying* to adjust and going, *Dude, like seriously? I can end all this any time I want, you know?* Four hours sleep per night is not something one wants to get used to. Though Tony is still snoring, the little shit.

I manage to get out of bed at 6am and go down to reception and there's nobody there. The sun is washing in through the many windows in the neighbouring computer room and there's no escaping it. I take out my Global Gossip card, which, if I forgot to tell you, is a kind of debit card for using the Internet and making phone calls. I go online, using my large head to create a shadow on the screen and therefore enabling me to see it.

So it's just me, the dawn chorus and the computers.

Suddenly, Pre-honeymooners David and Sarah, the quietest couple in the Southern hemisphere, trundle past me. Apparently, they have missed the sunrise. Damn it, I knew there was something I was supposed to miss this morning. There's an email from Marianne, a friend who's from Waterford. I had emailed her a couple of months back her to tell her that in early November I'd be in Queenstown, New Zealand, where she currently lives. She's telling me she's "sorry for the late reply" and that she thought she had sent a reply but it must not have came through. She says she will "hopefully definitely" be there in November when I arrive. Haha.

Some weird and random (random to me at any rate) hippie girl has just stormed in and I spot her through the corner of my eye. She's with another girl and I turn around to say hello.

"Hey...yu Oirish?" she asks me before I can utter a word.

"Yeah," I reply.

She's carrying a six-pack of bottled beer, some class of woolly hat and of all things, a smelly old pair of canvas slip-on shoes.

"Can I heeend these things in fo' Rhys Camarden?' or at least that's how it sounds to me.

"Sorry?"

"Je wooo'k here?" she continues. I nod my head from side-to-side. I'm actually speechless because she's plonked the stuff down next to my mouse. She asks me if I can hand them in anyway, once reception opens. Still half asleep, I tell her "Yes" but I add, "It's not open until seven and I'm going back upstairs shortly".

"Well, yu look like a nice Oirish goy an' I'm sure I cen trast ya."

Before I can reply to this, she's gone. The girl is clearly as mad as a sack full of ferrets or she's perhaps coming down from some trip or other, I'm thinking. I'm kind of annoyed at myself because I didn't tell her that I wouldn't do it. But now that I've given my word, I'm bound to it – like a mutinous, salty scurvy dog who's been chained to the anchor of a sinking ship for stealing the Captain's rum (Aye, that be it!).

I've returned downstairs, it's 7am and the guy at reception looks at me as if I'm the mad one and maybe I am. He carefully and suspiciously lifts the shoes and the hat from the counter and asks me if I can leave them "outside".

"Yu cin keep the beee's yasalf," the guy at reception tells me. I tell him that I don't want them as I head for the door with them in my hand.

"Oh, yu cin leave 'em in heee'e if yu want," he goes. I ignore him and keep on walking (he can either take the lot or nothing). Outside, I meet Beaver, who looks like he has just seen a ghost.

He has.

"G'day...whut da fack are yew doin' up this ea'ly?" I don't give him a definite answer because I don't know myself. We all pack up and Bobby is in a bit of a tizzy

90

because he can't find some Tin of Fruit (suit) – made of hemp, rice, paper or something. He has bought the thing for almost nothing in Borneo. Apparently, Bobby, an engineer, plans to use the suit for interviews and the like when he returns home to London in November. I don't know about London but if he goes for a job as a drug importer in Miami, a Columbian cocaine exporter or as a shady time-share realtor in Turkey, he should be all set. I have a lingering suspicion that he actually got a free mankini and Uzi machine gun in a consignment to, you know, sweeten the deal. Beaver, Tony and I wink at each other, as he shuffles off to reception to see if someone, eh, handed in his apparel. We leave him stew for a bit before we let him in on the joke. Tony had grabbed the suit and packed it away just moments ago at reception.

We head to Tin Can Bay, just kilometres away really, to feed some bloody dolphin or other. I put my Irish SIM card (I've bought an Australian one in Byron Bay) into my ridiculously decrepit mobile phone and there are, like, eight texts from my mother, Lily. Between Fraser Island and what-not, I haven't turned the thing on in days. There's also one from a friend back home, Anna. It's telling me of a local musician'a death. His name was Jay Barden and I know his girlfriend, Trish, quite well. Apparently he died peacefully in his sleep from a congenital heart problem.

Bed of Heaven to the poor guy.

So we arrive at Tin Can, just north of Rainbow Beach, before 8am and – only in Australia, I swear – the place is already packed. Actually, there's a bottle nosed dolphin in Dingle, Co Kerry, back home called Fungi. And for about twenty years or so now, tourists have flocked out to sea in these boat tours, to see him. It has occurred to some cynics that the original dolphin may have died, moved on etc and that the current Fungi is an imposter. I'm not saying a word; it's just what some cynics are saying. The dolphin here comes in to meet the visitors as opposed to going out to see him in a boat or whatever. The place is thronged with families, and kiddies, urged on by their parents; queue up for an age to feed "Mystique", the Alpha Male of his pod of "river dolphins". He is with his daughter (whose name I don't get) today and we can feed him for a Gold Coin Donation. That's nice of them. And you only give them fish that you've bought there too. The cafe/restaurant there seems to be doing a roaring trade. Oh, now I see that boat tours are being advertised. Of course they are.

Jesus, give me a break.

Mystique The Gay Dolphin, Beaver has rightly called him (Alpha Male? Mystique? For real?). Poor Mystique has had a chunk of his dorsal fin bitten off by a bull shark in a fight, we learn. The lady with the microphone warns us not to pet Mystique as he is protecting his females in his pod from other males of the species and from, well, everything else in the river really so he will likely be aggressive. Beaver rubbishes all of this. "Aggro? Bollocks...He's a fackin' dolphin fo' fack sake." He also says that Mystique was only caught by the shark because he lost ten per cent of his speed and that this was due to being overfed by the masses. I, for one, am with him on all of this.

(I will later post a photo of poor Msytique on Facebook but my friend Ruth will comment that she has little sympathy for his sort as they are "rapists" of some sort. I will comment that, for all she knows, the "kniiiick kneeck" sounds they appear to make could mean, "Hey honey, I'll meet you in the shallows in a while".)

After gorgeous banana milkshakes, orange juices, coffees and sandwiches, we're on our way again and by lunchtime we're in Miriam Vale, at the northern gateway to the Bundaberg Coral Coast and County Region. I get a large portion of lasagne with chips and salad, along with a (glass) bottle of lemonade for about $12 at a nice little cafè. Miriam Vale is a quaint little place but, like Kempsey and Gympie, I don't know how people live here. Though I do remember at times saying that about where I live in Ireland too. We're on the seemingly endless Dawson's Highway somewhere after Colliope (near the junction at Bruce Highway) when Beaver curses and stops the bus suddenly. We suspect that something's wrong with the bus. But there isn't. He tells us that a wedge tailed eagle – the "second largest bird of prey in the world", we're told – is perched alone on the branch of a tree. We walk back slowly, so as not to scare it off, and try to take pictures of the thing like the good little tourists that we are. However, he flies off suddenly (the bird, not Beaver) and although I zoom in and get one of the majestic bird in flight, it's not a great shot. My mind shifts to numerous friends and colleagues (professional photographers) at home who have sufficient equipment and talent to justify the stop.

Beaver starts telling us about the Banana Shire Yellow Cow and "what a loser he was" (long story). He's also boasting about Mount Morgan, where the gold mine opened in 1882. He proceeds to tell us that Queensland has the largest number of cattle head per area in the world but this is strongly contested by Lynne, the Canadian nurse who tells him that he's wrong; that it's Alberta in Canada. There's some good banter between the two as the debate moves onto coal and gold mining and who's the biggest, the brightest and the best! Lynne tells Beaver to go to Canada and see for himself and he replies: "Whoy would en Aussie go ta Canada? It's too blaady cold theee'."

That shuts her up (for a while anyway).

We stop at Bileola, the Aboriginal for "black or white cockatoo" apparently, in the heart of Queensland about thirty five kilometres East of Kirkroom Farm – a vast and sprawling oasis in the middle of nowhere really, where we will be spending a couple of days shooting, quad-bike riding, goat-herd herding, getting thrown from a steel bull, playing ridiculous party games and of course, drinking. It's late in the afternoon. It's hot and the air is dry. The place reminds me of one of those 1950s towns you would see in some of the Southern States in the US. I keep expect to see cowboys, miners and big-haired (former) Homecoming Queen-moms who played it safe by staying in town and marrying the quarter back who's now The Mayor, coming out of the steel-plated diners where they shared milkshakes as teenagers.

But I don't. I don't see the nuclear families that I suspect live here, either. In fact, I don't see much of anyone. Perhaps we arrived after the warning siren and I look to the clear blue sky above us, half-expecting to clap my eyes on a Mushroom Cloud for a nanosecond before the flesh evaporates from my very bones, which will almost immediately turn into ash. Bileola is administrative area for the Banana Shire, which, Beaver tells us, was named after the aforementioned yellow bullock again.

"Whad a LOOZA' (loser) thet cow was," he says again.

"This woy ta get yar Akruba Het moyte."

I follow. I've been looking forward to buying my hat, which will replace the baseball cap that just hours before was blown from my head as I absentmindedly stuck it out through the window of the bus to cool down. The way's now clear for the King Akruba.

Beaver and I are wandering around the shop, whose name I don't get, and in comes Trisha and Lynne. I end up buying this navy wife-beater – a kind of colloquial name for a singlet – vest with a white trim, a pair of brown plaid shorts with faint white and blue stripes in them. And Beaver's tempted to buy an Akruba but he seems to feel like he's cheating on the ancient one he's got in the bus, which was apparently attacked by an angered kookaburra and stitched up by his good self. It's slightly at odds with what he's told me already. "Ya don't wosh these hets; ya don't do enythin' wid 'em...it gives 'em characta'."

Anyway, I don't buy an Akruba as such, which is made from rabbit pelt. Instead, I opt for a Statesman made from Merino wool.

The farm, aptly named "The Cattleshed" by Beaver, consists of thousands of acres of dry and arid land that's home to countless goats and beige, humpbacked cows that kind of remind me of like dromedary (or single-humped) camels but that's more of an Asian thing. Whatever about the goats, I don't know how the scrawny cows can manage to survive the hot and dry conditions here but I guess that's where the humps come into play.

We're met by "Andy the Cowboy", who turns out to be (in turn) part adrenaline junkie, beer hound, cowboy and pure lunatic. We settle into our dorms, these wooden rooms with a veranda outside, and then go to the common area where the farm hands are cooking a mass of meat on a spit. We take turns in crouching down to pet this joey who has stumbled out of a makeshift pouch made from a pillowcase and in fairness, he is very cute. One of the girls working there is feeding him from a bottle and I'm wondering where his/her mother has got to. (I feel this question will be answered somewhat the following day when one of the Oz Experience tour guides will orphan – that's right, "ORPHAN" a baby emu. But we will get to that.)

Other animals that pop along to pay us a visit include an extremely clever sheep dog and Mini Moo, a sweet calf who comes up to lick you on the arms and legs with its sandpaper-ish tongue.

(The next morning I would become concerned because some of the farm hands would think it hilarious to feed her bread and toast. "Shi's not gonna see old age moyte," says Beaver.)

One worker, before dinner as we're sat around the large table, (apparently) picked up a cool-looking snake from the scrubs and I'm a bit apprehensive when I see him coiled around the arms of some of my tour mates. When it's my turn, I'm surprised to find that it's not slimey at all but dry, and though its skin is cool, it's not as cold as I thought it would be.

The bar has opened and the hardy cowboys and cowgirls there kind of growl or moan when you ask for a can of VB (form Victoria obviously) instead of Castlemaine XXXX, which is brewed in Queensland. *Hey, sod you,* I feel like telling them. *I prefer VB.* Then we're told that the meat is ready but they refuse to tell us what it is. I suspect that it's the joey's mother and I'm imagining the little one's sad eyes as I approach the spit. I take a low, narrow piece from a plate and chew on it. It tastes like lamb but there's a lot of chewing to be done.

Hmmm, tastes like lamb but is not as lean? Have you guessed it?

Yup, it turns out to be goat and I am surprised at how tasty it is. Anyway, dinner turns out to be a gorgeous meal cooked in a slow oven in the ground and consisting of tender roast beef, fresh vegetables and flowery potatoes. And after this, we're addressed by Alan, the owner of Kirkroom. He's dressed like an actual cowboy.

Alan tells us to go up to a nearby annex, "where ya can change yur clothes". There are three tour buses at Kirkroom tonight: our Sydney-to-Cairns tour bus; the Oz Experience *hop-on-hop-off* bus and the Cairns-to-Sydney version. As I may have mentioned, these buses are much bigger than ours so both buses basically outnumber us by three or four-to-one. We scour through a huge box full of the gawdy women's clothes and I end up with an ankle length maxi skirt (my sister will inform me upon seeing the pictures on Facebook). The blouse is shocking, I tell you. SHOCKING! The boys and I are striking overtly feminine poses for pictures on each others' cameras and when we get back to the yard as such, the girls who haven't opted for fancy dress – namely, the Germans, the Canadian nurse Lynne and Swiss Missus, Marianne – are doubled up in laughter at us. Of course, ever the entertainer-stroke-showoff, I jump up on their long table and stride up and down it with a tinny in my paw, basically dressed like a confused extra from *Blokes Back-Mounting* or whatever that movie was called. The lads have joined me and we are having a right old hoot.

We're called and we circle around Alan, who gives us a brief history of the place, the country and so on. He tells us to that the evening will consist of ridiculous party games; he will teach us how to crack a bullwhip and we'll take turns on the mechanical bull.

We sit around in the dusty yard, as the firewood crackles in campfires on its boundaries and the farm workers and tour guides drink and laugh in the background. We break into groups of six for a talent competition and our act involves an impromptu ballet performance while we sing *I Want to Break Free* by Queen.

The most outrageous and fun game of the lot requires us to break off into pairs and come up with a way to mimic a sexual act using a balloon. The balloon is placed between various body parts but on top of our clothes and we must burst it if we are to succeed. I'm paired off with Tony and let me just tell you that he is very *giving* with his performance.

We're led to a number of podiums set up in the grass beyond the dining area and I, along with five or six others, are given goggles and told to take to the podiums. So we do and we're cracking the air with the things. Apparently, the "snap" from a successful crack of the whip is the sound of the sound barrier being broken.

It's bloody hard, however. I start out well but then lose my rhythm and then Alan's suddenly standing nearby, barking orders and literally cracking the whip with us. I feel like telling him to *Fuck off* or something for acting the fascist. I'm standing there, on a podium on a huge farm in the depths of Queensland, dressed like a cross-dressing extra from the Little House on The Prairie with a can of beer in one hand, a whip in the other and a pair of goggles on my eyes.

I seem to have misplaced my dignity, though I suspect it may be swilling around at the bottom of my can of VB.

What the hell am I doing? I wonder – half afraid to ask it aloud because of the answers that I might get.

We make our way back to our seats and we're gathered in a semi-circle around the steel bull. The three buses will compete with each other and we all add our names to the list in the hope that we'll stay on the bull longer that our competitors. Tony's up first and does well, hanging on for about six bucks of the beast. Bobby betters this and hangs on for about eleven or twelve. I'm waiting for my turn when this curvy, curly-haired Scottish girl tried to get up on the mechanical bull, but fails miserably. A couple of attempts later and she's up but her momentum is such that she ends up shooting straight over its smooth leather back and onto the air mattress, which surrounds the thing. And there are calls for a strong chap to help out and the girls in our group bully me into it. So I go up and try to do so but my long skirt gets caught in the thing. I'm wobbling on the air mattress and it's not long before the two of us end up falling over. We fall over again and when I get up, there are long strips torn off the skirt. And the thing is hanging from me so I manage to get her onto the beast and I exit stage left – with laughter and clapping ringing in my ears.

You'd think with my erstwhile experience, that I'd have been something of an expert when it's my turn. However, this isn't the case: I end up on my backside after just three bucks. Three, damn it. And the winner, a wiry English young bloke in his 20s, hangs on for over twenty shrugs, which is awesome really. The tour guides take to the bull afterwards, all country boys who show us how it's done in style – standing, twisting and turning on the bull, which is now going at full throttle.

And to round off the night, we end up playing a massive game of Flip Cup. Nine contestants line up on each side of the long bench in the dining area and fill our cups. Starting at the top, the first drinker must down it all, then put the plastic glass cup or whatever on the edge of the table, on its head – flipping it onto its base. However, it

97

gets out of hand with the local lads – friendly but boisterous and as loud as fuck – getting messier than feeding time at a crèche. I get talking to the Scottish girl who I earlier (finally) helped get on the bull. And she tells me that she has a pacemaker and has an extremely serious heart condition that could cause a Cardiac Arrest at any time, God bless her. She takes my hand and puts it on her chest, and I feel the shape of a rectangular box, visibly protruding from under the skin. I'm humbled by her spirit.

DAY FIFTEEN

Today we'll be clay pigeon shooting, quad biking over a twenty-kilometre trail and spend a couple of hours mustering a giant herd of goats. We'll have to drive them across some rocky and scorched fields, stretching out over a few kilometres. And this is exactly what we do. Andy the Cowboy and Beaver take us up to the "firing range" in a couple of four-wheel-drive jeeps. I ride shotgun (pun intended of course) in Beaver's jeep and he tells me that he's "lookin' fooo'ward ta blowin' shid up" today.

And that, my friends, sounds good to me.

So we arrive at the range, next to one of the large goat pens that's devoid of the goats – waiting for people that look, smell and sound like us, to drive them home. We'll tend to them, following our shooting of orange clay discs. We're handed five cartridges (there are weaker and stronger ones, I get the stronger bullets) each and sign the disclaimer that's usually present before activities down under. Somebody jokes that it's the UK versus Germany in the shooting competition. *Don't disregard Ireland and Australia mate*, I ruminate in silence because I fear that they'll be famous last words. I haven't shot at anything with a real gun before. Only at zombies, terrorists and aliens in Tramore's arcades (Co. Waterford) and in computer games at my cousin Jason's house during my mis-spent youth.

Anyway, what prophetic words they turn out to be. All of us will step up to the mark, as it were, except for Swiss woman Marianne. True to her country's form, she remains neutral. We all take our pot shots at the discs that have been slung into the foreground thanks to the mechanical sling that has been unleashed thanks to the downward stamp of a fellow shooter. Andy encourages us and also gently teases us in

98

his own earthy and laid back fashion. Some shooters get one pigeon and others get two, and one even blasts three of the flying targets out of the sky. Andy hits four of the miniature flying saucers.

However, to my own amazement and probably to everyone else's as well, I shoot all five of them to pieces.

I can tell that Beaver and Andy are very impressed with my shooting. Beaver says, "Fack me mate; I've only eva' seen one piii'son do thet bifooo'e. She was a guuu'l (girl)...a liddle thing frum Korea or somewhe'e". Andy appears speechless (various other guides I hadn't met before will come up to congratulate me later on). I sound like a right show-off now, don't I? But if the premise of this book is to tell the truth, I must tell it – in so far as I can.

The English boys look astonished and gutted and the same time. I know it's in bad taste and I probably shouldn't have, but I couldn't resist it. "I knew the IRA training would come in handy over here."

They seem to get the joke. Ahem.

I remember other childhood shooting experiences. When I was very young, before I was even ten years of age, I remember making devices known as peg-guns. I watched my brother Tom – who would go on to serve his time as a carpenter in his later teen years like his father before him did – making them with his friends. I think he may even have made my first device for me. These things were made by hammering a nail into the top of a piece of 3×2 timber – probably White or Red Deal – and then nailing a peg (placed sideways) to the bottom of the length of wood. Some elastic bands are knotted together and one end of them is tied onto the iron hinge stolen from the inside of another peg. With the rubber band secured over the nail at the top of the peg gun, it is drawn down to the peg, the iron bullet now placed inside the peg's grip. It is tense and when the peg's legs are squeezed, the bullet is fired. These things hurt. I haven't seen one of those things for over twenty years and even though they were unsafe and have probably resulted in the blindness of some poor child somewhere, their probable disappearance is a shame. Kids today, eh? With their computer games and...and....er, nevermind. "Kids today?!" What the...? When did I become middle aged exactly? Some questions are best not answered. There were also the "galley banders", the old Waterford term for catapults. I remember buying the real thing, Black Widows they were called, in a local 'sports' shop. My childhood friend Brian and I would often fire marbles, ball bearings and occasionally stones at cats and birds, at one stage in our youth. Our shots were never successful, however. If I saw somebody doing that now, I'd be furious and disgusted. Little boys are horrible, aren't they?

I remember staying with my cousins in the very scenic Tory Hill (Bigwood, South Co. Kilkenny) once, just kilometres away from Waterford city but in the middle of nowhere all-the-same, as can happen easily in Ireland. I was in my pre-teen years and I was there for about two weeks one summer but the days seemed to go on forever and it seemed like I was away for months. And I swear the sun was splitting the rocks every day, even though I know that in reality it wasn't. Anyway, myself and my cousin Marcus, and his brother Keith who was a couple of years younger than us, cut down these Y-shaped branches from some trees with a hacksaw to make catapults out of them. I clearly remember them painting their devices in their county's black and amber stripes. Of course, I insisted on colouring mine in the white and the blue of the Déise (Waterford).

Meanwhile, back at the ranch, country boy Beaver tries his hand after me and also gets five out of five of the targets. So my prediction was correct: Australia and Ireland.

Then we're taken to the paddock and are assigned our horses. Mine, I'm told, is to be Chrissie. I can tell by looking at them that the huge, gorgeous well-tempered white Mayor is to be my horse. It turns out that Chrissie is a Gentle Giant, loves her grub but is extremely lazy. A tall blond girl from Northern Ireland whose name I think is Carol, tells me that I "need to be tough with Chrissie", a seven hundred-kilo horse whose whole head is covered in Molasses. Haha.

Lazy? Hungry? Gorgeous? Sweet? They have matched us too well, perhaps. The girl here tells me that I "need to give Chrissie a good kick in the sides" if I'm to "get her to do any work". However, I'm a big sucker when it comes to animals (Jesus, that's just sick, would you stop?) and I just can't bear to dig my heels into the animal. So, naturally, the adorable beast stops every few steps to feed on the sparse tufts of grass. And she also stops because...well, because she's Chrissie. I apologise profusely in the horse's ear with every little kick and I also tell her I'm sorry for being overweight, for the rocks under her powerful hooves and even for the weather. I know, I know; I'm a soft city boy. We start out about three kilometres away from our firing range – where we need to be – and we circle the herd, making loud cries such as "Yahhh" in order to startle the stubborn goats into movement. We cajole them into moving across the dry fields in hot weather.

"She's laughing at you Ciaran," Carol tells me with this patient smile. "Don't be afraid to give her a good kick with your heels. You won't hurt her – she's a huge horse." It doesn't register at first but I finally do just enough to keep her moving, all-the-while apologising profusely to the animal on our journey across the rocky fields.

When we get back to the paddock, I tie up Chrissie, hug her goodbye and then we wash up before heading back for a steak and salad lunch.

We're quad biking this afternoon. Well now, isn't this kind of like being on an outward bound/summer camp for troubled children or something?

(Imagine the sound of screeching brakes, NOW!)

They are charging us an additional $40 each to use the bikes. We're required to sign forms that include our credit card details. But hang on a second. "Fuck that – there's no way in Hell I'm including the correct details," I tell Lee, Bobby and Tony. I clearly forget that I don't have an actual credit card, though I do have a Bank of Ireland Laser card, all the good it's done me for over-the-counter transactions here. We give them fake details and then we make our way to the bikes, which are kept in a nearby pen. Sam, an Essex boy who isn't too bright, is teaching us the ropes, or the gears, or whatever you're having yourself.

We do a figure-of-eight around some tyres stacked metres apart and we go over a smallish bump so that Sam can grade us. Then it's the trial and the girls (Hannah, Trisha and Alexandre) lead the way. Then there's me, Tony, Lee and Rob. Andy,

Beaver, Lynne, Sarah, David and Marianne bring up the rear in a van. We rip ahead at a speed of up to fifty kilometres, then we stop, mostly because the slower people at the front keep braking. Reddish dirt covers our goggles, our faces, our clothes. Every breath means a mouthful of dust – dug up by the wheels of the bike in front – but we don't care because we are having such an awesome time. A guide from the northbound Oz Experience bus speeds off ahead of us on a scrambler motorcycle, and then he shoots back behind us before appearing alongside us again.

At one stage, when he's ahead of us, I see him ditch the track for the scrubs and long, scorched grass that's off-road. He comes back to us after a while – holding an emu chick aloft for me to see. "The bloody thang's jus' shid all ova' me aaaaaaam," he goes.

Our posse stops up at this beautiful, scenic spot where three of the farm hands on their quads have pulled off to the side. They have signalled for us to stop. The others in the van pull up next to us. I've got a thirst on me that could kill a camel and the lot of them are standing around – ignoring us tourists, drinking cans of beer and taking the piss out of each other as we burn up in the sun. If I'm honest, I can handle the thirst but I'm keen to get back on the trail. They stand there, congratulating the guide on "orphaning" the chick.

"The woife an' kids'll be stoked whin they see her," he tells them. "But the woife'll kill me if she foinds out how I god it." And that passes as humour out here. They laugh and joke about it – conveniently forgetting the reason why the bird has just shit itself.

After about thirty minutes we do get back on the trail – this is an utter disgrace. However, more bumps, dust and adrenaline soon make the matter disappear in the dust trailing behind us.

We have to stop at this cattle station because there are horses (with tourists on their backs) in the vicinity and we must wait for them to pass on.

We're taken back up to the range for more (optional) shooting at $2 per cartridge. Here, we can also take part in a goat-lassoing competition. Lynne and I, along with

Helper Monkey who was too hung-over to come with us this morning, choose the shooting option. Andy hands me five blue cartridges when it's my turn and I step up to the mark confidently. The tour guides gather around as Beaver tells them of my result this morning.

And then I miss every single pigeon. Five out of five this morning and now I hit zero/none/nada of the discs. I'm gutted.

"I've lost it."

They all offer theories involving wind, light and tiredness but I'm just annoyed with myself. Then the boys enter a lassoing competition but I don't because "I think it's cruel". However, this doesn't stop me from photographing them as they're put through their paces. They do well and are narrowly beaten by a group of Americans from the hop-on-hop-off bus but I think the lads were robbed. Ultimately, I see this as putting the goats through unnecessary trauma for our own selfish entertainment.

While this was happening, Beaver called me aside to tell me that he had to kill a goat. Apparently, the kid was almost dead on arrival into this world the day before and was in the pen, suffering. He told me that Andy signalled to him during the competition and then ran his finger across his throat to tell me he had just slit its throat.

"The little thing was jus loyin' there, facked," Beaver goes. "He points out the kids' parents to me and says: "Goats aaa' not loike humans or even otha' enimals – they'e not very mateee'nal."

For what it's worth, they didn't seem too upset. I'll go one further and tell you that they now, in fact, look like they couldn't give a shit either way.

To be honest, I'm not sure how to react here. These people are used to life in the countryside, except the countryside here is a different thing than "the country" back in Europe. Here, we are literally in the middle of nowhere. I'm sure there are vets in Bileola and the surrounding area but considering the vastness of the region, I doubt the vet is an option. And I'm doubtful as to whether they'd pay for him to put down some livestock. They don't wait for a second opinion here, this is rural Australia. One minute there can be life and a problem in the shape of pain for a suffering lamb or goat. Then there is death and no pain. I'm an animal lover but it's hard to argue with the logic.

So Beaver steps up to the plate for his party piece. He lays some canisters of Butane out on the range and we hide behind the fence as he unleashes one of the cartridges into the fuel, followed in quick succession by another. He truly is a great shot; there's a loud bang, a bright explosion and then all that's left is a line of fire across the scorched earth.

Andy the Cowboy is "Yee-hawing" loudly, as he gathers us around him in a circle for an "electrifoyin' finale". So, there are twenty of us, joining hands – he is in the centre with a crazy look in his eye and he's got a cattle prod in his hands. And, he *is* an "Aus'ralian". Oh well, it's clear to me that we're all going to die. Apparently, he's "gownna put" eleven thousand volts through our bodies in something akin to a "choyn roy-ek-chion". But we're not to worry because it's the "Amps that kill", somebody kind of half remembers reading somewhere but can't be sure.

This should be 'fun'. OH. MY. We're trembling. Scratch that: we are SHITTING ourselves.

I know what you're thinking but national pride is at stake here. I'm the only Irish person here amongst mainly English and American peoples. There's the odd German and Canadian but my main focus is the English chaps I've been touring with; Lee, Tony and Bobby. Can't have them thinking that us Irish guys are wimps.

Says Andy: "Now, listen caaa'fully...the chaaa'ge in this heee' caddle prod would be anough ta froy one piii'son and thet's just whad'll happen eff someone broyks the choyn (chain). Eff ya pull away...basically, ya'll make a circuit wid the graaa'nd (ground!) and the chaaa'ge will buuuu'n (burn) a fackin' hole in ya boot."

He warns us to take any electrical devices such as cameras and mobile phones from our pockets etc and to take off watches and jewellery. At this stage people start to drop away from the circle quickly. A mullet-wearing, earring-sporting Aussie boy of six or seven-years-of age pulls out, but astonishingly, not on the insistence of his father who's nearby. Less than an hour previously, the boy was firing the shotgun with Andy's help.

"And don't fo'git ta check thet ya hends eeen't sweady," he warns us.

"Aaaa' ya'll fackin' ready?" he asks. "Heeeya we gooooo."

And nothing. Tony is asked to hold one prong of the prod between his forefinger and thumb. And a heavy, mouthy, American-sounding girl with dreads grabs the other prong.

"You have GOT to be fucking kidding me," the London lad, Tony, tells Andy but he is ignored. So, after building the drama to an impressive height, Andy passes 11,000 volts through our bodies. I squeeze my partners' hands tighter yet. I'm sure I just heard bones snap but fuck it; here's no way any of this shower are going to let go and turn me into toast.

A quick, sharp pulse passes from my right to my left wrist within nanoseconds and that's it. The charge has passed through my body. Andy then organises a smaller circle and the boys are calling me to join them but I've already put my watch back on so I decline. Plus, I don't want to.

So Fat Dreaded American Girl turns around and says: "Come on...have you Irish goys got seeeand (I know, yeah! "Sand" apparently) up yore asses or sumethin', huh?"

But you should never corner an Irishman. "Nah, we just like to see Americans fry so poke yer beak out of it," I tell her. Everyone doubles up in laughter, especially Beaver. After this, Tony asks if he can be shot on his arse cheek because he's the kind of guy who would take one for the team. That's just the kind of guy he is.

He seems terrified, but he's also loving it. Tony slowly pulls down the top of his jeans and Andy duly obliges.

So today, boys and girls, we've learned not to go to the farm with the Bad Man and how to differentiate between Sadists and Masochists. Back at the camp, as the newbies queue for their roast goat at dusk, Fat Dreaded American Girl approaches Beaver, Bobby, Lee and I while we're having a drink. And she turns out to be a Canadian. Oops! Then she joins us at our table for dinner and is easily the loudest there. (I bet she is an American really.) She's sitting next to the father of the Aussie-mullet kid, while the boy himself and his sister are also there: the latter are lovely people, the salt of the earth. They're all having a right old natter and, although the girl hasn't been in the country long, she's telling us all (and anyone else who'll listen) about her plans over the next two years. "Blah-di-feckin'-blah", is all I hear. I've heard this story about 9,000 times in the past two-or-so weeks from various sources but talk about laying it on thick? I'm trying to learn to suffer Fools more gladly, I really am. It's easy to be cynical though. This is how North-Americans-who-pretend-to-be-Canadians talk and she seems like a decent-enough sort. Not sound enough to stop me and my lot legging it to bed, however.

It's 10.30 and everyone from my tour is sound asleep in bed, obviously exhausted after an event-filled day. I'm the only one still up, sitting on the veranda and smoking Long Beach cigarettes. I'm journaling the happenings of the past couple of days. I'm sitting, waiting for the Writing Monster to visit. Eventually he does.

I stretch my stiff limbs and slowly stand up, before making my way to the toilet and go over to the dining area to fill my water bottle. On the way there, I can see today's arrivals doing exactly what I did the night before. I see them through the corner of my tired eye but I don't look directly at them. I listen to crickets and campfire sparks on the way back to the cool dorm room – the gentle hum of the air conditioner and the snores, the only sounds filling the room now. And by about 11.10pm, I too am in the lad of nod.

6. Helper Monkey

DAY SIXTEEN

We're up at 7am and, even though it's the closest to eight full hours sleep I have gotten in almost three weeks, I'm shattered. Obviously my body is looking for more rest but it has had its lot until tonight. It's Sunday morning and we stop in nearby Bileola to allow Beaver get supplies for Carnavron Gorge, which really is in the middle of nowhere. Well, it's the middle of Queensland, or about 600 kilometres north-west of Brissy to be more accurate. Beaver will cook for us over the next couple of days at Carnavron National Park.

As usual, it's a gorgeous morning and here in Bileola I can finally get coverage for my phone. The place, named after Caernarfon in Wales, attracts about 65,000 visitors every year. I ring my sister Lorraine to catch up on the goings on back in Waterford and she can barely hear me because she's in a club. Not a club as such but a late bar named Ruby Lounge. She puts me onto Aisling, a mutual friend, and I can't understand a word so I hang up.

We move on and later stop near some lake or other and I'm eating chicken and chips from Chooks, a dodgy KFC if you ask me. The chicken here tastes just foul. I'm sorry, I had to do it. We're swapping stories of stupidity that we've witnessed in our lives (not our own though – ammo is the last thing these people need). Beaver tells us how, once upon a time on some other tour of "Austra'ia" while driving tourists along the coast, he took the piss unmercifully out of this bullish guy for asking him if they were "hoigh above sea level".

And Lee, who often works in camps for rich kids in the US, explains how the workers there used to tell some dopey kids to gather water "from the deep end of the pool and put it in the shallow end, to even out the water levels".

This reminds me of my youth, when I used to go camping with the De La Salle scouts out in Faithlegg, Co. Waterford. Some of the younger leaders, obviously bored out of their woggles, would send us off to look for "ice pegs" for the tents or "buckets

107

of elbow grease" for cleaning or, for the classic "long stand". Now, I don't want to be mean here but some of us knew what was going on but kept quiet so that the boys who weren't so bright would go looking for the objects.

We travel for miles and miles along the flat road up to Carnavron Gorge – spotting mainly wallabies as opposed to their larger kangaroo cousins. These are hopping about in fields near the road. Some of them are now at one with the road. Still, it must get boring for the marsupials out here. Roulette with cars and trucks seems to be where it's at.

Meanwhile, the Eucalyptus trees in the horizon give off a fervent blue hue, while the sun pierces through the branches and the motion of the bus causes the scene to flicker in the corner of our eyes, even through some of our eyelids when closed. There's a constant smell of burning bush and for some time, clearly in the midst of some dopey daydream, I think that there must be a fire somewhere. Also, I keep dropping my camera down the side of the bloody seats.

It turns out, according to Beaver at any rate, that the blue-ish film on the horizon could actually be smoke. "Ye, thet smoke could be frum thousands of miles awoooy."

Hmmm. Did I dream that?

We arrive and we're assigned our lodgings, which are these safari tents, or canvas tents with steel frames, zip-up windows and doors – all leading out onto some wooden decking with steps. We settle in, eat chicken salad for dinner, play cards and tease Lynne for "pretending to be Canadian" when she's "actually an American". Of course, we're on the goon again. Lynne is, in fact, a Canadian but sure why let that get in the way of a good ribbing. Anyway, she loves the attention and is well able to toss a few barbs back in our direction. Particularly in my direction. When I get bored (which, when it comes to cards, doesn't take long at all), I take the cards in hand. Lee has got them free with Brit lad-rag, *FHM* magazine, and I use them to tell the others' fortunes.

The cards have pictures on them of young nubile hotties kitted out in their undies, all in alluring poses. When I tell them what I'm up to, Lee seems very excited. Well, they're his cards and it's obvious that he wants to hear his name mentioned in the same sentence as the aforementioned young ladies.

I lay out cards for Lee and Lynne.

I tell Lee that he will become a boring accountant who will settle down in a boring yet respectable terraced home in Chiswick, London. He learns that he will get run over by his-then boring wife, Lynne, who has discovered that Lee is having an affair. He will survive and even recover from his injuries but alas, Lynne will leave him for one of the hot girls on the cards.

At this stage I can tell that Lee is disappointed at my prediction. But everyone else is cracking up.

I continue to tell him that he will live out his years wondering about what might have been in Australia if only he had managed to make a life for himself down under. This will lead to him living a life of quiet desperation, further leading to his early death from some lingering, painful condition. He will be buried in his favourite anorak.

Meanwhile, Lynne will marry her *FHM* Hottie. However, when she turns over the Death card, I'm left with no option but to tell her that she will die an untimely death after yet another crash in her Mini.

Helper Monkey, it becomes clear, "will become a crack whore who will give birth to seven children" – all of whom will have different fathers. Everyone is cracking up with laughter at that one. I can't recall what I tell Beaver.

Anyway, after a heated and drunken debate surrounding evolution, Western society, the evils of modern life versus days olden and spirituality, most of us head back to the tent I'm sharing with Lee, Tony and Bobby for some beers and goon. The lights at the dining area have been turned off at about 10pm. But it's gone 10.30 when we retire, having ignored the darkness, so enthralled were with the debate. Monkey is talking about her wheat allergy and Lee, obviously not hearing her correctly, asks her what it was that she has said. However, he doesn't understand the answer offered by Bobby and, to our amusement and curiosity, Lee tells him, "Look, I'm not asking you about your condom made out of bread mate; I'm asking about her allergy".

109

We're doubled up with laughter.

Then, a nagging neighbour comes up and asks us to keep it down.

We do try...honestly. The drinking and smoking continues and I misunderstand Alexandre at one point, insisting that she has a can of Pepsi (I bought a pack of twelve earlier in Bileola). However, she pulls her plastic cup away at the last minute so I destroy the table and her jeans with the sticky stuff and thankfully, she sees the funny side. Outside, as the low light permeates the campsite and surrounding vegetation, I spy a wallaby easily clear a distance of about thirty feet in three jumps.

I put my hoodie on because it's getting cold. It isn't long until we're all in bed, unconscious.

DAY SEVENTEEN

Tony's phone wakes me at stupid o'clock. I have a look at my watch and it's barely 5am. Bono is crooning about it being a beautiful day, though I couldn't agree less right now. The tune is nothing like that being played by the little man with the big hammer in my head. At this hour of the morning nothing is further from my plans than having a beautiful day so I toss and turn for the next couple of hours as the alarm goes off – the song playing again and again. And AGAIN!

Meanwhile, Bobby's phone seems to be competing with Tony's in the vain hope that at least one of them will wake from their slumber and go down to try and spot a Duck Bill Platypus in the nearby pond. I get up eventually, wrap a towel around my waist and try to muster up all the willpower that is mine to prevent me from murdering the London Lads in their sleep.

When I return from my shower to tent number twenty, David is taking pictures of a huge male kangaroo, which has stopped outside my tent to nibble at the grass. The marsupial is about fifteen feet away from my tent and he seems to be oblivious to our presence.

"His wife and baby are around the back," David informs me.

Daddy is chewing on the sparse tufts of sun-bleached vegetation and I don't know if it's the early morning light or what but his eyes, surrounded by eyelashes that would make your sister or cross-dressing brother jealous, look like those of a Kerry Blue dog. The kangaroo's arms or whatever are, I kid you not, bigger than Arnie's and his sleek rounded posterior – did I actually write that? – rests easily on two uber-powerful, spring-loaded legs that are coiled in easy athletic preparation for massive jumping. Hunched up, he looks about the same size as of a big man.

It's a humbling and majestic sight. *This ain't no wallaby*, I tell myself. I decide against telling him that I'll be eating his cousins later.

Anyway, I get dressed and hop off for breakfast consisting of Coco Pops, fried eggs, bacon and tea. Then, we leave for our hike up around Carnavron Gorge. We stop a short distance up and Beaver tells us about the oldest tree in the world and also about Eucalyptus trees. We're literally roasting in the morning Queensland son, baking in our sweat like a chicken in an oven. We are all the worst for wear but in good enough spirits all-the-same.

We climb about one kilometre to the escarpment. I start to show serious signs of my age (I'm between ten-and-twelve years older than Bobby, Tony and Lee) and general malaise, as I pant and push my way up the steep incline over 300 metres of wall-like steps. Tony stops about fifty metres above me and asks if I am okay. It's not intentional on his part I'm sure but it immediately makes me feel like the granddad of us four. I try and make myself feel better by imagining that Lee is taking time out from his career as a semi-professional soccer player, while Bobby nearly made the last Olympics, such is his gymnastic prowess. And Tony, well, he has climbed anything worth climbing in Britain and Ireland. Actually, none of this is a million miles away from the truth. Not one million; no way.

I console myself that, at the very least, I should be sweating out the goon from the night before. I'm a bit surprised – after all the steps – that there is another small incline and a 700-metre walk to the edge. When we get there, us boys pose in various positions over the barrier at the edge – overlooking the magnificent gorge –, pretending to be hanging from it and so forth. However, none of this can happen until we take pictures of Lee, who has insisted upon completely stripping off, as he does his Tarzan impression.

"Quickly, before the others get here," he tells us.

I'm groaning and my head is buried deep in my hands. *Why me, oh woe is me.* Hundreds of metres below us and as far as the eye can see, lies an expanse of dizzying green. There's absolute silence apart from the roaring quietness and the occasional echoing "Coooee", "Beaver is a bollocks" or whatever comments we send shooting down from above.

On the way back down, relieved at having made the strenuous journey up, I meet three ladies who are easily in their 70s, striding steadily up towards me. My heart sinks as it dawns on me that they are able to maintain a three-way flowing conversation. I must be in terrible shape.

We rest at the bottom, eat oranges. When we get back to the dining area, we make some wraps. Some of us sit around relaxing. I sip from a can of VB and, stretching out on one of the long benches there, I nod off.

I wake up and about twenty minutes has passed. I go to check my emails on a computer that has possibly the worst Internet connection on the planet. Although, considering where we are, I'm not too surprised. Paying $3 for fifteen minutes here is just like throwing the money into the gorge. I go back to my tent to relax and catch up on some writing before I head over for yet another shower before dinner.

I go over before 6pm to help Beaver to cook up some "snags" (or long pork sausages), steaks that come from a cow and those of the marsupial variety. Oh, and there's salad, and veggie burgers for Monkey as well. I'm surprised at how tender and juicy the near fat-free kangaroo steaks are. After some chocolate cake and the obligatory washing up, we're sitting around and drinking goon. Goon, in case I neglected to mention, is a type of wine concentrate. Although it's closer, chemically, to nitro-glycerine I suspect. And oh, it costs about $12 for five litres of the stuff. When I bought my first box, at a Bottle Shop (as they call them) in Rainbow Beach, the guy working there warned me of its potency.

"Aaah ya gunna put somthin' through thet mate?" he asked me.

"No, like what?" I enquired.

"Lemonade or waduh (water)."

This was before I had actually handed over any money. Alas, only when the cash register hand rung, did he tell me of its toxicity. But when I asked as to why he didn't warn me of this important fact before the purchase, he just said: "Aw well mate, ya've jus boughd it now so..."

Bastard.

Anyway, we've taken the goon out of the "Esky" (that's a cooler, to you and me) and we're drinking it like water. On the way to the toilet I ask a Kiwi woman and her English expat friend for a loan of their lighter. On the way back, the Kiwi, who looks like Mother Theresa on holiday, tells me that her husband is from Belfast. "His name is Green," she tells me, as if I had asked. The English woman, who has been living in Aussie for thirty years, joins in and tells me that her husband is from "somewhere in Cork beginning with the letter T". So I'm wondering if I'm supposed to play a guessing game with her or if she actually needs help with the location. It turns out to be the latter.

"Togher?"

"No."

My poor drink-addled brain struggles to come up with other place names in Co. Cork beginning with the letter T, when she says, "I got it".

"Tyrone," she goes. Okaaaay...but I don't have the heart or the inclination to tell her that Tyrone is actually in Northern Ireland. Though, maybe she's not totally mistaken: it could have been one of the other two husbands. She has yet to divorce hubbie number three but she assures me that the papers are in the post back home in Brisbane. She warns me of Karma in life, which lends me to guess that she hasn't been the most faithful of people in the past. That she's been a bold girl even.

The natural light leaves the chilled, spring sky and the processed light goes out at the dining area at 10pm. So, against our own better judgment, made earlier when we were far more sober, we decide on a party back at our abode, tent number twenty. We go back and finish yet another carton of goon that the lads have bought and, as is the custom, the box is made into a helmet. It is made by mine own hand and I place it onto Helper Monkey's head. Tony and Bobby go for a shower, which I find very bizarre. Lee is laid out on the double bed he has commandeered and he is goon-ed out of his skull. There's just myself, Monkey and Trisha sitting on the decking outside my tent. Helper plonks herself down on my lap, as I demand another cigarette from her. I am being demanding here but I've run out and there is nowhere to buy cancer sticks for miles and miles around. And, she is *my* Helper Monkey. Plus, I've been drinking the dreaded goon.

I go a step further and tell Helper and Trisha to "get out of my apartment" and to "go home". Of course, I can't remember any of this clearly. I learn about the last bit the next day from the girls, who find it amusing in the extreme. Helper takes pleasure in telling me how I went in, got undressed and got into bed. However, not quite: the girls charged in when they heard a "loud thump" and tried to get me off the floor. When I eventually got back into bed, I only went and fell out again. The girls gave up on me and left, apparently. They left me as I was – with my top half hanging out of the bed, my elbow resting on the floor. However, when I woke up some hours later, I was fully in bed. So 'progress' was obviously made.

The girls think it's all hilarious and take the piss unmercifully.

At least now I know why it's called goon. I half-expect to see a picture of myself on the front of a box of the eejit-fuel sometime soon.

DAY EIGHTEEN

We are to meet for breakfast at 6am and of course I'm late. Lee comes into the tent as I open my eyes and he tells me that everyone is packed up and waiting at the dining area. When I get there, Beaver is packing up the esky and he says: "Oi've jus' told the boys thet 'I hope Ciaran loikes livin' in Carnavron Go'ooge 'cuz wa' loyvin' (leaving) now." The little shit.

David, my Saviour, takes pity on me and produces a tea bag from his pocket. I scrounge some milk and sugar from the good folk at the neighbouring table and I make tea with the boiling water from the boiler. Sa-weeeeet!

So I take a can of lukewarm Pepsi on board and we're off on our nine-hour drive to Airlie Beach. From here, we'll spend a couple of days here before sailing around the Whitsundays for a couple of more days. On the way up the road we spot a lone backpacker – who easily looks to be in his early sixties – hitching a lift. He's literally in the middle of nowhere. And he looks German. We also pass the site of a crashed truck, while the vehicle was recently towed away, according to Beaver. Nasty.

We stop a couple of hours later in God-Knows-Where for diesel, and I buy a pie, a packet of crisps and a bottle of Powerade. We push on but I get bored and I can't sleep so I hop up to the front to keep El Beaver company. And, as a conversation with the great man himself normally goes, we touch on everything from music, religion and philosophy, to women, booze and drugs.

Lest I forget, my phone, a Nokia that has been with me for some five years and has subjected me to ridicule from my friends because of its shabby status, has finally packed in. Beaver has "ab'aaat six phoynes" so he kindly lends me one of his, another Nokia model; until I hit civilisation where I can buy a new one. And alas, in my sleep-deprived state and with my drink-soaked brain, I've only gone and left it in the tent at the gorge.

I'm feeling sentimental because the old Nokia and I have come through some scrapes together. One of these happened twenty-one months previously. My friends and I were out having Christmas Drinks in Geoff's [Bar] in Waterford, which is one of the more known bars in the city. We agreed to move onto another pub, Nicky's, on Mayor's Walk. But I got caught talking to somebody or other – as has been known to happen – and the lads were pissed off waiting. So they left. I had placed my old phone on the table and it was still there (minus the lads) when I returned. I should mention here that the plastic cover on the aforementioned mobile was broken. And, nutter that I am; I had even used sticky tape to hold it together. I could afford a new one. I could have easily bought a new cover. But I did neither of those things.

Anyway, I thought I'd just ring the lads to make sure they were headed to Nicky's. But when I tried to do so I found that the buttons, those raised ones on a rubber mat of sorts if you will, were gone. I had a few drinks on-board so it took me about half-a-minute to figure out what had happened. They kept ringing me too, though of course I couldn't answer the bloody phone. I left the bar and turned left up John St. and then saw the lads turning the bend up Newgate St. Bastards. Of course, when I got there, I was a great source of amusement to them all. Suspect number one, Leonard, was laughing the loudest.

He didn't even deny doing it when I challenged him on it.

We stop at a city actually named Emerald, a quaint and wealthy Queensland mining town. Can you guess what was mined here in days olden? As I've said, Aussies aren't the most imaginative when it comes to place-names and so on. While here, Lynne buys some hats as presents for loved ones back home in Canada and I find some bathrooms at the train station. I finally spy a coffee shop, cafe or whatever and it reminds me of a US diner but, with reassuringly expensive wares – surely to remind travellers and locals that, Yes, one is in Emerald.

I order a large cappuccino to take out and I'm charged €5.70, which ain't good value, let me tell you. Some hours later, we are driving north and we're drawn in my "Beaver Mountain", to the right on our horizon. Hang on, WHAT? Did our tour guide just name a mountain after himself? What turns out to be Peak Downs (apparently there's gold in them there hills!) doesn't seem to get any closer for some time but then, strangely, it's literally on top of us. I check Beaver's face but there are no winks or knowing nods, no slight upturn or even twist of the mouth either. In fact, there's not even a trace of self-consciousness to his face when he tells us how a mountain is "noymed afta'" him.

When I ask him what it's really called, he continues: "Beaver Mountain." Apparently, in case you asked, which you didn't but then again neither did I for that matter, some tourists christened the mountain thus after the tour bus broke down near there.

Riiiiiight so (edges nervously towards the door).

We stop for lunch at some "royde haaas", as Beaver calls it, and I imagine that the ghost of the late, great Patrick Swayze is busting heads in there. But the place is basically a filling station that sells hot food and it attracts a mixed bag. These seem to consist of holidaying families, truckers, mullet-loving locals and other commuters. And then there's us.

I buy some class of chicken or fish cake that has lots of broccoli inside it and is truly disgusting, and so is the vanilla milkshake but the chips are okay. Deep fried broccoli...a sneaky way to get some vitamins and goodness into the kids eh. Cue duelling banjos. I don't see too many fresh fish items on the menu but then again, we're well over one hundred kilometres from the coast – and in the middle of nowhere in Queensland – so that's understandable. Though of course this distance is virtually nothing in Australian terms. In fairness, Australia is one of the few developed countries in the world where you can drive at a fair clip on a road as the crow flies for nine hours and still remain in the same state.

Eventually, we reach Airlie Beach. The eucalyptus trees on the run in are sparsely populated and then all bunched together, before they fall away and reveal lush greenery – the palm trees springing forth, telling us that water is not far away. Clean streets and well-designed residential spaces clear the way for the houses and apartments that, from on-high, overlook the sea of partying tourists ebbing and flowing along the strip below. But the houses on the hills flanking the resort are surely the reserve of the rich and famous. Beaver drives us to our lodgings for the evening, Club Crocodile.

We amble into a curious cubbyhole called Paddy's Shenanigans and of course I hate it. Then, it's on to Mama Africa's, a nightclubby kind of joint that stays open until 5am apparently. One of the younger girls gets upset because of some minor drama that has been propelled into the stratosphere with, more than likely, numerous

Jägerbombs. We make sure that she's okay. Bobby and some others take her back to Club Croc – and Tony and I head back into Africa's. Outside in the smoking area are numerous beefcake blokes – all sporting wife-beaters and casual shorts, big-tongued trainers and baseball caps. Most...actually, all of them sport tattoos and some wear chunky neck chains. The lot of them seem to be out of it, the atmosphere here is tense and aggressive.

We meet two Kiwi barmaids who recognise us from Beach Bar and we engage them with ridiculousness. The last thing I remember of the club is challenging the taller one to a dance-off on the floor. Imagine, if you will, Derek Zoolander versus Chrissie Hynde on speed. Not that either of us were but...!

We all end up on the street at some ridiculous hour and Tony and I decide to get rid of the idiotic pair after the Chrissie lookalike stupidly spits some chewed up crisps on my arm. Perhaps this is some weird southern hemisphere mating ritual or maybe she was reared by wolves but alas, it's time to say goodbye.

7. "Cetch of the Doy"

DAY NINETEEN

Today, we will go sailing around the Whitsundays – the name given to a group of islands off the east coast that's close enough to Airlie. My pirating skills will be called upon at about noon when my band of scurvy dogs will commandeer a vessel and take to the High Seas.

For now, we're ushered into a shop that sells didgeridoos and opals. Beaver has assured us that it's the finest collection and most reasonably priced selection of both in the land. Well, in Airlie Beach at any rate. I'm seriously dehydrated and I've had my fill after about twenty minutes but we're still in the place about one hour later and Beaver's commission, I suspect, like my boredom, is growing by the minute. Eventually we leave and make our way to some place nearby where we can book our diving on-board the yacht. However, my honesty is not rewarded and I am not allowed to dive because of state laws. I must, apparently, get a letter of clearance from a doctor. Why? Because I absent-mindedly admitted to having asthma, albeit a controllable, low grade of the condition.

Beaver introduces me to his girlfriend and then tells me to "Shad ap Ciaran" as soon as I speak. It's presumably for her benefit so I jokingly pick up the little guy and pretend to shake him around like a dog might a rabbit. For her benefit you see? Haha. We go to some Mall nearby and order some pizzas at a unit there. I'm annoyed when it takes over forty minutes, and after some prompting, for her to deliver it. Unusually, it's not the hunger that annoys me but the fact that we're left with just fifteen minutes to buy our booze for the sailing trip. However, we do manage to get sixty cans of VB and ten litres (two boxes) of goon to keep us afloat (or drown us!) on our three-day, two-night voyage. We also get a twelve-litre drum of water. Honestly.

Down at the harbour we sign our documents before we're greeted and welcomed on board by Locky – a loud-yet-chilled and lean-yet-deceptively strong Aussie in his late twenties or early thirties. He's a good enough laugh but he rarely smiles and looks completely different without his sunglasses, it turns out. So we board our sleek vessel, dragging our booty alongside and beneath us. I keep my personal effects to a minimum and I have only one pair of board shorts, my swimming shorts, a towel, two tee-shirts and toiletries. Alas, I forget to bring underwear. *A likely story, Creep.* Who said that?

We're baking in the October sun; the heat is stifling. (There's something wrong with that sentence.) The hangover is kicking in.

"G'day, welcome abooo'd," yells Kane, our Skipper.

Kane is a no-nonsense, chilled and butch Aussie. He's an amiable chap. Shy of six-feet tall, he's stocky, has clearly had a broken nose and looks like he could handle himself in most situations. Including the crew, there's over thirty of us onboard the vessel. Lou, a sweet and chirpy girl from Essex in England, smiles and welcomes us aboard as Dave, an understated English bloke who's "trying to get a job with the touring yachts", makes up the crew. I'm surprised when I find out that he turns out to be "working for his board" on Boomerang. Eh, fuck that!

The Southern Cross Sailing Adventures company's information leaflet thingy tells us that Boomerang raced under the name Ondine VII and "achieved great success" such as winning the World Maxi Series Race, plus "winning races in the USA, Japan and New Zealand. Incorporating a "sloop design", Boomerang is 82 feet in length and built of carbon fibre with a mast extending 110 feet above the deck. So far, so good. She was competing in "tough ocean races, such as the Auckland to Suva Race", up until late 2001. But in November 2001 Southern Adventures bought the yacht in New Zealand, fitted a new interior and in May 2002 she started her Whitsunday sailing tours. So now, it seems, Boomerang has been put out to pasture. She ferries tourists around the islands, the barrier reef and so on. Along with a teak and ash timber floor, Boomerang has full galley, three bathrooms and an equal number of dining tables, a lounge area and double and single berths, for twenty eight guests and four crew.

With our engine still on, we plough through the turquoise mass, squalls of white foam rushing up to meet the stern as it cuts through the water. Kane and Co. are clearly in their element now as they move away from land and, probably from the eyes of their bosses. They change out of their uniforms and the skipper lights up a cigarette as he tells us about the boat, the islands and so on. Diced fresh fruit is brought around on silver trays, shortly before we go snorkelling. We don these weird stinger suits, which makes me feel like a diver from some random 1960s Sea Monster movie. However, they'll apparently protect our vital organs (!) from being stung so I'm down with that. The masks and snorkels come next, as do the fins. Kane organises us into three groups: those who consider themselves competent swimmers; those who have some experience in the water and those among us not too confident in the drink. I'm in the first dingy-trip out – the "Adventure Group" – as are Bobby, Tony, Lee and David. On Locky's instruction, we put our hands over our masks and tumble backwards over the edge of the rib, like Navy Seal Commandoes. Of course you are lads – just like Commandoes.

We spend over an hour scouring the reef below for fish that seem to be asleep or themselves on holiday. I spy a school of blue flecked fish with yellow tails that follow me along the coral. They surround me as I move and even though they move quickly in avoidance of my fins, I can feel them around my feet. Then, I'm underwater. I turn over and propel myself along on my back as the fish follow, moving my arms close at my sides in a circular motion to aid my movement. Suddenly, they're above, below and around me and it's an amazing sight. I think about trying to surface for a moment to try to contact Lee or Bobby, who both have waterproof cameras but I decide against it; opting to savour the majestic sight alone instead. I surface and swim about eighty metres to some reef and to more snorkelers, taking in the last thirty or so metres at speed. I want to see if the fish will stay with me. I sink below and watch the water from my wake settle and, lo and behold, the same school are there.

I find out later that these curious fish are called "Yellow Tailed Rangers" or something.

Shortly afterwards, we see a couple of Parrott Fish. They're aqua and red, and they look stunning. The coral below looks soft in parts, hard and brittle in others. I'm tempted to dive down and snap off a piece but I remember that it's forbidden and I respect the wishes of our crew in the end.

In the shallower parts, of course, you can stand on the coral (you're not supposed to) but that's the last thing I want to do and so of course it happens. I graze my foot on a jagged part of it. I barely feel it to be honest and I'm surprised when I look down to find that the coral is fairly ugly at this spot. Let's just describe it as raw beauty. Large and bulbous masses of spongy coral give way to sharp and spikey branches that jut out at irregular angles. I'm hovering gently over a particular section when, just seconds later I find myself metres away – over completely different vegetation. Suddenly, rays of light sear past me and into the dark watery depths beyond some shelf. It truly is a living organism and like life, it becomes clear that its components cannot be neatly boxed away.

Locky comes back for us in the inflatable and the younger, more slender lads can hoist themselves up onto it from down below, just by using the handles on the sides of the vessel. I try twice and almost succeed on the second attempt but I fail. So, with the help of Locky's reaching arms and with not some inconsiderable effort from yours truly, I find myself wriggling on the deck like a fish out of water. "Cetch of the doy moyte," he tells me.

"Tell the girls that."

When we board Boomerang again, one of the girls comments on my bleeding foot, which I suspect will hurt more later on than it does now, once the numbing effects of one-hour-plus in the water wears off. I tell anyone who will listen that the blood pouring from the savage gash in my foot is a result of a shark attack (adding, of course, that the shark came out all-the-worse for his foolish move!). Kane seems to enjoy the tale anyway.

We shed our suits and laze about on deck – sipping cans of beer in the early evening sunset. The crew have brought out a snack of messy nachos and we all get stuck in. Smooth sounds emanate from the speakers and the boat is steadily cutting through the water. As you can imagine, life isn't too bad at the moment. It contrasts boldly with the work we were tasked with earlier. Some of us were made to work at raising the sails. Four groups of two were placed at the centre of the yacht for grinding or gybing or whatever the hell it's called. It basically involves the grinders facing each other and bending over these winches. You know the score; there's handles on the end of these shafts that work the same way as pedals on a bicycle. Grabbing a handle in each hand, the slaves must rotate them in a circular motion on our skipper's commands – first one way, then the other. Meanwhile, three others will use their body weight, along with every aching muscle in their torsos, to tug on a line in the assist to raise the sails. It's technically called jibing the jib-jab, tacking-the-trim, hanging-the-ticktacktoe – ah, here, look; I haven't a feckin' clue, okay?

Anyway, they say, write about what you know, so here it goes. I'm laying on the deck and I raise my can of VB to Tony as the sun – like a giant, juicy orange – sips slowly beneath the horizon. We're waiting for a dinner consisting of chicken pieces smothered in a peanut satay, salad, rice and garlic bread. In the run up to dinner, as the light is sucked out of the blue sky, I take this time to inform the girls of their duties and I tease them unmercifully about which of them will be bringing me my dinner; who'll be doing do my washing up and so on. They'll need to wait on me hand-and-foot, they learn. At the outset, it's clear that the Canadian and English contingent aren't sure how to take such outlandish cheek. English girls, Emma, Claire, Rachel, Thuay and both Canadian girls whose names I can't seem to remember, are shocked, horrified and apparently disgusted when I tell them that "you can decide amongst yourselves who will bring me my dinner tonight". The others, I inform them, can "do my washing up afterwards".

"And if you can't decide among yourselves, I will do it for you," I go on. Emma tells me that I'm "just like" her brother, "who's also a male chauvinist pig" and I thank her for the compliment.

But don't get me wrong, the girls are actually loving this.

And in the end, would you believe that I end up having to do my own chores? I tell the girls how disappointed I am in them and the craic continues. We lads, having drunk our quota of seven cans of lager for the night (we've rationed out our drink do you see?), are now getting stuck into the goon. This will leave us with eight cans each tomorrow night. There's a group of ten playing drinking games such as Ping, Pang, Pong and it's obvious that I'm the eldest here. I'm also the only non-English person there (until the Canadians, Tazzy Tim and his mate David come along). It becomes tedious for an old codger like myself so I mosey over to Monkey, Trisha and a young Italian bloke, Tomaz.

When I go back, Thuay and I break away from the group awhile. We're stretched out on our backs as we scan the vast panorama above us. It's probably the best view of the stars that I've ever seen. And it's quite different to the views we get in the northern hemisphere.

I'm looking for the Southern Cross – instead of the Big Dipper. It's October so it's probably below the horizon or something. Either way, it's an awesome view of the Milky Way. An endless navy ceiling is dotted with faintly-blinking bulbs as elsewhere, prominent and barely-visible pinheads of light mingle and look like trails of paint casually flicked from a paintbrush onto a navy canvas. We exchange what information we each own about it. However, I don't want to mislead here. It's not like a scene from *Dawson's Creek* or *The OC*: it's not at all romantic, cheesy or worthy of cringe, and it has little meaning to us on that front.

I eventually stumble down to my bunk. There are many competing snoring sounds below deck; the music, voices and laughter drifting down from above. The only light down here in the cramped, stifling space is that coming from the stars and moon – beaming down the gaping hole that allows access to the dungeon.

DAY TWENTY

That ain't workin' – that's the way you do it – money for nothin' and your chicks for free. The irresistible guitar riff that follows this, hooks me in and alas, I can court no more sleep. The music is loud, the sunlight washes down into the dungeon from various orifices on the yacht's deck and from the corner of my eye I can see Lou preparing breakfast as sailors all around me wake from their slumber. It's a surreal scene.

After breakfast, we're told to take a stinger suit before we're ferried into Whitsunday Island in the RIB. From here, we'll trek to glorious Whitehaven Beach. We're told that the removal of the fine, white sand from the beach is not allowed.

Except, of course, unless you're from NASA. Fact. The sand, the finest in the world apparently, is used for making special telescope lenses. That's the official line, though I prefer the conspiracy theories that are running through my head regarding same. I imagine some creatures that look like a mix between the aliens from the movies Cocoon and ET, popping up from the sand for lunch.

It's not often that I think about the area in between my big and second toes. However, I can think of little else at the moment: my flip flops have indeed waged war on my feet. So I take them off but, between the red-hot sand and the bits of branches sticking out of it, there's pain. Even in Paradise. However, it's worth every painful step along the trial down to the beach because, when we finally make it there, we're met with a spectacular scene. We walk some distance down to reach the water's edge – a fine line separating the blue and white blankets. We're supposed to don the suits but there's little chance of that happening. In our excitement, we run into the water. We're like kids. The lads and I throw a rugby ball to each other, the girls scan the clear shallows for a "Tiffany Ring" that one of them has apparently lost. It is finally found.

Afterwards, we lay on the beach and regenerate – the sun warming us to our bones. And I don't feel too healthy. The drinking is definitely taking its toll on my body and mind. After about an hour here, we make our way back to the pick-up point. I've been good enough at painting myself with sun block (or so I think) and the fact remains that there's little escape from the sun. And patches of red are appearing on my torso. Lee bursts out laughing at the design sprawled across my chest and stomach, so I've obviously been a tad careless in applying it. I've also been wearing the Akruba, which I've almost lost to the drink a few times. At one stage I have my fellow deckhands scattering along the deck chasing the thing as it tries to make good its escape from my sweating head.

After lunch we go snorkelling at another location, a much better place for the activity. I'm swimming along the surface, my face down in the water, and I seem to see faces in the coral. Happy faces, sad faces, angry and contorted faces. I'm a bit perturbed at all of this. However, I shake myself out of it and swim to another location. I was born to the water – a creature of the deep, at one with its wishes yet locked in a brave battle of wills against its desires. I command thebeautiful winged coloured creatures to accede to my wishes, obey my orders. The fish follow me wherever I go.

Jesus, what? I struggle to break free of her hold on me; my inner monologue telling me that she's sucking me in with her rich, lingering promises. Raising my head above the surface, I notice that I've drifted quite a distance from the markers, realising that I need to get a grip here. And that's the hold the reef has got on me. Perhaps I've had too much sun, too much sea, too little sleep and way too many drinks over the past few weeks (little do I know that I'm only touching the tip of the proverbial iceberg here!). Maybe all of these are involved in a conspiracy to fudge my thought processes. It's an unreal existence but oh, such fun when it is!

I swim to the RIB and ask Locky if I can swim back to the yacht, which is about 600-700 metres away, and he is thinking about it for a few seconds. "Naw mate, theee's too meny otha' yachts araaaand."

So again, he pulls me onboard, again telling me that I'm the "Cetch of the doy". Bet he says that to all the boys!

However, and maybe as a consolation prize, we're allowed us to do somersaults and backflips from the side of the boat into the water about eight feet below. Feeling instantly better than I've felt all day, I swim under the yacht and am greeted by relaxed and curious Batfish as I frolic in an underwater paradise, almost as far away from home as I can be on this planet. I'm having a Ball of a time.

Later, in the early evening as the clear blue sky starts do darken in small increments and looks like it is smeared manically with marmalade, we engage The Broom Stick – the old enemy, apparently – in competition. However, when both yachts sail side-by-side across some strait but at a distance close to one kilometre apart, the 'Stick chickens out. It's clearly because she's getting a royal arse-kicking. There's some work to be done in making sure the Boomerang gets the most out of the conditions: we're all working together at getting the sails raised and the boom in position.

Kane is in his element. It's clear that ferrying landlubber tourists around the 'Sundays gets boring for the crew, particularly for our skipper. He skilfully guides the yacht into the wind, seemingly reading the conditions expertly and applying subtle turns when necessary. David, a Triathlete of some experience, and I are grinding at the bow and it is exhausting work as it's an activity that requires short bursts of explosive energy. After a while, when the Broomstick (awful name for a yacht, don't you think?) yet again plots a different course to apparently tell us that she's thrown in the towel, we go back to the drinking.

But not before we give them the "Boomerang salute". This is something that we will do to any and all that dare cross us on our voyage. We engage said vessel with waving and cheerful pleasantries. And when the yacht is lulled into a false sense of security – and upon Locky's instruction –, us lads drop our shorts, shake our white touristy arses in the air and shout, "Boomerang!"

Back to the drinking and we're suddenly interrupted by something close to hysteria at the stern. Porpoises can be seen surfing in the wake of our surf for some nautical miles. They can be seen just below the surface before disappearing, then reappearing in huge leaps into the air with enviable agility and ease. Of course, everyone is vying for position to get pictures of the awesome sight, as the family continue in our surf, free-loading little bastards that they are.

Oh...Porpoise is it? A Porpoise and not a Dolphin, huh? Hates that.

Jokes aside, Kane gets worried when over ninety five per cent of the human contingent onboard is at the stern and calls us all back. We also take pictures of the sunset and it's a truly majestic sight. Yet another unsuspecting yacht passes by, as we take our position at the edge of the vessel and shake our pasty booties in their directions.

We eat spaghetti bolognaise, salad and garlic bread and after cleaning up, we're up on deck for our second night of drinking and related capers onboard Boomerang. Tony and I try to enliven things up by inviting ze German girls to join us for our "Techno yocht pardy". I'm wearing my flowery boardies of course, with a black hoodie and white-rimmed sunglasses. Tony and I look like two hooded Thunderbird puppets on speed. There's much merriment on deck, apart from a few cross words between two rough-looking English ladies, who I suspect are vying for the attentions of the skipper. I decide against sleeping on deck and stumble down to my bunk.

When I awake a couple of hours later, I'm wrapped around a certain young lady. Nothing has happened, though if it did I would hardly tell you now, would I?

DAY TWENTY ONE

It's some hours later, I've opened my eyes and realised that I'm back in my own bunk, which is just as well seeing as we're sleeping in such close quarters.

Lou is, yet again, preparing breakfast. I eventually come around and decide to arise from my pit. I'm wrapped in a sheet because I'm actually sans apparel. That's right, as naked as the moment I was born. The reasons for this are purely practical, honestly. I decided against sleeping in my shorts because I've got to wear them again today and, as I've already told you, I am travelling light and forgot me bleedin' underwear.

Anyway, the sheet is slung around one shoulder and basically covering me from the chest down. I resemble Julias Ceasar, Marcus Aurelius and Co. In fact, the erstwhile Roman greats have taken possession of my persona, so I decide to go seek my counsel, Tony. However, I only go and stumble, momentarily dropping the sheet, much to my embarrassment. Unfortunately, Lou and one of the Canadian girls are on hand to witness my downfall. Agape, the Canadian, looks at me and then Lou.

Both suddenly burst out laughing and Lou takes the opportunity to encourage my face to turn as red as my sunburnt neck.

"Have you got nothing on under there?" she asks. But a gentleman would never discuss such things with a lady. So I speak on the matter at length.

I don't really. But I do have lukewarm tea with cold toast and vegemite and head up on deck. Oh, I did dress myself beforehand of course. There's a final snorkel on offer for those of us that want to go but I know it can't top yesterday's outing. It's also a rush-job and I'm quite sunburnt, and in peculiar places too. The factor nine I've being using is obviously not strong enough for my current needs but then again, nothing short of a pit full of factor 100 probably would be in this heat.

We sit around on the deck and at 8.30am, we head for dry land again. Most of us sit on the edge of the yacht, as it cuts through the water – our legs dangling some feet away from the surface yet still getting splashed.

Then, we are sailing into the wind, moving into the centre of the boat on Kane's instruction. We're told to brace ourselves and for some time we cut through the water at an angle of about forty five degrees. I'm near the hatch and I look down to see Lou below, more-or-less falling into the boat at an opposing angle in order to remain on her feet. It's a weird sight – kind of like a scene out of Batman or something. Of course, I'm talking about the 1960s (Gay) Batman series here and not the much darker movies that would come decades later. The last time I saw things at this angle was about fifteen years ago when I absent-mindedly drank some mushroom tea at a party in Tramore, Co. Waterford.

It's exciting enough and the scenery is beautiful. We're several kilometres away from Airlie Beach, which is looming larger on the horizon with every glance. Kane is shouting but I can barely hear him. All eyes turn to the bow, to me. Locky, picking his steps carefully but at an impressive enough rate, makes his way down to me and asks me to assist him with unfibbering the jibbit. Oh, you know; the lowering, unpinning and folding of the sail or whatever it's all called. Just two days previously, I helped him to fibber- to pin it on and to raise it. But this feels more like two weeks later. I'm wondering why this is. Is it that whole days spent on the water can seem like longer. That sailing hour after hour with little concept of distance can have an effect on our experience of time, or just that we've packed so much in over the past couple of days? Hey, we could be in some Australasian version of the Bermuda Triangle.

Either way, I don't mind working (if that's what you'd call it) under these conditions...in fact; I enjoy it because I've always felt comfortable around water.

We reach dry land, bid our goodbyes to our crew and swap our Facebook and email details. My ATA group hooks up with Beaver and we're on our way to

Magnetic Island. We pass through Townsville and I'm in agreement with Beaver's unimpressed take on the place. However, mine is not a fully formed opinion, as we don't even stop there.

It's late in the evening (dusk is fast approaching) when we arrive at Magnetic Island for what is probably the most pointless leg of our journey north to Cairns. We'll spend less than fifteen hours here, at this kind of communal hostel area that overlooks the beach. I'll go one step further here and add that our sole purpose in being here is to seemingly make up the numbers, and to keep the cash registers ringing of course. Their sneaky, staggered happy (small "h") hours will not keep me from my slumber tonight.

Upon disembarking the coach to the hostel here, the driver, who's a bit of a pain in the arse it has to be said, almost drives off with our bags. He only stops when we bang loudly on the coach as it pulls away. He comes out and stands there, in his weird and stupid, long knee-high white socks and short-shorts. Shaking his silver-topped head, he actually glares at us for a few moments. Finally, the penny drops and he apologises to us, opening up the undercarriage for us to unload our lot.

"Sorry guys," he repeats over and over again, after some time. The scene is reminiscent of a bad episode of US TV programme, *Lost*.

We're assigned our dorms and take the chance to shower before getting something to eat and of course, drink. Some of ze German girls are less than happy that they've not arrived in time to take in the sights (namely, some gorge or other that has Koala Bears). The girls are particularly keen to see the bears as they have had a Koala-less free trip so far.

I, on the other hand, couldn't give a shit. I've seen the sleepy buggers in Victoria. Plus, my aims are: shower – food – pint and bed in that order. Actually, I don't even care about the pint to be honest. Anja tells Beaver that they have arrived too late in the evening to see the sights at Magnetic and he tells her to stop complaining and make the most of it or words to that effect. (The next day, he admits that he was in the wrong and shouldn't have argued with her, fair play to him.)

130

After some dodgy nachos and a couple of pints of Tooheys New, I'm fit for bed. So I go back to the dorm and sit on the edge of the bed and after a couple of lines, I fall asleep – pen in hand, hovering over my journal.

I have little memory of this but Bobby comes in after about ninety minutes and I wake up, groggy. He's telling me that I was half asleep and still struggling to write.

Apparently I've just told him that I had been trying to scribe down the word, "Experience" but that "Dolphin" kept appearing in its place. (When I look at the entry in said diary, the letters "exp" are followed by a long scrawl resembling a line where my hand had obviously lost all control of my pen. A dolphin would have made a better Fist of writing it.)

DAY TWENTY TWO

Bobby, Tony, Hannah and Patricia have joined ze Germans in successfully tracking down the Koalas at an unforgiveable hour. Bobby laughs as he tells me that he was clueless as to what I was on about last night. That makes two of us then. I get up, pack and go over to order a fried breakfast called "The Hangover Cure" even though I don't have a hangover. Then I top up on my Global Gossip phone/Internet card and phone my mother. It is not yet 10am here and therefore post-midnight – some nine hours before – in Ireland. But it's okay; she is a bit of a Night Owl. I eventually get through.

And she drops the bombshell.

The world has shifted. Time stands still as she tells me that my old friend Alan Symes, from Stradbally in Co Waterford but who now lives outside Auckland, has hit the international headlines for the wrong reasons.

Apparently, his two-year-old daughter, Aisling, has gone missing. She tells me of reports expressing suspicions that the toddler has been kidnapped from the garden in Angela's parents' home in Longburn Road in Massey, Waitekere. And that's all I know, for now.

Alan attended Newtown Secondary School around the corner from my family home in St. Alphonsus Rd and we became instant friends when he joined the Civil Defence in Waterford city in 1990. We were trained in First Aid and would go on various "duties" together at events around the city and county. On a couple of occasions at least, he stayed in my house after these duties when he had no way of getting home to his rural abode, quite a few miles away.

After subsequently leaving Waterford with his mother and sister some nineteen years ago, he settled with them out in the sprawling Auckland suburbs. Alan and Angela met, married thereafter and later had two daughters, Caitlin (5) and Aisling (2). Sadly, we never got to meet up in 2005 when Alan was last home and I was living in Dublin – some two years before little Aisling was born – because our schedules didn't agree.

Lily, that's my mother, has told me that the story is big news back home and seemingly, everywhere else too. We were out of touch with each other and I'm due to track Alan down once I hit Auckland. I knew that he had been working in security at Auckland Airport and that was to be my starting point in a week's time.

And now this.

We take the ferry back to the Australian mainland and then we're on the road north again, so I'll have no Internet access for the next few hours so, until then, I can't find out the latest.

I'm blown away. My mind is reeling as we take in the final leg of the journey. What in the name of God could have happened to little Aisling?

We're about an hour away from Cairns ("Kaaaaaaaans") when we stop of at the "Croc faaa'm" (farm) as Beaver so eloquently puts it. It's situated about ninety kilometres south of Cairns in a place called Innisfail, North Queensland. As we ruck up to the Johnstone River Crocodile Farm, we're greeted by Brett, who has a small, lazy lizard on his arm. That's small by Aussie standards: the thing is about a foot long from snout to tail. We all get our picture taken with the little dude and I'm a bit reluctant.

132

But he doesn't move much at all and even feels like a stuffed toy on my arm. I'm a bit surprised at the texture of his skin, pretty much as I was with the snake at Kirkroom.

Meanwhile, Cory is inside getting the crocodiles ready for the feeding frenzy, I mean, meet and greet with ATA northbound. In we go to meet Henry, who, at more than four metres in length and weighing in at over 400kgs, is a sight for frightened eyes.

Growing up, as I did, with three sisters, I have often overhead statements such as, "Did anyone see my mock croc bag" and "Yeah, it's mock croc...do you like it?" And so on. (Yup, I grew up in the 1980s...how did you guess?)

However, the sight of Henry poised, camouflaged in the green grass and as stiff as the proverbial Mock Croc (bet you thought I was going to say "statue"), is enough to make the hairs on the back of your neck run for cover, never mind stand up. His mouth is ajar – apparently he just loves North European 'meat' – and if you stood there long enough, you would be forgiven for thinking that he wasn't around. And this, my friends, is the point of it all.

He's loving the sun of course.

So Brett goes into the pen and teases Henry with a lump of coarse and hairy pork in pretty much the same way that a child would a dog. He's holding it up and then whipping it away at the last minute, just before Henry's terrifying teeth get to grips with his snack. Akin to a performing seal, Henry jumps time and time again – his upper and lower jaws smacking together and making a low wallop, as air gets trapped inside. We learn that crocodiles mouths are not watertight but that the species has a palatal valve in its throat. The valve obviously prevents water from entering the throat, oesophagus and trachea of the croc when it's underwater and allows the predator to capture its prey. Although they generally eat their catch on land, they can also keep their heads aloft while in the water and swallow with the aid of a series of flicks. We're also told that Henry's bite equals about 3,000lbs of pressure per square inch, which is far greater than that of a shark, for example. Imagine placing a 3,000lb weight (one inch in diameter) on a one-inch area of your hand or foot. Now imagine that pressure applied across the entirety of the beast's crushing mouth. Yeah, I know! Never mind square inches; you'd have a bloody square, flat foot after that.

Lee is asking inane questions – there are many – and of course he wants to know, "Who would win in a fight...a crocodile or a shark?" Ridiculousness aside, Cory tells him that a croc probably would in the *given* circumstances.

Then we meet Marco and Cory tells us that *he* (Henry, not Cory) only keeps his mate in the pen for reasons carnal in nature. The ball and chain, whose name I don't get, comes up to say hello to us. She is lighter in colour and MUCH smaller. If Marco wasn't getting any, he'd probably kill the missus if she annoyed him or started nagging him about not walking the human or whatever constitutes domestic chores from a croc perspective. He'd likely crush and drown her by giving her one final Roll before tearing her flesh apart with his savage teeth, in much the same way he would with any other prey. And that, my dear friends, would be that.

But this is no ordinary croc farm, which doesn't sound too ridiculous in Oz, let me tell you.

Because these crocs are in jail! That's right: JAIL! All of the crocs at the park are "problem crocs", and Henry himself is here because he ATE the tastier half.

So, on we go, learning the difference between kangaroos and wallabies. I feed a kangaroo some cereal pieces and I am surprised at how gentle they are. We also see an alligator, which is much smaller than Henry and Marco are and has different colourings. When we reach the dingoes' pen, I'm surprised to see a large, round bird with a black body and a blue neck and head with red trim. On top of its head is a long and hard helmet which we assume is for warding off predators and competition. And, aside from the fact that it's used in charging an enemy, it's also used as a speaker of sorts for the weird sound it makes. This bird, a cassowary, is a cousin to the emu, we're told, and it will bury its head in its chest and let out a low, vibrating thud as it shakes comically. Cory taps the fence repeatedly and the bird duly obliges. His outer claw is used for fighting and could disembowel a human with a kick.

Aha, niiice cassowary...attaboy! I take a closer look, and there's no sign of Rod Hull. I'd be more afraid of Hull's questionable crotch-grabbing than disembowelment if I'm being honest.

Cory's crouching inside the pen now and the dingos; the lovely, playful dingos come running up and jump up on his shoulders. Others clamber for attention and even come up to the fence to lick our fingers, as we reach through the fence to stroke them. The fence comes up to my shoulders, which means that I'm one of the few people present able to rest their arms atop the trellis fence.

So, I do.

But I only notice the two electric wires running behind the top of the fence just as the 240 volts speeds through my body. Ouch! The others burst out laughing when I jump back, shouting loudly. Bobby, who is standing next to me, is laughing with particularly gust.

"That was hilarious," he offers. *No, Bobby...if I thumped you right now, that would be*, I feel like saying. Cory tells me, as if I don't already know, that I have created a circuit with the ground, especially seeing as I don't have the appropriate footwear on. I look down and notice that I've stepped out of my pain-inducing flip flops and I am standing in clay and leaves. I tell Bobby, the Engineer, that even though the 240-volt shock was about one-quarter of that we experienced with Cowboy Andy at Kirkroom, I felt this surge a lot more. The little know-all reminds me that it's the amps (or milliamps) that kill. Well, bearing his earlier laughter in mind, perhaps I could tell the judge that it was his big mouth and not my shotgun that killed him.

We get to Cairns in and check into our hostel, Calypso, on Digger St. and I'm sharing a dorm with Lee, Bobby, Tony and some strange middle-aged English woman who has come down under to take part in some weird type of Triathalon. At the hostel, we have dinner and drinks: lots of them. We're having the Last Supper as our ATA northbound tour has officially ended. We chip in a few bucks each and give it to Beaver after dinner, in thanks for all his help on the tour. Our own contributions aside, he really has made it a worthwhile trip. I hang out with him and some of his tour guide pals for a while and we have a laugh. Beaver tells me that he plans to "doy [do] Route 66" in March and he asks me if I fancy accompanying him. I tell him that it's a great idea, even though we both know it's not going to happen.

I'm going to miss this bloke.

I slope off and finally I get to a computer. A huge search for Aisling is underfoot apparently, with Alan joining in. The reports are suggesting that the toddler could have been kidnapped. Police want to talk to an Asian women, the last person seen talking to the two-year-old in the Symes's Waitakere neighbourhood, according to a message from my sister Sharon on Facebook. According to 3news.co.nz, "Known child abusers and sex offenders are now being targeted by police in West Auckland as fears grow for missing toddler Aisling Symes may have been abducted". Fuck. In the story on their website, Area Commander Inspector Gary Davey "said police were visiting known sex offenders or anyone with a criminal history of kidnapping or child abuse".

I'm feeling useless here in Cairns. My flight to Auckland is scheduled for October 16th and I'm trying to rack my brains as to how I can get there, maybe use my skills as a journalist to help with a media campaign to possibly find Aisling.

I don't even have an email address, let alone a phone number.

This evening, the gang go to The Woolshed and I join them because I feel my brain will explode with questions if I stay behind and brood. Here, one of the girls in our group joins us blokes in some drinking games and all of a sudden, she collapses on the floor. Tony and I manage to get her outside with the help of some of the doormen and she seems to come around into a semi-conscious state so we take her to a medical centre around the corner. At this stage, she has become aggressive and is screaming.

However, the male nurse/orderly at the centre is worse than useless and we have to wait almost an hour for a doctor to arrive. When he finally comes, the medic seems clueless as to what to do and simply gives us a letter for the real doctors at the hospital.

We call an ambulance and it takes ages to arrive, then we join our friend on the journey to the hospital. We wait another couple of hours and the doctor, a friendly young Australian woman and a real medic, finally tells us that our friend will be okay, after being put on a drip and being kept in for observation. She tells us not to feel too bad, as the girl, whose name you're not getting, was obviously drinking shots secretly throughout the night. This, apparently, resulted in her upset, confused and agitated condition and not, as we feared, her drink being spiked.

Tony and I eventually get back to Calypso. It's about 4am and we're knackered. And way too sober.

DAY TWENTY THREE

We awake some two hours later, and the lights are all on. Lee is sitting on the edge of Tony's top bunk – directly opposite mine. "It's okay Lee; it's okay," Tony is telling him. "That's your bed there," he says, pointing at the bunk below mine. Lee looks out of it because he is out of it. And, the mad bastard has to get up to do a bungee jump AND a skydive today. He doesn't seem the type to be involved in taking psychotropic or hallucinogenic drugs but it does appear that the drink, the lack of sleep and the latent fear related to him throwing himself from some tower or jumping out of a plane at 15,000 feet in the following hours, have pushed him over the edge, if you will.

I'm half asleep. What a day. Funny things happen all the time – in the midst of tragedy and vice versa. I can hear Bobby telling Lee to "get up"; that there's a bus waiting for him outside the hostel and that "Yes, it's 7.35[am] now". Weird Middle-aged English Triathlete Woman is turned into the wall, still asleep or pretending to be, perhaps all-the-while shaking like a shocked and hypothermic child of nervous disposition who's laying on a washing machine. Well, wouldn't you be if you'd just witnessed such a carry-on?

Apparently, after Bobby couldn't get Lee out of the cot following five minutes of trying, he finally wakes up. "Shit, it's 7.40, I'd better go," he shouts...or words to that effect.

I *actually* give up.

It's Sunday lunchtime and Tony, Bobby and I are strolling along the busy waterfront in Cairns. Despite a dizzying array of choices, we settle for a pizza and glass of vino combo on offer (for a reasonable $15) and sit on the strip, trying to put our minds back together as we look at the thousands of people passing us by. The masses are walking up and down, buying souvenirs as presents, presumably, for their loved ones back home. The more adventurous of them are booking skydives, barrier reef dives and so on.

I break away from the boys after lunch to do some shopping, passing all the bars on the waterfront and almost getting killed by a car at one stage. The bars are thronged with groups of youngsters – tourists, locals and year-out settlers I guess – all with groovy hairstyles and sporting flip flops, shorts and tee-shirts.

Of course the sun's shining ☺

I find a quiet cafe and sit in a hidden corner with my cappuccino apple strudel with cream. I write in the journal for about two-and-a-half hours, which to me is therapeutic and productive, and it helps me to get my head around the madness of the past couple of days. I leave and go to buy some boomerangs and fridge magnets for folks back home. If it was just sticks I'd bought, I'd save on the stamps by throwing them up to Ireland and take my chances. But they're boomerangs so they'd come bac-nevermind! I do apologise.

I stop at this English sweetshop and buy some cola cubes and then I play a video game in a nearby arcade. I've travelled to the *other* side of the planet and resemble an adult in appearance, yet I seem to be seeking out a Sunday afternoon that belongs in Tramore over twenty years ago.

The girl who lost the plot the night before has moved to another hostel and will be flying out of Cairns for Perth in the early hours of the following morning. However, she takes the time to seek out Tony and I at the hostel as we're having some dinner, and she thanks us for taking care of her following her meltdown about seventeen hours ago. This evening, we are entertaining these two Cambridgeshire lasses, Emma and Becky, at Calypso. Another girl, Bethany from Wales, has joined us. A sneaky joint is produced from somwhere at the end of the night and, because it's mixed with the beer and the goon, there are some casualties. Then, it's time for bed. In four-and-a-half hours time, we'll get a shuttle to the port nearby for snorkelling and scuba diving on the Great Barrier Reef.

DAY TWENTY FOUR

A herd of buffalo couldn't have dragged me out of the bed when the alarm went off so of course, the shuttle nearly leaves without me. But I do make the next one and, although we've paid $35 deposit of $179 for the day-long trip, we must pay the balance when we board. So, I must get to a bank machine and if there isn't one at the port here, I'm pretty much screwed.

I go inside the terminal to find an ATM and fortunately I do. However, the machine just won't accept the card no matter what I do. *Fuck!* It doesn't seem to fit the slot (I know, I know; said the actress to the Bishop!). It's awfully annoying, especially as there seems to be a monkey on my shoulder. I turn around and there's Daniele...AGAIN! Unbelievable; everywhere I go lately, she's there. She's starting to bug me a bit – constantly telling me not to be late and to make sure I do everything her way, ze German way. So when I eventually get the card to work for me and go outside to meet the others, she once again reminds me not to be late, all the while tapping at the face of her watch. How can I be bloody late if I'm standing right next to her, while we're all waiting to board the vessel?

Enough is enough.

"Mind your own business," I tell her.

We pay our outstanding sums, board and then queue for tea, coffee, fruit and sickly sweet muffins. Bobby and Tony are signing paperwork for their scuba dive but I'm not. I was told that diving is verboten in the twenty four-hour period preceding a flight (for health reasons) but the *Ocean Free* crew, who are far too cheery and in the face for such an un-Godly hour, tell me that I should be okay as long as I wait twelve hours to fly. And I will be flying at 4.30am the following day, which I'm told will be about twelve hours from the final dip. However, I've already ruled myself out so I've not made financial provisions (and so on) to do so and it costs a further $100 or thereabouts to dive today. I've come to terms with it, as I've been told that snorkelling out there is actually better than the diving so that's good enough for me.

It takes us about ninety minutes to reach our destination, an island sandbank in the middle of the ocean. I go up on top of the three-tiered yacht to take in the sights and find it weird in the extreme, in the approach, to see a long and lean sandy coloured mass appear on our horizon. The *island* (okaaay!) is being lapped with gentle waves on all sides: we learn that the mass will more-or-less disappear soon enough. In groups, we get into this glass bottom boat and we're taken to the sand. It's not yet 10am and, sand and sun aside, there are over thirty people engaged in a scene reminiscent of something from docu-movie, *Flight of The Penguins*. I half-expect to hear Morgan Freeman's low, smooth voice as an accompaniment to our every move.

We waddle precariously on the sand up to our ledge in the middle of the sea. However, the clear, turquoise, lukewarm water is just knee-high – for me at any rate – and remains so for quite a trek. Tony, Bobby and I break away from the main group, many of whom are wearing "snorkel jackets" (lifejackets to you and me). Others are grabbing hold of other ring-shaped buoyancy aids. This group is being led by Becca, a tanned and super fit woman in her late 20s, I guess. She's bubbly (veering on bursting at the seams actually) and she's Hot (with a capital "H"). Becca will lead this group along a gentle current that will bring them back to the boat, hundreds of metres away.

Anyway, us lads get out in front and wade through the shallows and out into the coral. Patches of the stuff appear sporadically in the water below us, which is so clear, you'd basically snorkel it without the mask. Well, if the salt didn't sting your eyes into submission and the breathing aid held itself in place, that is.

I imagine that the exotic fish swimming below view us as giant birds in their watery sky. Then my mind drifts to the sharks that will strip the very flesh from our bones. I tell myself that sharks don't like human meat and almost as quickly that, after a quick bite, the shark will let go of the relevant body part...leaving us to bleed to death no doubt. Sweet Jesus, what are we thinking!

But these worries are all a waste of time and energy as the only sharks that inhabit these here parts are harmless Reef Sharks.

Down we dive, our faces sucking the masks into it – our eardrums feeling tighter with the increase in pressure as the water gets incrementally colder. No matter how cold this gets, it's still nowhere near as low in temperature as the surface water in the Atlantic and Celtic Sea around the Irish coastline, I can assure you.

I see the same species of fish that I've already spotted down and around the Whitsundays. Apparently, over one thousand species of fish inhabit the reef. Some of those we see turn out to be called Yellow-Faced Angelfishes, Coral Trout and Fusiliers and Nemo, sorry, I meant Clownfish.

I'm surprised to see a perfect bulbous mass of deep royal blue coral among the various forms on the reef. I signal to Bobby beneath the surface and he goes towards it with his camera. And then I see a giant, vivid, star-shape of the same colour on the bed. It looks like a Starfish to me. I remember reading somewhere that coral is actually categorised as an animal and not as a plant.

Further on, I spy a giant shelf of coral that has a deep crevice splitting it in two. On the surface, one of the crew, an English bloke, tells me that Reef Sharks and Stingray live in under the watery cave. I take in a lungful and dive down to the crevice without getting too close. Perhaps it's irrational but I feel as if I'll be sucked in...or more likely that the scaly green arm of some Sea Hag will reach out and pull me into her deathly clutches, from where I'll spend an eternity catering for her every need.

Her EVERY need! Shudder!!!

Anyway, I do see a Stingray and I even find Nemo. There are black-and-white striped fish and many different sandy-coloured types that have cleverly evolved so that they are camouflaged by the bed. The drag here is quite strong; you could be drifting along, minding your own business, dive down mindlessly and come up much further away than is expected.

When I get back to the boat, I'm surprised to find dozens of shiny fish swarming around the water near the ladder. I get a bit worried when I see them swimming towards me – I'm underwater, keeping a close eye on them as they speed past my mask.

I surface and find some of the crew throwing pieces of prawn into the water, encouraging the feeding frenzy.

"Keep ya fingaaa's in mate," I'm warned.

"Eh thanks," I reply, as more Sparkling Emperors (apparently!) swim around me.

I climb up onto *Ocean Free* and help them feed the little creatures and watch as others approach in the same reticent way that I have. Those of us not diving then pile into a glass-bottomed boat for a tour. We see an array of fish including a large turtle, swim under us.

We're told about the various species of fish, such as Clownfish who can apparently change sex. I'm kind of blown away by this. When the female of the species in their particular group dies, the male dominant male steps up to the plate and changes sex. That's right, becomes a female. But the thing is, they're all born males anyway. AND, they are A-sexual, which basically means that he/she/he/it doesn't get he/she/he/it's rocks off in the reproductive process. No clowning about, but it's little wonder that Nemo did a legger. The poor thing was obviously in the depths of an identity crisis.

I'm sipping a can of VB throughout and when we return, get stuck into a buffet of cold meats, prawn and salmon.

Some of us again go snorkelling this afternoon, while others laze about in the sun on the decks above. Two large clams, about fifteen feet below the surface, catch my attention. They belong, to my mind, in some 1960s watery adventure caper. And, I spot a giant turtle below. Actually, I'm swimming above two divers who do. So, there's the turtle that's scraping the bed, then the divers above them and me on top. The turtle does a U-turn and loses the divers. But not me. I take a big draw of air and then a long dive down. It's just me and the turtle now and it's awesome. I surface and gesture to the boat, about fifty metres away. "Turtle," I shout. You kind of have to – it's part of the deal really. After a while, we lose sight of it and I swim back to the boat.

I'm up on the middle deck and restless, so I jump off the rail and into the drink about seventeen feet below. I'm actually preparing for the top deck, about thirty feet above the turquoise, watery mass.

"Hey, no jumping from the boat," says this kind-of weird girl who took us on the glass-bottomed boat tour.

I'm trying to place her accent but I can't: it sounds like a cross between Eastern European and Italian (I'm thinking of Dracula with Italian enunciation). It's hard for me to take her seriously because she looks uncannily like a bloke I studied Engineering with in college back in Waterford, a lifetime ago. When I do get on board, our Skipper, Rob, waves me over. He has a serious look on his mug. Oh shit!

His face evolves into wry smile.

"Sit in the cornaaa' (corner)," he tells me. "Seriously mate," he goes on, "no jumping...because if they all troy it, someone will creck their head opan or break tha' nick."

Fair enough.

We get back to dry land and say farewell.

Tony, Bobby and I walk back to Calypso and Bobby is going on about how much better the reef is here than around the Whitsundays. And that's a fair point but he's kind of annoying me by going on and on about how much better the diving was, compared to the snorkelling, and I suspect it's for my benefit. It's just bullshit really, all things considered.

Back at Calypso, a smelly pile awaits me. I have fucking loads of laundry to do. Basically every stitch of clothes in my backpack needs washing. And when I re-emerge and meet the others in the bar, Becca, from earlier, has taken up Tony's invitation. She's here with the gang there. Eight from my ATA tour are still at Calypso here in Cairns and most of them are at our table, along with Emma and Becky from last night. Everyone, bar Helper Monkey and I think Danielle, are leaving

Cairns in the next twenty-four hours. We are all exhausted and the group drops off, one-by-one, after extending their generic goodbyes.

I have booked a seat on a shuttle to the airport at 3.30am. I'm caught up in a dilemma of sorts. I could stay awake and risk getting drunk with the others who are leaving at a more civilised hour in the morning or, go to bed and risk falling into a coma and therefore miss my flight to Auckers. There's talk of going to The Woolshed. Compared to other nights, I've hardly been drinking at all and I switch to water at 12.30am. The English crowd, Lee, Bobby, Tony, Becca and Emma are all singing Disney songs from their childhoods, which ended a lot more recently than mine, let me tell you. I'm considering taking a chance and going to bed, because the childish singing is really driving me mad. Michael Schumacher wouldn't have me arriving at 'Mad', quicker than this awful shite.

We go back to Bobby and Tony's dorm and shortly thereafter, I leave for my room. I'm sharing a room – and a bed would you believe? – with Lee. Hang on, hang on...we only decided to do so because we wanted to save some valuable dollars...he would be basically getting to bed when I'd be leaving.

And that's what happens. I say goodbye to them all and rest in the room for about an hour or so.

DAY TWENTY FIVE

Lee comes in shortly after 3am, as I'm arising from my crypt. I drag all my stuff outside and sit down to have a cigarette as I talk briefly to an American girl, Ksenia (*Proun*, Kesenia) who is staying in the room next door with her brother.

It's time to leave, New Zealand beckons. However, while I'm waiting for my shuttle, I check Facebook and my sister Sharon tells me that little Aisling's body has been found in a drain near her grandmother, Angela's mother's house. According to an article by the NZPA (New Zealand Press Association) dated October 12th, "The body of a child was recovered tonight from a drain at a West Auckland property near where toddler Aisling Symes disappeared a week ago".

"Firefighters, using concrete cutters, and police had been excavating on a property since 6am on Ponmaria Rd, a Henderson street connecting with Longburn Rd where the two-year-old was last seen a week ago."

So many questions.

The taxi I've ordered comes along and I have to sign off. What does it all mean? Was she murdered? Did Aisling just wander off and fall down the drain? When I arrive at Cairns Airport, the gates are not yet open. I dump my bags at a seating area and I pump some coins into a payphone to call my sister, Lorraine. I get cut off but try again. Lorraine tells me that the details remain unclear and that it's now thought that the two-year-old did wander off and that her death could have been the result of an accident. I know it sounds terrible, but I'm kind of hoping that this is the case – considering what the unspeakable alternatives are.

I go to the check-in area before walking down to the departure area and lie down across some seats near Gate 25. My flight to Auckland leaves in ninety minutes. I put my Akruba over my face, telling myself that I will avail of the opportunity to catch forty-or-so winks.

Then, there's blackness; I'm literally exhausted.

The next thing I know, I'm being shaken awake by two chaps from Qantas.

"Are you Ciaran Muuu'phy," one of the men asks me.

"Y-yes, I am," I tell them, completely out if it and not knowing where the hell I am.

"You need to boooa'd the plane Mista Muuu'phy...they're waiting for you to do the safety demonstration."

Wait! They want me to do the safety demonstration? Alright then, but I hope they're not expecting too much.

So I run down to my gate as fast as I can in my sketchy footwear.

"Get ya boooa'ding pass," I'm told. I fumble frenziedly in my bag and, after some difficulty, I find it. I don't meet anyone and the only noise entering my ears is the "flip flop" reverberating around the tunnel leading onto the plane. If I were to tell you that it was my "thongs" (*aka* flip flops, down here) making such a noise, I think my Irish and UK readers would get the wrong impression.

I eventually board the aircraft and, after being subjected to some class of smart remark or other from a steward, I find myself seated next to an Irishman in his 40s who wants to make conversation. But I don't want to; I want to sleep.

A couple of hours have passed when I awaken, in plenty of time for the landing in Sydney. Though I only have about ninety minutes before leaving on my connecting flight to Auckland. One long walk-coffee stop and-short sit-down-in-the-airport later, it's time to take off again. Then, it's a hop, skip and a (jumpy) jump to Auckland.

"It's always rough coming over the Tasman [Sea]," says my neighbour. This woman, a hardy Kiwi in her early 70s I guess, tells me that both of her sons are journalists. One of them reports for the *Newcastle Herald* in New South Wales and the other is a freelance like my bad self. She also has two grandchildren who have recently "greduaded from Uni' with Jeeee'n-lism degroys (degrees)".

I have to fill in the relevant documentation and get kind of worried when I realise that I still have a sawn-off – you thought I was going to write "shotgun", didn't you – bull's horn that I took from Kirkroom Farm in Queensland. I forgot that I had the souvenir until now. I've disinfected it but if I'm caught with it I could be in deep shit to the tune of up to $100,000 and/or face up to five years in prison for failing to declare biodiversity risk goods.

No Bull!

I can't help remembering various episodes of Border Control and I envisage myself being rugby tackled to the ground by some huge Maori woman working in customs. Ouch! By the way, no bulls were harmed in the writing of this journal. I found the erstwhile horn discarded on the ground back at the ranch.

It's quite a bumpy flight, in fact, one of the worst I've ever experienced. Well, apart from an Irish-bound flight through a storm over Chicago nine years previously.

146

Anyway, it's early in the morning and this woman is skulling (knocking back, hammering, or whatever you're having yourself) the quarter-bottles of vino. As an Irishman, I feel it my duty to keep up with her but I stop after three. I know that Kiwis boast, almost as idly as the Irish, when it came to drinking but this woman is ridiculous. It's certainly a good introduction to the natives, culturally speaking of course. Perhaps it's the turbulence over the Tasman that causes the drinking, and the reason why the country is relatively unspoilt by the human footprint.

So, we have a drink and a laugh and Hey Presto, we're in Auckers.

I get through the checks and am surprised that, along with my manbag, my backpack must go through the X-Ray thingy at the airport (again) in the nothing-to-declare or whatever on the way out.

I have something to declare: I have a bull's horn on me but – What do you mean that's disgusting? – No. I forgot I had it. It's dirty but I'm going to give it to you right now – Huh? Keep my voice down? – Come with you Sir? Hey, am I under arrest or something?

Shudder.

Aotearoa, or the land of the long white cloud, is, along with Patagonia and southern Chile, the most southerly inhabited land mass in the world, according to Gunther in *Inside Australia and New Zealand*. With an area of 103,736 square miles, it's similar in size to Italy. The combined length of the two islands – North Island and South Island – is about one thousand miles and while the South Island is bigger by about fourteen thousand square miles, the north has roughly two-thirds of the population. The climate here in New Zealand is temperate and oceanic, and though the hot winds from Australia and the cold ones from Antarctica generally lose their gust on their journey, there's over one hundred inches of rain per year in places, though generally between twenty and sixty elsewhere. In relation to its main cities, the Capital, Wellington, was found by merchants, Christchurch by Anglicans, and Dunedin by Presbyterians. And Auckland was founded by pirates.

Perhaps the latter is my spiritual home.

147

I've made my way to airport security and have made enquiries about Alan, who doesn't work there anymore. The man working there connects me on the phone to a very helpful fella, Matt, in the "Av Sec (Aviation Security) Control Room". Matt, in turn, tells me to email a manager there, Peter. (And later, when I do, he sends Alan on my details. Alan, in turn emails me his phone number and so on).

On the bus into Auckers, as I've christened the city, I'm dozing and I must be tired or sick or something because I'm ignoring the glad eye of a hot Brazilian girl (I discover). In fact I am exhausted. Screw this, I'm treating myself to a hotel room.

After taking a quick look at my *Lonely Planet*, I decide on Elliott St. and hence my course is chartered. The radar is still on – I get a nice King-sized double bed with fresh, clean sheets in a room with an en suite, at the Best Western President Hotel. Normally it costs $155 I'm told but the night manager there gives me the room for $125 when I feign disinterest because I know that the place is fairly quiet. Sa-weeet!

He tells me that the *Black Eyed Peas* are playing in town tonight. "Really?" I reply, not even trying to hide my disinterest.

I strip and experience a severe bout of vertigo after so many road, sea and air trips over the past month. In fact, taking the elevator, so shortly after landing, has me wavering on the edge (pun intended!). Staring out of the window at the bungee-ball on the street opposite, I smile as I think, *Only in New Zealand*. I forward my watch to local time – two hours ahead of East Australian – and I make myself a cup of tea, place it on the locker and then fall into the bed. Suspecting that I'm too tired to take a shower and possibly, to sleep, I stare at the ceiling, my eyes adjusting to the dusk.

It's 7.30pm local time. Perhaps I could manage an hour or so and explore the city at night when I come around.

8. "A Theck Egg-cent"

DAY TWENTY SIX

The digital display on the alarm on the locker is blinking *5:45am* when my eyes land on it upon waking. It takes me some minutes to get my bearings. It's amazing how effective clean sheets can be as an aid to good sleep. I turn over and sleep once more.

After about two hours and thirty of your earth minutes, I arise from my crypt and turn on the TV, switching and settling on the news. Aisling's death is the first item and I learn that residents have asked the local authorities in the Waitakere neighbourhood, where the tragedy occurred, to close the drain on Longburn Rd. Their failure to do so gives rise to claims of negligence resulting in the toddler falling down it, as she was found thirty-six metres away from the manhole and into the storm drain.

According to the news bulletin, Mayor, Bob Harvey, has "last night told Close Up" TV programme that four previous complaints about the manhole had been lodged with the council. He has said that he's "more disappointed than angry...I don't think it's a time for anger". Now, far be it from me to take him out of context but that's easy for him to say now, isn't it?

I get up, shower and go to reception. The young man there tells me that I need to pay $155 for that night but I want to pay $125 again. I explain my case but he stands firm. And there's a bit of a polite stand-off before the manager interjects and tells his minion to yield.

Bargaining works.

I buy a couple of postcards at reception, then leave and go to Denny's, a restaurant on Hobson St. – a couple of blocks up the hill. So I'm a Waterford man in a restaurant on a street named after the erstwhile Waterford man, William Hobson. An endless supply of tea is brought to me, along with bacon, (questionable) 'sausages', beans, scrambled eggs, toast, orange juice...oh, and pancakes with maple syrup. It all costs me just $17 (roughly €8.50).

The U2 song, *One Tree Hill* from *The Joshua Tree* album (1987), starts playing and I'm tempted to go and have a look, seeing as I've just found out that the subject of the song, *i.e.* the hill, is located here in Auckland. In fact, if you check the sleeve of *The Joshua Tree*, you'll see that the album is dedicated to the memory of Greg Carroll. This man was a U2 roadie from New Zealand who was killed when a motorcycle crashed. Legend has it that the kiwi was taking the motorcycle back to Dublin from Waterford – for a band member – when it crashed. Weird.

Maungakiekie, the hill's Maori name, obviously, stands at 182 metres and offers "amazing 360° views", according to my trusty *Lonely Planet New Zealand*. At the summit lies the grave of John Logan Campbell, who "gifted the land to the city in 1901, requesting that a memorial be built to the Maori people".

Well, the least he could do really, seeing as it's their feckin' land really. It gets weird: there's no tree.

Up to 2000AD, a "Monterey pine stood at the top of the hill", while this was a replacement for "a sacred totara that was chopped down by British settlers in 1852". Maori activists first attacked the tree in 1994 and again in 2000, leaving a stump.

The Maori occupation of Auckland goes back 800 years, when initial settlement "concentrated on the coastal regions of the Hauraki Gulf islands", until the isthmus was cleared for food growth. With a population of 1.2 million, Auckland is a "conurbation formed from four main urban municipalities", according to *Lonely Planet*. "Auckland City proper includes the central isthmus and Gulf islands", while the others are Waitakere City (west), North Shore City and Manukau (south).

Nearby is an Internet Cafe that I avail of, and I get sucked in by Facebook for about an hour, as per usual. I've decided on the Auckland Art Gallery, where works by Goldie (*Charles Frederick, O.B.E.*); his interpretation of the Maori culture etc. are on display, over One Tree Hill. Upstairs, the Rita Angus collection is on show and I spend about ninety minutes here. I'm no critic but her use of colour, hard edges, metaphor and her particular stance on modernisation, are all intriguing. It seems that Byzantine Art and

Cubism were among her influences. And she certainly seems to have been a fan of the female portrait, leaving one to believe that Rita was a feminist, fair play to her.

The IMAX beneath Sky Tower is full of teenagers of Oriental and Maori lineage. A barber on Lorne St. wants $20 to shave my head – normal for Ireland, expensive by New Zealand standards I guess. A Swedish Barmaid, at O'Carroll's Irish pub on Vulcan Lane, suggests that I try a pint of Red Lion ale. It's not normal to find me in an Irish themed pub anywhere but I actually went in fancying a pint of stout, before I changed my mind. The Occidental – one outlet of a Belgian chain of "beer cafe(s)" – next door, with its smells and its mouth-watering menu, has persuaded me to indulge in its mussels dressed in garlic and leek with chips smothered in mayonnaise. The Belgian classic costs me $19. Not the cheapest but there's a lot of grub. While I'm waiting I order some weird, rich-red beer. It tastes of cherries and I'm disgusted. I hate cherries!

I'm walking along Queen St., the wrong way, I'm told by the know-it-all but helpful American students who I ask for directions. I disagree in the extreme: it's not possible to be going the *wrong* way. Is it? If I walked into a gun-toting gang at the street's end in this direction, perhaps they would have a point though.

A couple of hours ago, I was told to check out a comedy night at the "comidy clab ap the stroyt [Queen St.] samewheee'e", by some Kiwi woman at an information desk at Base Hostel.

"Can you tell me where the Comedy Club or Comedy Centre is please?"

"Oh, The Classic...you're going the wrong way" she replies. "It's that way, I'm afraid," she goes on – pointing in a southerly direction along the long street.

She adds: "It'll take you about ten or fifteen minutes."

And she was right.

I pay $10 at The Classic to see ten comedians, which is great value, anywhere. The deal is this: you don't know what you're going to get. This is the place where up-and-coming comedians (and their down and leaving colleagues, I expect) come to test out their material. On a rainy Monday night? How bad? Hang on? Is it Mon – no, it's Tues – wait, maybe it's still Su...oh sod it, whatever!

This small, ginger guy with a goatee beard (or Moe or whatever you're growing yourself) comes out and introduces himself. He asks if there are any Aussies present. Some brash bloke, who has been heckling him for the past couple of minutes, falls into our host's trap. And our MC basically tears the guy a new one. Ouch! His name is Jamie Bowen and you'd better watch out for him because he's coming to get you.

Jamie Bowen to Aussie Heckler: "So, why the fack did you come to the one country in the wuuuu'ld (world) where ya not wontid?"

Ouch! The Aussie is trying to fight back but the laughter drowns out his reply. Memo to self, don't fuck with the guy holding the microphone.

Jamie asks if there's anyone else from out of town.

I raise my hand.

It goes as follows:

JB: "Whe'e ya frum moyte?"

CM (me!): "Ireland."

He seems to neither hear me nor understand my accent. Someone from the front of the audience prompts him.

JB: "Oh Oi'land? Whit paaa't?"

CM: "Waterford."

JB: "Uh, raaaight moyte...(turns to audience)...we'd bedda be noice ta the Oirish goy or he'll probably bomb the shid oud of us.

(More laughter)

What? Hang on, he can't say tha –

JB: "So, what's ya noooyme?"

CM: "Ciaran."

JB: "Olright Ciaran...(turns to audience again)...Jeeesas; his voice is tuuurnin' me on jast listenin' to 'im. Whad a theck egg-cent...(turns back to me)...I'm haaa'd listenin' to ya moyte 'en I'm nod even goooy (gay)."

And everyone's having a great time, including me.

Jamie leaves the stage and the first of the comedians comes on, and the second and so on. It's a mixed bag in fairness and Jamie pre-announces them before they fly or die.

He turns his attention to me once again.

JB: "Sooo, eny ladies in heee'e like Ciaran's egg-ccent?"

And some of them cheer. Memo to self: *they're mostly in the first few rows!*

JB: "Sooo Ciaran...does the New Zealand egg-cent on a guuuu'l (girl) tuuu'n you on?"

CM: "Not as much as the Aussie accent does."

So there are good-natured boos and hisses, mostly from the first few rows.

JB: "How long have ya bin here?"

I think for a few seconds.

CM: "26 hours" (I immediately tell myself that it's been more like 28.)

JB: "Aaaa' ya serious (he says laughing)?" An' ya thought ya'd come to a comedy show?"

CM: "Yeah, I'm doing a tour of Australia and New Zealand; reviewing comedians."

And there's more laughter.

He's talking about "Keewoy (Kiwi) ingenuidy" and he asks me what I know about New Zealand. I tell him that it's got nearly the same population as the Republic of Ireland, gets lots of rain like Ireland does and has lots of sheep, although more than Ireland. With the sheep reference, I have just given Jamie licence to go to town on me. But he didn't. Aha...you see...an Irishman would never slip up like that.

Anyway, he tells the audience to give me a round of applause and they do. I'm touched. HEY, I heard that!

It's weird. Some of the acts that mess up on stage are actually the funniest. And some of them go down like the proverbial lead knickers. Although an impromptu rap act by the last comedian, Steve Wrigley – accompanied by Bowen's Beat box –, is very funny.

I go to this store-come-Internet cafe on Queen St. and check emails and Facebook. And there's an email from Alan so Peter has obviously contacted him with my details. It's brief, naturally, and I can't believe he's even had the presence of mind to email me, considering the personal hell the poor guy must be going through. So, he's given me his mobile and home numbers and has told me to call him. And in the morning, I will definitely do so. I'm feeling nervous, now regarding what I'll say to him. What can I say, what could anyone say?

I sink a few in the appropriately pretentiously named Cassette Number Nine Bar back at Vulcan Lane. I noticed the Indie bar (of sorts) earlier, and told myself that I would return later to check it out. It's full of Kool Kiwi Kids – the Auckland alternative set – and Oriental Emos for want of a better description. The majority seem to be up their own arses but it definitely beats the Globe Bar, below the ACB Backpackers hostel on the corner of Queen St. and Darby St.

Good little boy that I am, I get to bed before 4am.

DAY TWENTY SEVEN

I wake up after 9am and I really need to get my arse in gear here. I have to check out and I've loads to do. I lie in bed, watch TV, have coffee and watch more TV in that order. After 11, just before I get into the shower, Reception calls to see if I'm on my way down. Sometime after the shower, they call again but when I again tell them I will be down within minutes, I can once again tell that they don't believe me. And who would blame them?

I'm sitting on the edge of the bed, towel wrapped around my waste, just staring at the back page of my diary – where I've written down Alan's numbers. When I finished my MA at DCU, some five years previously, I began working freelance shifts for the Irish tabloid, The *Irish Daily Star*. Here, like all the other news reporters, I was a few times called on to make the Death Knock. This kind-of involves, if you will, cold-calling the friends and relatives of (mostly) people who died or were seriously injured in tragic circumstances. Anyway, it's something I just decided to stop doing very early on.

154

I remember it being a difficult and harrowing thing to do, but it's not a patch on how I feel right now. What makes it all-the-harder is that Alan's an old mate, and apart from a couple of emails a few years previously, there hasn't been contact for almost nineteen years. The thing is, I had intended contacting him anyway.

The poor guy. Jesus!

My heart is doing ninety to the dozen – as we say back home – when I lift the receiver and start to punch the digits. I call Alan and he sounds strong and coherent. It all goes better that I thought it would, probably because he does most of the talking. Alan's rattling on and it's quite understandable. He gives me his address and tells me to get a bus out if I can. He would drive in and pick me up but he doesn't trust that he will get himself there in one piece. After checking out, I go to this nearby restaurant on Victoria St. and dump my backpack and man-bag in the corner (though keeping my Akruba-that's-really-a-Statesman on my bonce), before ordering a BLT, orange juice and a cappuccino for breakfast. It all comes to $16, which is more expensive than Denny's but the food is of much better quality. You know the type; sustainable and organic stuff. The surroundings are nicer too, though in an earnest, middle-class, self-conscious way. I remind myself that $16 (€8) represents good value in terms of what I would pay back home. I also chastise myself for thinking in these terms.

There's this alert, trendy couple who, seriously, look like they're in their late-thirties but I suspect are about ten years older. The fresh-faced, sporty-looking pair greet another couple who have just come in the door. The male of the latter couple is dressed for a business meeting apparently, but business Kiwi style, I guess. He's wearing these weird patent shoes, a loud and colourful tie, purple waist jacket (covered with a fleece of the same colour) and these drainpipe trousers made from a kind of waterproof-looking material, if you can imagine such a thing. She's wearing an expensive-looking red coat and stilettos of the same colour.

They're eating quiche and drinking coffee. It turns out that their daughters are in the same class in school. I'm thinking, Bourgeoisie urbanites. Afterwards, I go to the aforementioned hostel. I book a double room, ditch my bags there and walk around a bit before making my way downtown – with a view to getting a bus out to Massey.

It's after 2pm. The family home, as I've just said, is in Massey, which is deep in the Auckland suburbs, miles and miles away. However, I'm a bit apprehensive as a bus strike has been going on over the past few days. The workers have reportedly been "locked out", which I find a bit bizarre in this day and age.

It's just stopped raining but it's not cold. The rain has given the road and pavement this bright, clear sheen; capturing and reflecting the natural light and that coming from the car headlights as it does. It is warm, still overcast and the air is somewhat muggy. I sense this kind of electric charge in the air (you know...the one you get just before you see lighting cracking the sky apart!). I'm walking down Queen St. towards the bus terminal near the harbour and I stop to buy flowers for Angela and a teddy bear for little Caitlin. A woman, in the mall near the terminal, tells me that she has little left because so many people have bought flowers for the Symes family.

The woman moved to Auckers with her family some three years previously and set up her business here. She says that she loves it here and I don't doubt her – though I'm sure there are some important things about running a business down here that, as an employer, she's had to become familiar with.

Live & Work in New Zealand by Susan James tells us that last year, in 2008, a "legal minimum hourly wage of NZ$9 applies in this country" for workers aged sixteen to seventeen. A wage of NZ$11.25 applies for employees aged eighteen and older. From discussions I've had here, the country's workforce is not known for being the best paid, though the standard of living is considerably less than in the UK and in the Republic of Ireland.

There are eleven public holidays here in New Zealand – separate from and additional to annual holidays – while workers are entitled to a paid day off on a public holiday it would otherwise have been a working day. If these days land on a weekend, when the employee does not work weekends, the holiday "transfers to the following Monday or Tuesday". An amendment in 2007 to the Holidays Act 2003 means that workers are employed to four weeks annual holidays – an increase of one week. Interestingly, part-time employees "may agree with the employer that holiday pay will be included in the hourly rate, although it must be shown as a separate amount". Meanwhile, untaken annual leave and "lieu days must be paid out when employment terminates".

Employers, including partnerships, companies and non-profit organisations, themselves cannot operate in any market without first getting an IRD (Inland Revenue Department) number, though sole traders can use their own personal IRD numbers, while information on this, taxes and so on is available from www.ird.govt.nz.

Salaries in Wellington and Auckland are considerably higher than in the rest of New Zealand, so says Susan James. This reflects the higher living costs in these cities "as well as the higher stress and greater responsibility routinely associated with these positions".

Only Down Under I swear. Paid more for stress? Am I missing something here? I need to re-read this: surely, being able to pay the bloody bills is less stressful than being unemployed or working for the equivalent of €5 per hour.

Anyway, salaries in the rest of the country might be up to twenty per cent lower, "but it is difficult to find exactly equivalent jobs to make precise comparisons as industries and work pressures vary so markedly".

Ooookaaaay.

I need to send a postcard to my sister, Sharon in Germany, so I call into an HSBC outlet nearby to ask them to point me towards a post box. And like I already said, the funniest of things can happen in the midst of tragedy and vice versa. There are two glass partitions at the counter. On my left is a woman in her 60s and on the right is a young beautiful girl in her 20s who is of Oriental lineage. I'm walking towards them and there are no other customers there and they're both smiling at me, eyeing up teddy and the flowers, wondering which of them I will go towards. The older one pipes up first so I go towards her and I trip up on the way. So I get the whole, "You shouldn't have" and I tell her that I didn't necessarily *fall* for her, and the younger girl laughs and I feel embarrassed.

Then, I get the same thing at the ticket desk in the terminal, but this time from a man who says it as if he was the first person to ever say such a thing in similar circumstances. I'm at the wrong window, it appears (well, I'm wrong, and not the window but you get the picture), so he refers me to another window and I get the same good-natured guff from the girl working there too.

Is this *The Truman Show*?

It's 3:26pm and I must go outside and run a block over because the bus is due to leave at 3:25. I take Bus 058 to Bellringer, which is "just up the road" from my destination, Carillon Place in Massey.

And it seems that the Kiwis take a similar view to Ireland regarding time because the bus is still there when I arrive, at 3:30. The bus driver appears to be a Maori woman approaching sixty. I sit at the front and I tell her where I need to get off and she assures me that she will let me know when we are near. I can tell that most of the passengers are regulars and she seems to know them all. So, after driving for over ninety minutes (yes NINETY!) and a few eyebrow-raising queries from yours truly in relation to my stop, I disembark.

I walk around the hilly, leafy suburb until I find Carillon Place. In fact, a couple of policemen are getting out of their car to enter their house and I ask them where the Symes abode is and they tell me. Again, I'm wondering what I'll say when I get there. A boy, who seems (quite rightly) to be oblivious to what has happened, is playing in his front yard across the road. I believe children should be protected against such things in so far as they can be.

I ring the bell and wait for the door to open. And suddenly, Alan's tall frame appears in the porch. We say nothing but we embrace. I walk across the threshold and I tell him that I'm so sorry for his loss, which is a common Irish greeting on such occasions. Again, I hug the lovely Angela when we're introduced and it's clear that she's exhausted, as is Alan. The house is absolutely thronged with flowers and cards; pictures, candles and teddy bears. For a moment, all I see are flowers and cards and it is indeed heartbreaking. But not as much as it is when he shows me the shrine he has put together, and braving another onslaught from a wave of grief, he tells me about the centrepiece, a Fathers' Day card that both Aisling and Caitlin made some months before. Their pictures are on the front.

Caitlin plays with her doll in the middle of the living room floor, seemingly detached from the tremendous tragedy that has befallen them all. However, I suspect that it is a childish coping mechanism: a natural buffer and a construct designed to replace the expression of the feelings that her words cannot yet facilitate. It takes a great effort for me to swallow the sobs that threaten my grip on things. Alan tells me how his "precious angel" wouldn't want them to be sad and that his little "adventurer" was "always happy and smiling". Alan and I catch up and I can tell that, aside from the obvious, he is glad to see me. In this moment my selfish thoughts for my own comfort evaporates, and I can see that I am a welcome, momentary distraction. His mind is racing and he almost seems in good spirits, before yet more grief washes over him, knocking him sideways. In these moments, he hugs Angela or Caitlin in close to him; tears streaming, kind and softly spoken words of whispered consolation exchanged between them. But the couple still have time to play the gracious hosts and I feel as if their humility could swallow me whole when they offer me tea, coffee, biscuits, sandwiches.

Alan and Angela's extended family are there, including Alan's sister, Aithne (*proun*, Et-neh) and her pre-pubescent son, Hamish. Alan I talk about this and that and in another context, all of this would appear like a reunion of sorts: two Irishmen sharing the happenings of the past twenty years and so on. His grasp on Irish life at present is impressive. And his ability to talk of such things in the circumstances is testament to his strength as a man. Alan shows me photographs of them all skiing, along with various snaps of other family holidays in recent years. After three-and-a-half hours, I tell them I must leave. I decline their kind offer of dinner, as the last bus into the city leaves soon. My tour of New Zealand begins tomorrow, hours before little Aisling will be laid to rest. Alan invites me back to stay with them for a few days, once the tour is over. I tell him that I would love to but that I can't commit to it. There are hugs and goodbyes with Alan, Angela and Caitlin and Aithne. Then I leave. I'm humbled that they Symes family can be so hospitable at such a horrendous time.

What strong, courteous and amazing people.

It's approaching 7pm and I'm waiting uncomfortably for the last bus into the city. Light rain visits me sporadically and at these times I pull the black hood (from my hoodie) over my head as I try in vain to take shelter in the low bushes near the bus stop in the pretty suburb. In my low state, I imagine that the passing locals and those living in the surrounding houses think that I'm the Grim Reaper himself. After about fifty minutes, the bus arrives and two hours later; following a change of bus, I'm back on the city streets.

I'm at a loss this evening and don't really fancy being alone so I seek out Knesia, the new Yorker I met briefly at my hostel in Cairns who told me that she would be arriving in Auckland the day after me. I find her phone number in the back of my journal and call her in a payphone (I still don't have a mobile after leaving mine behind in Carnavron Gorge). I've been having problems using coins in payphones and an annoying female voice has told me to buy a call-card thingy. So I bought a $10 phone card but the bloody woman is now telling me to call back later or to use coins. AAAARGH! I go back to shop, explain my predicament to my foreign salesman whose English has suddenly and mysteriously evaporated, and finally I get some coins. Taking a deep breath through gritted teeth, I plunge them into the machine and get through. Only to get cut off. I eventually get through to Knesia's Aussie number again. Then I get cut off...I've run out of coins. When I get through again, it turns out that she's in her hostel, a few hundred yards away.

Sweet Jehovah!

Ksenia and her brother Tussla, they are of Ukrainian lineage apparently, are drinking at Fusian, a bar at their hostel on Fort St. in the CBD. There's a free glass of wine and some class of curious liquid that some masochist describes as "beer", on offer to the hostel's inhabitants. The offer ends just as I reach the bar so I've been spared. However, that's only partly true because I buy a disgusting type of Monteith's that I have not yet sampled. As I taste it, I imagine some mad, evil "MWA-HAW-

HAW-ING" Scientist filling a large vat with rats' piss and yellow pack washing-up liquid.

Here, at the hostel, the Ukranian-American siblings are drinking with some woman, a small and ultra-thin woman of about fifty from Newcastle (UK) who I later need to shake off. I can't, for the life of me, remember her name. And there's a younger woman, Emma from Essex in the UK – a place which, like Limerick in Ireland, gets a bloody bad press that I suspect is largely unwarranted. (In fact, Emma will end up touring most of New Zealand on my tour bus.) All of us, except the lady from Newcastle (in the UK) it seems, are concerned that we need to get up for touring in a few hours.

We say our goodbyes. However, I'm not tired or drunk so I end up at Globe below my (ACB) hostel and end up drinking with a couple of girls, lunatics from Cork and Limerick. They're dancing with this very heavy, peroxide-blond (apparent) Afrikaner who grabs me and says, "Come to me Paddy!" I escape her clutches and hang out with some Air Hosts and Hostesses from Dubai Airlines. These are from various locations in Asia and are great fun. The women are real stunners too.

Great, now I can't find my alarm clock. I persuade the clerk, a bloke from Cork, which is my neighbouring county back home, to give me an alarm call at 6.30am, less than three hours time. He tells me that it's not something they do there but he does agree...fair play to him.

DAY TWENTY EIGHT

After dragging myself out of The Cot – a double bed, the only bed in the room – I quickly wash and stumble downstairs. I find my Kiwi Experience (tour) pick-up point at 7.10, which is leaving time. I ditch my bags against the bus and I run across the road to a Dunkin Donuts outlet for a large cappuccino. I go back and get on-board and our driver, a Kiwi in her 30s I reckon, asks me for my documentation. This is proof that I've paid for my trip really but I tell her that when I handed it over to the guy at the travel desk in ACB, he forgot to hand it back. She asks me if I'm sure and I tell her that I am and she's cool with that but that we'll have to stop off at the office and sort it out, I'm told.

There seems to be mostly English backpackers on-board the bus. There's an Irish guy called Matt, who turns out to be from Co. Kilkenny, and only about twenty kilometres away from my home in Waterford actually. There are also two sound blokes, Ben and Mike, from Wales. I'm sitting at the front of the coach and Fly, our codenamed driver, is giving us the rant about Auckland and I'm only half-listening because I'm thinking about Alan, Angela and Caitlin, who must say goodbye to Aisling today. When Fly takes off her headset, I get the real lowdown on New Zealand and she asks me about my work. We're also talking about her, then me, then her again. It passes the time.

We also talk about stereotypes and she goes on to tell about her time living abroad. She explains how she has lived abroad for four years, mainly in the UK, and how she felt the draw homewards once hitting her thirtieth Birthday. Her friends in Paihia were largely settling down into marriages and baby-making relationships at that time. And she tells me how she regretted it and how most of the company's drivers are "splet (split) in tha' (their) moynds", which I guess is different to having a split personality as such. I tend to agree with her analysis though.

For my part, I tell her about my diary and about what's mainly on my mind at present: about little Aisling.

Not forgetting to share the funnier parts of my journey so far, however, I spill the beans on the bag-forgetting incident at Melbourne Airport, falling asleep at the airport in Cairns and she's laughing in recognition, if nothing else. It turns out that on a recent trip, there were two Irish guys who "jas' kipt fo'gittin' their shet", missing activities through sleeping in (known as "sleeping it out" in Ireland) and so on. Of course I take the opportunity to let her know of my theory: mainly that us Irish are always distracted by our genius; our focus landing always on art, literature and things scholarly in nature. She buys it, or perhaps she's just too polite to say otherwise.

I explain to Fly, or whatever her name is, how the terrain on the way south to Wharangi (*proun.* Farangi apparently) is similar to Ireland, though more dramatic.

162

The vegetation looks similar to home as well, lending me to believe that both countries are separated in equal terms from the equator. The North Island is about 40° south of the equator, while Ireland is over 50° north of it.

Endless and sudden hilly pastures; lush, green and dotted with sheep, remind me of fertile zits that have popped up from nowhere. In topographical terms only...the scenery is surely worthy of nicer imagery or metaphor.

We pick up some people in Wharangi and again head north, this time to Paihia. On the approach, I'm amused to learn that Russell – one of the islands making up the Bay of Islands – used to be the scene of much drunken debauchery, gambling and fighting. The pirates were largely to blame (of course they were!). I'm laughing because, you see, I have the Russell blood. My mother is a Russell.

Fly-or-whatever seems to have these weird and secret hand signals for every commercial vehicle that passes us: she has a different sign for every type of vehicle and for the truckers; she splays her fingers wide and turns her hand sideways. We arrive at Paihia and pay for the various excursions and activities that we've booked through Fly on the relevant forms, on the bus from Auckland. Most of what I now call *my* group; the Welsh pair, along with Englanders Joe, Andrew, a girl named Alex and Tash, are going north to Cape Reinga tomorrow. I've booked The Zephyr tour, which means I must pay a further $89 to indulge. So I do, also paying $80 to go parasailing the morning after.

Some of the gang are finishing their trip at the "top bit" (Cape Reinga) in the north – the opposite of us who are starting north and going south. A number of those on my bus are going to Russell on some boat tour. They later come back disappointed and $89 lighter in the wallet region.

Meanwhile, I crash in the dorm I'm sharing with Alex, Joe and some others, for a few hours.

We meet for a BBQ consisting of these disgusting beef sausages that Kiwis seem to like and afterwards we play drinking games. Then we go to these cheesy late night joints down the road. I arm wrestle Ben, who's ten years younger than me, in fantastic

163

condition and I swear it, it takes all that I have to put the bugger down. I'm spent afterwards, my arm hurting badly. We're both wrecked. He demands a rematch at a further date. Some of us need to go to an ATM and on the way we're a bit intimidated by these groups of large hooded Maori types – hanging around outside – who appear to be wholeheartedly embracing American gangster culture. It surprises me when I try to take out $320 and the receipt indeed shows that I have withdrawn $320 when, in fact, I get $330 cash.

We hear reggae music pumping from this trailer so we stop by because he is selling burgers.

"Je want some bacin (bacon) in-ya brid (bread)?"

"Sorry?" I reply. "Oh, no thanks."

"Je want some soce on ya biiii'ga' (burger)?"

Of course I should reply, "Sweet as broooooo," though my grasp on the wonderful Kiwi use of the English language is not up to speed just yet. On the way back to Pipi Patch Hostel, we take a detour to go skinny-dipping in the Tasman Sea. I'm reluctant, in much the same way that I was in Oz, though I join them in the end. The dipping consists of running into the water up to waist level, while covering our various bits and pieces with our hands. Alex, the baby of the group who is just eighteen-years-old, has suggested it and is first in. It's all just a bit of harmless fun really. She laughs as somebody takes photos of us all. However, she objects to anybody actually including her in said snaps because she "will be a politician in a few years time" and doesn't want the images ending up in some publication or other at a later stage.

I hope she's not directing that at the *ethical* journalist amongst us.

DAY TWENTY NINE

It's not yet 7am and we're in a Fuller's coach. We're hungover to bejasus and Barry, our driver, is driving us...well, up the bloody wall if I'm honest. He's only being paid to drive us to Cape Reinga. Here, we'll see the northerly tip dividing the Tasman and Pacific seas and on the way back, we'll go sand boarding before returning to Paihia.

We'll spend a second night here, "as the Koiwi Bus does nut, I'll repeat thet one mooo'e toime; does nut, go daaa'n (down) ta Auckland on Sadurdoys".

Whin ya get ta Cape Reinga, Barry goes on, you will pat one foot en front of the otha' to walk daaa'n the steps...some of ya will put ya left foot forwaaa'd, while othas will choose to stip owff the bus using the' roight foot fiii'st.

Honestly, this is (almost) the way he talks to us – for up to twelve hours of our Saturday. To be fair, Barry is a lovely man and does his utmost to ensure that we have a great day. Impressively, before we left Paihia, he went around the bus to each of us; asking us our respective nationalities and immediately greeting us in our native tongue impeccably. Chinese, Japanese, French, Welsh, Swedish and even Indian folk, were speechless at his efforts.

However, saying that he tends to get bogged down in the finer detail is probably understating it to the point where it's not actually said at all. Today, my lot are as sick as a planeload of Catholics en route to Lourdes. Ben, Mike, Andrew and Joe – along with fellow Irishman John Kelly and his motley crew who are finishing their tour of Kiwiland at Paihia – are feeling the worse for wear following a night of ridiculous drinking. Of course I include myself in this category.

In agreement with some of the lads, I ask Barry if we can stop somewhere for coffee, as breakfast has not yet been consumed. He risks death by telling me (albeit politely) that he'll "see" what he can do for us at 9am, some ninety minutes hence. Our driver sticks to his itinerary like superglue. Like superglue on magnets. Like superglue on magnets bound together with Velcro. He picks up some other passengers before we go see trees or some other bullshit at the smelly Manginangina Kauri Walk.

I'm sorry but I need my coffee.

He's telling us that we must hug the Kauri trees "en order to "foyl' (feel) bedda' by the followen' mornen'". And this, to me, is kind of (totally!) missing the point: we need sustenance to make us feel better THIS morning. However, it's a short trek and the gorgeous clean air helps us somewhat. I'm not sure how it helps, exactly, but this is what people say in these situations, is it not?

I stumble, back to the bus with my fellow tree-huggers and we head to some little bakery for some pies and coffee, the mandatory morning meal of the antipodean man. Or is it? The Brits love their pies too, so next time you're at a soccer match in the UK and the crowd starts shouting, "You fat bastard, you fat bastard; who ate all the pies?" at least you'll know the answer. Australia and New Zealand did. Both are awash with Bakeries. After stocking up on pies, sambos, sausage rolls, coffees, soft drinks, juice and water, we're on the road north again. We were told to also buy lunch at the bakery if we must, for there is no shops or whatever in Cape Reinga.

The topography in the north, like I implied earlier, is more dramatic than London's West End. It is so, so beautiful though, and isolated even more so. Of course Barry drones on, providing us with the soundtrack. He tells us about what we are going to do, what we are doing and what we have done. He tells us that he's going to leave us to our thoughts, but he doesn't. Not for a minute. We spot pink sheep and Andrew is VERY excited. He's excited, that's all I'm saying. I borrow Ben's ipod – I don't possess one – and I listen to Pink (I know yeah!) and Green Day amongst others. On the approach to Cape Reinga, we are told that "this is the laaast fellin' station in the nooo'th" and "thes is the most nooo'therly post office and" – MOTHER OF GOD!

The scenery, like I said, is breathtaking. Rolling vegetated woodland is dotted with patches of sand and rock. Though, for the life of me, I don't know how anybody could actually live up here. It is so, so isolated. I'm thinking, *This place is definitely due a Wolf's Creek!*

Barry tells us that Cape Reinga is a place where you can silently tell your deceased loved ones of your troubles and so on. And he tells us about how his own son died some years earlier. He goes quiet then, and I feel bad for taking the Mick earlier. That'll be the Catholic in me; I must do something about that little fucker one of these days.

We arrive at Cape Reinga in Northland and unfortunately the visibility is not great. It's bordering on shit, in fairness. We start out on this trek down to the Cape Reinga lighthouse and I childishly carve out my initials on a bench (if you're ever there, have a look for it). You'll find the letters *XX*, as carving the letters *C* and *M* is horrible.

166

Anyway, we get down to the lighthouse and we're snapping away. There's one of those signs – you know the sort that point to various destinations in the world such as Tokyo, London and so on. We take pictures of each other in *that* pose, whereby the subject puts its hand across the forehead and pretends to be looking out to sea towards the homestead. We are on the headland, staring out. To our right (east), is the Pacific Ocean, while the Tasman lies due west.

And after some time we head back the coach. We're taken to these massive sandunes for sandboarding and up we go. The strain is considerable – I'm out of condition at the moment – so it's a strenuous hike. The aim of the exercise is to run, throw said board on the sand and jump on top of it, before hurtling headlong down the dune at a ferocious speed. We should lift the front of the board out of the sand and lift our feet up, in order to increase the speed, Barry tells us. Those who wish to slow down must dig their feet into the sand.

On the bottom of the dune is a stream and if we gather enough momentum, we'll skim across it for some distance. If we are unsuccessful, we'll probably get a mouth full of sand. And fair play to Barry, who's easily in his mid-fifties, he goes off first and gives it socks. I, however, get a mouthful of sand because I lose control of the board. I put this down to the fact that my shoulder's gone into spasm for the second time in the past week. I stop at the base just shy of the stream but because of my sore shoulder, I will not be going back up for a second attempt. Mike and some others go up for a second go and Andrew manages a third trip down the sandy hill.

On the way back to Paihia, we stop at the Ninety Mile Beach – which is actually more like ninety kilometres in length but hey, this is New Zealand. We're picking some Tuatua, which are cockles, albeit much larger ones than those found in Ireland. Barry shows us how to dig for them at the wet, sandy shoreline and how to prize them open. Some of us, me included; eat raw, salty, sandy ones. This reminds me of one of the few childhood memories that I have of my father Tom, who died suddenly when I was four. The taste and the texture is the same as the ones we picked all those years before in Woodstown, Co. Waterford.

I never liked cockles.

We fill a large bucket, which will be dropped off at an old folks' home on the way back. Barry tells us a very touching story about how they'll be used. Apparently, in said home, an elderly gentleman living there has gone senile and, Heaven help him, he refuses to dress and leave his room. Unless they tell him they have some Tuatua for him. It turns out that if they tell him there are copious amounts of the shellfish in the kitchen, he will wash, dress and come out to basically, get on with his day.

It's a touching story: it would warm the cockles of your heart (Sorry, I just had to!).

On the way back, Barry's telling us about driving a four-wheel-drive vehicle on sand and unsurprisingly, I fall asleep. When I wake up fifteen minutes later, he's still banging on about driving on sand. So, the ipod is back on and when I take out the headphones some time later, he's droning on about fish and chips.

AAARGH!

He goes, "Eff ya wunt ta git one piece of fesh with ya cheps, then do so. An' eff ya wunt two pieces uf fesh with ya cheps, thit's nut a problum eitha'.

"And insoide the fesh shop, ya'll foind cutlery and ta'ta'e (tartare) sauce...so just geve me ya' orda' an' Oi'll reng it in for ya, okoy?"

One of the lads suggest that perhaps Barry is used to a more mature audience and I feel as if I've aged about fifty years just listening to him. We get to the shop, in the middle of bloody nowhere of course, and the food is gorgeous to be honest. And it's cheap. One piece of fish with chips costs just $7. Alex reminds me that I have to pay for her food also, having lost a drunken bet with her some seventeen hours earlier. Apparently, I bet young Alex that she would not be able to do the splits and pick up a box of cigarettes using just her teeth. And of course she did it. It's coming back to me now. So I pay for hers too. A bet is a bet after all.

When the rest of us are full to the gills with the grub (pun very much intended), Andrew eats everyone else's leftover fish and chips. Well, those belonging to our little group at the back of the coach. It's unbelievable, I've never seen anyone put away food the way he does – and he's in his early-twenties so it doesn't even reach his waistline. The little shit.

We arrive back at our Paihia hostel and jump into the hot tub there. Then I spend about ninety minutes online. I'm trying to think of things to do that don't involve alcohol because tonight, my dear readers, is to be the first night in over a month where I won't drink.

And it must be the sea air because we're all in bed by 10.30pm. Will miracles ever cease?

DAY THIRTY

Our eight-bed dorm is full now, and because our neighbour Ben is now sharing Alex's bottom bunk opposite mine, there are nine sleeping in the room. Two of my dormies are still out – there's a French guy asleep in the bed above me and an English couple in the bunks behind me. The guy, who looks a bit like Skeletor from 1980s cartoon, *He-Man*, is on top, while she is below. Of course she is.

Anyway, at some stage in the night, Skeletor starts clapping his hands and counting randomly. Ben gets up out of the bed for the toilet as the guy is coming out of the bathroom and he's like, "one, nine, eleven...six, four, two."

He adds: "Yes mum; ride 'em all day long."

Then, I crash again.

At some stage in the night, I'm woken by some bloke going, "Ciaran, they' givin' out man...ya'll have to lie on ya si-ed."

"I am lying on my side," I tell him, though I can't make out who *him* is in the dark.

Ben is telling me that he was the mystery figure who was trying to stop me from snoring hours earlier. Hmmm, I was sure it was one of the strangers in the dorm. He tells me that he was talking to Skeletor about me. Apparently, he just kept going "Fucksake!" with Ben telling him, "Alright; naw point in wakin' everyone else up aswal (aswell)...he is asleep after all."

That's when Skeletor said, "Alright mum". The context was lost on my sleep-soaked brain. However, I wasn't imagining the numbers thing, according to Ben, who

169

also had words with the French guy above me for shaking the bed violently in efforts to wake me. We have a good laugh at how he tells the story. He's a funny chap. It turns out that Skeletor, a total stoner, was out of it on some concoction or other. And I was totally sober pre crazy sleep-snoring. Let the indulgence of one and the abstinence from the other act as lessons to you, kids. Hmmm.

Ben, Mike and I go for breakfast in a cafe nearby: the place is called Lips. In New Zealand, you don't ask; you just go with the flow. Trust me. I opt for a bacon and egg triple-decker sandwich with hash brown and beans, glass of tomato juice and a large pot of tea. However, the owner only charges me $15, a good $5 less than the menu said it would, "because it's Sunday". This would cost nearly twice that back home...i.e. €15! Now, you see, this kind of thing just doesn't really happen in Ireland anymore. The Kiwis remind me of the Irish pre-Celtic Tiger – the name given to our particular economic success story, before the attitude, the snobbery, the hangover in the form of recession of course. During the Tiger, our egos became even more inflated than our fiscal growth.

Afterwards, at 12pm, I go down to the jetty for my parasailing. The fellas operating the thing are very chilled out and friendly. The younger guy straps me into this harness, puts a lifejacket on me and asks me to go to the back of the speedboat. I stand on this platform and I'm attached to this line – a hydraulic winch. The sail, a kind of parachute really, is filling up with air behind me and I'm holding onto this steel bar. Then, when the winch line is slackened, I let go and I'm floating gently upwards. The two Taffs are standing at the tourist offices near the water's edge, looking at me. I can see them get smaller and smaller as I rise higher and higher. Parasailing is quite a gentle experience really and not, as I'd imagined, such an adrenaline-rushing activity. Then I look back, and the boys have disappeared. Everything is getting dark, a huge shadow engulfs the bay. I look up and there's a massive pair of lips closing in on me. A huge tongue comes rolling out over sharp teeth. AAAAAARGH!!!

Lips, aha. Ahem.

Anyway, the sun casts sparse, dark patches around clouds and over the turquoise blanket below me. And while my own shadow has long since disappeared; the parachute's own projection looks like a pineapple ring or a donought that gets smaller with every passing minute. Occasionally, the sun disappears behind a cloud and there are a few drops. The wind lifts and so do I. At the trip's zenith, I'm 800 metres above the water. I can see the bay dotted with islands while in the background a dark, jagged line runs along the horizon and I quickly realise that these are mountains of varying elevation. Akin to a 3D painting of sorts, I'm breathing in some of the rich natural landscape on offer in New Zealand's North Island.

We're boarding the Kiwi Bus again before we snake our way back down to Auckland. Some of us are staying in ACB in Auckland again.

I share a dorm with Tash, Mike, Ben and Alex. We lads go down to the Globe Bar below, while the girls prepare dinner for the four of them. I've decided to go it alone because I have a craving for nachos. We end up playing pool with two French sisters who are mysterious at best and otherwise, liars.

Along comes "Mike", a seedy-looking little Aucklander with an extremely loud shirt. On closer inspection, I notice that the thing is covered with playing cards. He tells us that he's lost, "aw, a couple of hun'rid (hundred)" on the poker tables at a local casino.

Well, it is Sunday afternoon and he doesn't appear to have a wife or girlfriend to waste the money on.

I go back up to the hostel and prepare nachos, which don't turn out as I planned. After uploading some photos onto Facebook, I ring the mother back home in Ireland to let her know that I'm still alive. When I get back to the room, it's nearing midnight. I don't even shower or change out of my shorts. But I will in the morning.

I'm thinking that there seems to be a large Maori population in Auckland, though I'm wondering where they came from. And I learn from *Australia & New Zealand – Economy, Society and* Environment by Robinson, Loughran and Tranter, that New

Zealand has gained almost half a million people through immigration during the 20th Century. Little wonder for a country that is 'new' in terms of the development of its cities and its settlement. According to the book: "It is widely accepted that New Zealand's immigration before 1945 was based on a 'White New Zealand' policy, similar to the 'White Australia' policy.

And as a member of the Catholic Irish contingent, I'm interested to know that, particularly here; there "was a deliberate bias against" my lot. So, until the Second World War 96 per cent of Non-Maori New Zealanders were of British origin. Racist as this may sound, numerous schemes were introduced and from the late 1940s to the 1960s, the 'White New Zealand' theme continued – focussing mainly on immigrants from Britain and Northern Europe. In the 1970s there "was a surge of net migration to New Zealand". They also continued to come from Australia, North American and the Pacific Islands.

This continued until 1987, when the Immigration Act "specifically removed discrimination based on race and national or ethnic origin".

DAY THIRTY ONE

We're on the Kiwi Bus again; this time with a swollen, heavily-tattooed Maori. I warm to Buzz straight away and I'm wondering if he was in the well-known Kiwi gangster movie, *Once Were Warriors*. In fact, Buzz looks like he would fit into any gangster scene, anywhere. He is giving us the lowdown on New Zealand as we head south east to Thames, before going due east and through a little village called Tairua, which, Buzz tells us, was once the site of a fortified Maori village known as a "Maori Pa". Then we go north across the Coromandel Peninsula to Mercury Bay.

On the way down, I get talking to Kieran, an Engineer from Co. Cork who has not-long-since completed a three-month driving tour of the entire coast including a drive into the centre of Oz – from Darwin to Ayer's Rock. I actually thought that he was English, even though he was wearing a New Zealand international rugby (league) jersey. His first words to me, while we stopped off at a pick-up point in Auckland, indeed involved drink. He was new to the bus so he hadn't really been speaking to anybody but he clearly picked up on my accent.

"Fancy a pint?" he asked me, nodding towards some Irish bar across the road.

It was shortly after 9am at the time.

I looked at him as if he were half-mad because the thought of facing drink at that hour of the morning is repulsive, even to a good Irishman like myself. I only saw him as half-mad because a) he is Irish and therefore, the thoughts of a pint or nineteen are therefore, surely only rarely far from his mind b) he is on tour abroad and suffering from the mother of all hangovers and therefore in need of a cure c) he is from Cork – I rest my case. Jokes, Corkonians, jokes. Anyway, we understand each other's shorthand impeccably. Thankfully, the bar was closed.

We were due back on the bus again so we finished our coffees and embarked.

I get talking to two perky, peroxide-blond girls from Canada. Chantelle, it turns out, has just finished her biology degree, while Kayla is a fitness instructor. Kieran tells me that he's "doing the north island" (!), Auckland to Wellington and back again – as long as he can get back to Auckland within two weeks for his flight back to Sydney again, where he's currently based. Small world that it is, he studied civil engineering at the Waterford Institute of Technology (WIT), where I studied manufacturing engineering many moons ago. He obtained work experience working on the new bridge on the Waterford City Bypass with a Spanish construction company. And, he's waiting in Sydney for a US working visa to go to Texas for them, as they are looking for English-speaking Engineers there. He talks about jumping from gorges in the Northern Territory and about driving around the country with some German girl he met in Perth or Broome or somewhere.

Kieran points towards his big toe: there's a tattoo of a camel on it and he swears that he woke up one morning, not remembering having got it done. So, the amber nectar or Indian ink fairies were at him then. It transpires that he got drinking with some blokes who dared the big eejit to go through with it. He says that a couple of days later, when the fog had lifted, he finally remembered the tattoo artist stopping every few minutes, so uncontrollable were his fits of laughter. He was also in a serious paragliding accident in New South Wales a few weeks prior to this, while his Instructor fractured his skull and the pair had to be airlifted from some isolated patch of beach.

We've made a couple of stops to pick up some people and then we're on the highway south out of Auckland when some girl stands up suddenly and mutters something to Buzz, who dons the headset and tells us that she's only gone and taken the wrong bus. You can tell he's pissed off but he doesn't make much of it. Some drivers would! Now, far be it from me to slate anybody for being forgetful or careless but...over ninety minutes into a journey and she's only just discovered this?

Fuck. My. Life!

We take some exit or other and then we're back in the city, dropping her off again. We're on our merry way again and I'm teasing the Canadians to pass the time – a pastime that will catch on. They don't like being confused with Americans. Who knew?

We stop along the peninsula at Hot Water Beach, to dig our own hoot pools in the sand apparently. Ben, Mike, Kieran and I don't bother, however, instead choosing to play some form of American rugby. This is basically playing rugby with an American football, throwing the thing with one hand over the shoulder at times when we are too far apart to pass it rugger style. The ingredients of this particular game include two Welsh and two Irish men, all of whom will have previously felt the heat of battle on the rugby pitch. All four should be extremely hungover and at least one of them (me) should have excruciating pain in his shoulder for some reason. The aim of the sport is...er, boredom relief.

I'm feeling drained and I'm struggling to keep up with the others – most of whom, as I've already said, are on average more than ten years younger than I. Some part of me is literally dragging my body and mind through the day: my chest is fucked and so is my head, while my body is feeling worse.

After a while, we go stomping around others' pools and these are so hot that we jump from one to the other – searching and finally finding patches of cool water where the pools are being fed by a stream coming down the cliff nearby. We look on in awe and secret admiration at those masochists who can bear to laze around in the pools, their torsos red-raw in appearance from the heat. After nearly an hour, we go back up to the beach shower and wash the sand off our feet. We're eating ice lollies outside the shop at the edge of the beach and a local sheep farmer there nods at his grandson, who pulls up at the seated area on a quad bike. His daughter-in-law owns the place, it turns out. He starts engaging us, looking curiously at the American football and asking us where we're from.

"Wales and Ireland," he learns from me.

A smile appears across his face. I swear I could slap it as I anticipate his next words.

"Sew....wotcha thenk eh the All-Blecks?"

He's a friendly chap and he goes on to ask us what we're doing in New Zealand. He tells us that he owns most of the land – a couple of thousand acres, probably – around the area. We say goodbye, as we spot the others boarding our coach. So, after some hours driving, the duration of which I've spent listening to Swedish Andre's ipod (*Creedance Clearwater Revival*), we're finally at Cathedral Cove.

It really is beautiful. A track allows us access to Gemstone Bay, Stingray Bay and the cove. I don't want to sound like some scribe from days of yore, but I'm in no position to appreciate it all because of a certain imbibing malaise. We've stopped at the carpark here and the bus is then locked and the others go down the various walkways to have a look at the beaches and cliffs. I have Alex's ipod and I want to be alone so I break off from the various groups so that I can be. I'm walking down and Andrew is hot on my heels, trying to get in my ear. He's doing nothing wrong in fairness to him but, as I've said, I want to go it alone. He's a talkative chap, is young Andrew. He appears to finally get the hint because when I reach the rocks on a beach below, I'm alone. Some of the crowd have decided to go kayaking but I didn't. I sit on a rock and watch them being led in around some natural arch or other. I wave at them but they either ignore (or more likely don't see) me. The little fuckers.

175

The place boasts white sandy beaches, containing water that looks like a swimming pool in colour, and it is flanked by trees and cliff faces of varying elevation. On the way back up, my spirits lift a little and I manage to stop and take in the stunning scenery across the bay. I even take some pictures with my image-capturing device. When I get back to the car park above, some of the lads are throwing the ball to each other and I join them, only stopping when the pain in my shoulder makes this impossible.

Finally we arrive at Turtle Cove Hostel, a smallish hostel in Mercury Bay that is run by a married couple. It costs us $26 per night plus $20 deposit for our dorm keys. Kieran and I have opted to pay $7 for a spaghetti bolognese dinner that includes garlic bread and the promise of seconds should we require it. Ben and Mike, along with Alex and Tash, are preparing their own meal. I don't see the point; they're trying to save money but they've paid $7 each to make fajitas.

Anyway, we get a couple of bottles of Speights and play pool in the 'bar'. The small table is more curvaceous than a room full of glamour models, while the pink cloth is ripped to shit. It looks like a couple of angry bears have played on it just before we arrived. Most of the nets in the pockets are torn to bits so that the balls fall to the floor, once sunk. It's all hilarious and so, so New Zealand. The dartboard is harder than a scouse ale house. It has dried sufficiently so that the relevant missiles refuse to be housed there. Even momentarily like. Instead, they're likely to end up in someone's foot, eyeball or whatever you're having yourself. The "20" section on the board has actually grown out over the wire or, more likely tried to make an audacious bid for freedom. The dart board and pool tables are next to each other and, alongside the entrance into the bloody joint. So, it's basically a health hazard.

But that's not the best of it: the owner walks into the Bar and says, "Ouch". Sorry, let's try again. The owner comes in and grabs himself a beer. However, when we ask him if we can purchase one for ourselves, he just asks, "Where's the beer guuuuu'l?"

When we don't answer, he says, "Sha'll be en, en a bit".

And he's right; she does come in – about ten minutes later. The beers are just $4 and there's even a fifty cent return on the empty bottles. We thought it would be economical to bring back about a dozen or so of the little brown chaps at a time but we're only allowed to bring up one each per purchase.

There is dinner, there are seconds, there are more beers and there is laughter. Then, there is sleep. I get talking to Leeds girl, Emma, who's wearing a Sonic Youth t-shirt. She tells me that she didn't know that SY are a band. She "jus' laaaked (liked) the tee-shuuu't".

I feel old. Bedtime.

9. The Wheels on the Bus...

DAY THIRTY TWO

So today it's on to Rotorua. And we pass thought Hobitton. We see a little Hobbit house with a statue of Gollum or Sméagol or whatever you'd call the cretinous little shit, outside of the place.

I couldn't really care less about anything Lord of the Rings (LoTR)-related, if I'm honest.

It's lashing out of the heavens, as us Irish would say. We have an hour to spend here before we hop back on the Kiwi Experience bus again. I'm wearing flip-flops, shorts, a navy wife-beater tee shirt and my Akruba hat as I wander around town – looking for somewhere to buy a waterproof jacket. If they aren't used to looking at such a sight, they're not doing a good job in hiding it. No luck on the jacket front, not even in a Farmers store, which is a...eh, fashion store. I pop into a Subway for lunch on the main thoroughfare and Andrew's there. A mother-and-daughter (it's obvious) are standing at the counter, rambling on and laughing their heads off like a couple of schoolgirls. Andrew is prattling on about cookies and ice cream and iced buns. I'm terrified that he will start rabbiting on about fluffy bunnies (get it?) and so on (see what I did there?). Dear Lord above us all. His speech gets faster and his voice gets higher and higher with his rapidly increasing excitement. It's like a scene out of the BBC comedy show, *The League of Gentlemen*, and I'm morto.com. Thankfully, he gets served and fecks off. I breathe a sigh of relief as I sit at the table next to the women. He's outside now, filling his water bottle with the large coke he's just bought. I think he thought that I would leave with him.

The three of us are just staring out at him. "He's on my tour," I tell them. They look at him and then at me.

I change the subject.

"Can you tell me where I can buy a waterproof jacket?" I ask them.

"Theeey's a place on the cooornaaa'," the elder of the two women tells me. Then, she just gets up and heads out through the door.

However, she returns in less than a minute with this all-weather fleece-lined sports jacket and just, like, hands the thing to me in this understated way. As if it's the most natural thing in the world.

Bay of Plenty Motors is emblazoned on the left breast in orange. Otherwise, it's black.

"I used to work theee'e," she explains, obviously noticing the surprised look on my mug. "It's olright," she continues, "Kiwis aaa' loike thet."

"Yo'll pick up a chick in thet jickit," she says. I'm taken aback at her generosity and thank her profusely. Yeah, I'm thinking...but what kind of 'bird' exactly?

Oh, a Kiwi. I get it now.

It's mid-afternoon and we've just checked in at our Base Hostel in Rotorua. We're going on the Luge ride which, in this case, is hurtling down a huge concrete concourse in a tiny, rubber-wheeled cart. The group consists of Alex, Ben, Mike and Kieran; along with Leeds folk, Emma, Naff and Chris. It costs us $28 each for three goes.

I'm having great fun but the trolleys, not even the larger ones, are not designed for tall people. They operate on a push-pull system, pushing the T-bar at the front forwards to go faster and pull it backwards to brake. However, my legs are too long so, I can't get the bar back far enough or quickly enough to stop or slow down adequately. This nearly gets me killed on the bends but more importantly, costs me the first race – on the beginners' course. Fittingly, the Welshies are wearing the red helmets, the Englanders don the blue, while Kieran and I pop on a couple of green ones. Alex comes first, and does so again on the Intermediate course. Naff and Chris come next, so, England is the overall winner. Wales come second and we Irish lads come in Paddy Last ☹

Rotorua: Te Rotorua-nui-a-Kahumatamomoe or *The Second Great Lake of Kahumatamomoe* for long; is in the Bay of Plenty region of the North Island. *Roto*(lake) *rua*(two) is a city with a population of almost 56,000, while the district

179

(Rotorua or *Second Lake* District) has an estimated population of nearly 69,000. It's 230 kilometres south east of Auckland and eighty kilometres north of Taupo. Rotorua has seventeen lakes, and is a popular spot for fishing, swimming. And other activities such as waterskiing are popular in summer.

Whakarewarewa Forest, known as *The Disneyland of Mountain Biking*, has some of the best mountain biking trails in the country.

Rotorua is known for its geothermal activity, meaning there are hot mud pools, hot springs and geysers. Often known locally as Sulphur City, the smell of hydrogen sulphide emissions is stifling. In case you're wondering; it smells *just* like rotten eggs. Lots of them. In fact, the sulphur deposits next to the southern end of Government Gardens are known as Sulphur Point and this area is particularly smelly.

No sooner have we arrived back at our hostel when we must leave for our meeting with the Maori chiefs at Tamaki. We're picked up by this tall, mean-looking Maori with an extremely long-winded name. It begins with Mark spiralling off into some unpronounceable Maori-speak before ending in something sounding like "short". On the bus, we learn that his grandfather is from Co. Waterford. His grandfather came from Dungarvan, about forty kilometres from my home in the city. It takes us about forty minutes to get to the Maori village. During this time, Mark tells us how he's a "Real Man" because he plays rugby. He says "Kia Ora" about a thousand times on the way, before he tells us that it means "be well" or "be healthy".

Mark tells us that a "Chief" will be picked from our "tribe" to represent us at a ceremony before dinner. The chiefs will face the Maori warriors, as they threaten us with contorted faces and gestures, in a pre-dinner ceremony. The warriors will perform a Hakka for our chiefs and will lay down a peace challenge for them, which, if not taken up, will probably result in our annihilation. A branch will be placed on the ground – by the warriors – and this must be picked up by our chiefs, if this fate is to be avoided.

Anyway, on the way in, Mark tells us that our Chief should be tall, handsome and a talented singer...a "real man". So naturally, everyone on the bus looks at me. But

Mark says it should be Kieran because he's wearing an Ireland rugby jersey. Well, I can't object on those grounds now, can I?

We enter the village when the Maori women sing to us; we're told we can take photos but must otherwise keep our hands in front of us at all times. And of course, we must remain silent. So, I'm kneeling down, taking some shots, when I'm tapped on the shoulder. I turn my head and see a black shape in the corner of my peripheral. I ignore it, assuming it to be a jealous tourist. However, it turns out to be a tiny Maori woman, who reminds me that I must stand during the ceremony. I duly oblige – a bit embarrassed if I'm honest.

We're taken around this carefully cultivated Maori village, from where the Chief and his minions issue arrogant boasts, warning that they will take our women from us. Afterwards, we're taken to this large timber hall, lit with candles and heated with these gas heaters. The Maori tribe perform for us; singing and dancing away on the stage. The dreaded Hakka ends the performance.

We go to a dining hall and get stuck into mountains of food, which has been cooked in a slow oven in the ground throughout the day. There's roast beef, chicken and gorgeous lamb, breads, pastas, fish and vegetables, bread and butter pudding and cheesecakes for dessert. It's all delicious.

Then there's a trip to the gift shop of course, where I buy a carved wooden book mark and key ring.

So the rituals we've seen today would have been those that New Zealand's colonisers would have faced. Speaking of which, the British influence on the country was underlined almost 150 years ago. The Treaty of Waitangi in 1840 fortified British Rule, though twenty years later the Maoris – obviously horrified at legal wrangling and being pressured into selling their lands – burned down the British settlers farmhouses and with this, a bloody war had started. Twelve years later and the Maori Wars had ended, with the settlers gaining most of the country's land following the loss of about two thousand Maori lives and one thousand English. The real damage to the Maori, however, was the introduction of diseases such as Typhoid and Tuberculosis.

So how did New Zealand get its curious Maori inhabitants, and where did they come from anyway?

Many 19th Century scholars recorded different Maori stories about reaching New Zealand from Polynesia. That's according to *Maori Tribes of New Zealand*, by Te Ara, the Encyclopaedia of New Zealand published by David Bateman. The book says that a man by the name of Percy Smith calculated, from listening to Maori histories, that they had "migrated together in 1350AD, in one 'great fleet' of seven canoes". "According to Smith, they had then conquered the Moriori, who he said were a primitive Melanesian race already living in New Zealand."

But it doesn't end there. "In the 1960s, errors were found in Smith's research for the Great Fleet story", it appears. Recent scientific evidence includes DNA analysis, and the radiocarbon dating of archaeological sites and it "is now believed that the Maori arrived at different times" and from "several points in East Polynesia late in the 13th Century".

From the 1920s, scientists had proved that Chatham Island Moriori, like the Maori, were descendants of the original Polynesian New Zealand settlers of the country. "Moriori had migrated to the Chatham Islands some time after 1300AD, possibly around 1500."

Gunther, in *Inside Australia and New Zealand*, maintains that the Polynesians were probably Asian Caucasoid and "modified by Mongoloid and Negroid blood as they moved eastward through Indonesia and Melanesia to the Pacific Islands of Hawaii, Tahiti and Easter Island". They became expert canoemen who were capable of travelling a few hundred miles in canoes carrying 250 people. Interestingly, he also says "it is known" that there were two Polynesian civilizations in prehistoric New Zealand – one of which, he explains, was a "Stone Age culture based on hunting the moa", while the other is the "more advanced stage" of civilisation found by the Pakeha (or Europeans). He says that the Maori peoples were traditionally agricultural, artistic, religious and warlike. They cultivated sweet potato, the taro root and the yam. They also ate fern roots, birds and fish.

And they ate one another.

I have to re-read this part. Apparently, it was not uncommon for them to keep people in pens in order to "fatten them up", while the "notorious cannibals" allegedly ate "all shipwrecked sailors".

Captain Cook gave his account of the Maori in *An Account Of The Voyages Undertaken By The Order Of His Majesty, For Making Discoveries In The Southern Hemisphere (Vol. III)* by Commodore Byron, Captain Wallis, Captain Carteret and Captain Cook. He says that "the stature of the men in general is equal to the largest of those in Europe...stout, well limbed...but not fat" and they were "also exceedingly vigorous and active" with "manual dexterity in an uncommon degree". Their "colour in general is brown; but in few deeper than that of a Spaniard, who has been exposed to the sun, in many not so deep".

Eh, right so.

The women, according to Captain Cook, "have not a feminine delicacy in their appearance, but their voice is remarkably soft". He goes on, however, to say that "like the women of other countries," the female Maori exhibits "more airy cheerfulness, and a greater flow of animal spirits, than the other sex". The hair colour of the Maori is black, and "their teeth extremely regular, and as white as ivory...the features of both sexes are good; they seem to enjoy high health". Cook said that the Maori treated each other with "the tenderest affection, but are implacable towards their enemies, to whom, as I have observed, they never give quarter".

In his journals from March, 1770, Cook gave a general account of his experiences of meeting the Maori in very tense circumstances. "When they came within a cable's length of the ship [in their canoes] they used to stop, and the Chiefs rising from their seat, put on a dress which seemed appropriate to the occasion, generally of dog's skin, and holding out their decorated staff, or a weapon, directed the rest of the people what they should do."

He said that their words were "almost unequivocally the same. *Haromai, baromai, barre uta a Patoo-Patoo oge*: "Come to us, come on shore, and we will kill you with all our Patoo-Patoos."

They would begin their "war song and dance, as a prelude to an attack, which always followed", he wrote. This dance, clearly a Hakka, consisted of "violent motions, and hideous contortions of the limbs, during which the countenance also performs its part: the tongue is frequently thrust out to an incredible length, and the eyelids so forcibly drawn up that the white appears both above and below, as well as on each side of the iris, so as to form a circle round it...". The "horrid dance" was always accompanied by a song" that was "wild indeed, but not disagreeable", while "every strain ends in a loud and seep sigh, which they utter in concert".

Yup, this dance is the God and every-international-rugby team-in-the-world fearing Hakka. Either that or they were nursing addictions to speed.

Eh, we've just been fattened up at the village and where is this bus taking us, exactly? *(Swallows hard)*

Mark rambles on manically in various accents and languages from all over the planet. Actually, on the way out here he greeted us all in fifty six languages while now, on the way back to the hostel (hopefully); he is encouraging us all to sing a song in our respective native tongues. He appears to be going mad. He starts standing up and sitting down while driving – singing his version of *The Wheels on the Bus* or whatever it's called, as we circle a large roundabout six or seven times.

It goes like this: "The bus droiva' will lose his licence whin the Police cetch up with hem; Police cetch up with hem; Police cetch up with hem...the bus droiva' will be arrest'd whin the police see his droi-vin'; he'll neva' be allowed on the roads again."

And an "A-ha" moment duly arrives: in this moment I realise that he must have the Irish blood. An Irish lunatic mated with a Maori woman and spawned a boy or girl, I'm not sure which. This person then parented a child...this crazy bastard! Polynesia be damned. The, eh, best of them mixed with Co. Waterford men.

We're at the Lava Lounge, next to our hostel, Kieran and I take on Ben and Mike in an international pool competition. We beat them 2-1. So that's revenge for losing to them at La Luge earlier then. We rule at sports. Well, of the pub variety.

184

A creepy guy in his 60s, who's lurking around in the shadows on his own, gets thrown out after touching Chris on the crotch. Jesus! He's being eyeing up all the boys all night (so he likes men, that's fine; whatever floats your boat and everything). But Chris rightly complains him to the management and he gets thrown out. And proper order too.

Apparently the weirdo was a regular at the bar. Time to leave.

DAY THIRTY THREE

So we leave Rotorua for Waitmomo and I offer to cook an Irish Stew for the Magnificent Seven; for the two Welsh boyos, Kieran, Alex, Tash, Andrew and yours truly.

There are some activities on offer today, including The Abyss (abseiling in dark caves), dark water rafting and the Ruakuri Walk near Waitomo. However, every item of clothing in my bag needs cleaning, I'm cooking the others dinner plus, I'm tired. So I pass on the clipboard.

When we stop for lunch, I go shopping for ingredients for the meal. I buy carrots, parsnips and turnips, an onion, diced beef potatoes and of course, butter. I also grab three packets of oxtail soup. And oh, I buy eight cans of Guinness for the Welshies and The Chef to drink. The ingredients come to $47, which works out at about $6.50 per diner. The cans come to about $30, a bit expensive by New Zealand standards – though it is an import here and works out at roughly the same price that it would in an Irish supermarket.

We arrive at our Waitomo hostel and I get down to my domestic chores. The packets of washing powder cost me $1 each and the washing and drying machines cost just $2 per 40-minute cycle. I load up the washing machine, and then the dryer about forty five minutes later. But when I come back to take out the clothes, they're still wet.

Not damp, wet! After I set the machine in motion again, I go back to the kitchen and when I return once more, the clothes are still ringing. Ben and Mike are waiting for me to finish with the tumble dryer. They tell me that they'll stop drinking their

185

beer long enough to go find the caretaker, inform him of the problem and get me a refund. The caretaker gives a refund AND, cheerily offers us the use of the industrial dryer in his utility room free of charge while he fixes said machine. That's New Zealand for you. Ireland is still like that too in places, by-the-way.

Meanwhile, back in the kitchen, the cooking utensils are scant. I have to juggle between whatever pots and pans I can find in order to get dinner cooked for the others. Residents are coming in at various times to cook their own food and I'm like an Army or Prison Chef, cooking for the hungry masses. Finally, about thirty minutes after schedule (and a lot og eye-rolling behind my back, I expect), dinner is served. The gang seem to like it and there's plenty to go around so both of these fears are quashed. We wash up and return the cutlery to Reception and get our $10 deposit back.

It's about 10pm when I meet Buzz and the others at Curly's Bar on the huge hostel campus. The place has two pool tables – one is broken – and a dart board. There's also a smoking area. Here, we meet four Irish teachers who are doing the rounds in a camper van. We all have a good time here, taking the piss out of each other.

We're followed back to the hostel by these creepy Kiwi blokes we met at the bar. Of course they're following the girls – we can hear them shouting at us as we trawl through a wooded field of some description in the dark.

We shake them off and head straight for the games room. There's a TV, a pool table and a deck for smoking on, outside. Kieran has had the foresight to buy a 1.5 litre bottle of vodka and 1 litre bottle of Coke. The Welshies, Ben and Mike, have also bought a bottle of vodka and have Sprite. We're already well-on but we intend getting absolutely hammered. Ireland, including Nicola from Meath, takes on Wales with English Emma in a pool competition. My mouth loosens. A lot. When Mike starts bridging his hand to take his shot, his fingers curve naturally. And, under the yellowish light, his smoke-stained fingers remind me of a bunch of bananas. I proceed to calling him "Banana-hand" and "Plantain fingers" for ages and though he's not impressed, Ben finds it all hilarious. I know, I know: very mature. When Mike stops to tell me, quite justifiably, to "Fuck off," I tell him that he is "*actually* Terry

186

Griffiths", the most boring snooker player of them all. Mr Griffiths, putting it mildly, never rushed himself and, he too was a Welshman.

After a while, when Mike and I are wrestling each other to the couch, the lights are turned off. Hey, I heard that. Ben and Nicola, who I keep calling Grainne for some reason, continue playing pool in the dark. Mike and I, totally plastered, start singing rugby songs. Mike teaches me *Bread of Heaven* or whatever it's called, and we sing it about six or seven times in a row. We then move onto *Ireland's Call*, *Flower of Scotland* and even an impromptu version of *You Can Stick Your Fuckin' Chariot Up Yer Arse* – for the benefit of our English friends. But we don't mean any offence...they see the funny side of it. Vodka is spilled and I find myself cleaning what I suspect to be diced carrots out of my jacket collar at about 4am. I left the jacket on the couch – perhaps I shouldn't have tackled Mike so hard, though he swears that he wasn't the puker. That's fine, but I'm still the pukee.

I scrub hard.

DAY THRITY FOUR

I wake up this morning to find my cellmate, Andrew, rolling up his clothes and putting them carefully into his backpack – like the good little Boy Scout that he is. I shower and when I'm putting the key into the lock to my door, Emma comes bouncing down the corridor. I'm naked, except for the towel that mine own hand is holding in place.

"A'll rip that off yuh," she chirps up in her broad Leeds accent.

"I know you would."

And of course who would I be to stop her.

Arriving at the bus, I'm told that I'm five minutes late. However, I'm not the only ones, as Buzz tells me that Kieran, Ben, Mike, Alex and Tash have not yet appeared.

I offer to go get them.

The door is unlocked. I turn the handle, enter and I'm greeted by four corpses, laid out on slabs in their crypt. The room is pitch black, the smell of alcohol would drop a horse. Ben pops his head over the duvet and I advise him that Buzz has promised to leave without them, should they not be ready in thirty minutes.

Meanwhile, I board the Kiwi bus and we drive to the Ruakuri Reserve for the thirty-minute walk that I missed out on yesterday. The fresh air is agreeing with me. A gentle climb on the trail reveals a serious of curious limestone rock formations, while the inviting caves and native vegetation ease me back into sobriety. I even manage to smile when French girl Maitena takes a couple of pictures of me.

When we go back to pick up the others, Kieran is with them. Shit. Completely forgot about my fellow Irishman: talk about leaving a comrade on the battlefield.

While clambering on board, they all look well-shook and a bit sheepish. We move off, stopping for coffee and pies after thirty minutes or so. It turns out that Kieran slept on the couch in the games room, even though Reception gave him a double room because he was last to check in yesterday. I know New Zealand is the *other* side of the world, but rewarding tardiness in this way seems to be kind of backward.

About twenty minutes after we set off again, Kieran approaches Buzz. I'm sitting alone in the front row so he sits next to me. Apparently he has forgotten his glasses or, lost them. And his phone. (He finds his glasses in the bottom of his bag later on in the day. This sounds suspiciously like me – maybe Fly was right about us Irish folk being so engrossed in things scholarly that we forget about the 'minor' details of life...i.e., the day-to-day stuff. It's either that or the drink.)

A brief stop for a short walk at Huka Falls on the Waikato River, New Zealand's longest river, leaves me breathless. There's not much conversation. I suspect it's for two reasons: a) it's bloody loud, rendering it near impossible to make an audible sound with our mouths b) our pie holes remain open only, such is the raw and awesome power in motion before our eyes. The charging, raging foam climbs over itself in the rush along the canyon, which is only about fifteen metres in width. Meanwhile, the angry bubbly and beautiful mass relents in parts to reveal large patches of clean aqua-coloured water. I have never seen anything like it before. It is a truly majestic scene. Running two kilometres north of Lake Taupo, the falls are up to eleven metres in height here. The almost perfectly cut channel that contains the frothy, angry mass, was forged as a result of a volcanic action. The word "huka" literally means "foam" in Maori and the volume of water flowing through it can reach up to an astonishing 220,000 litres per second.

After about twenty minutes, we push on to Taupo, whose lake, at 616 kilometres in circumference, is the largest in New Zealand (if not Australasia). It's basically big enough to fit the whole of Singapore into. Lake Taupo is said by some experts to be the location of one of the largest volcanic explosions in the world. And it happened circa 186 AD. According to our Kiwi Experience guide book, it promises to be the "Adventure Capital of the world". I don't know about that but I do know that it's a beautiful spot.

Taupo has a population of over 22,000 people and sits on the shore of the great lake.

It's raining now as we check into our Base Hostel, one of the nicest I've seen in New Zealand, actually. So where do Kieran and I head straight to? Yep, straight to Irish pub, Finn (not "Fionn" mind you) McCuhal's, directly across from our hostel. I spied it through the window from my bottom bunk in the dorm.

We order two pints of Kilkenny – with Guinness heads – and the Welshies do the same when they arrive. English couple, Carly on Crutches and Spanish-born Antonio join us also. It's pissing down and I stay for four pints, on a Thursday afternoon in Taupo. A couple of hours later, I re-emerge from my dorm and head down to Element Bar in our hostel for a barbeque. I realise that I've left my Bay of Plenty jacket in Finn's, so I run back over to get it. It's been handed in and thankfully, my camera is still in the pocket.

Back at Element Bar, at our hostel, the barmaid asks me if I'm a driver because I've just ordered a Coke. "No," I tell her.

"I hope y'aaaaa (you are) cuz the fuzzy (fizzy) staff's (stuff is) free." I'm tempted to tell her that I'm on the fuzzy because my mind is fizzy. Then I'm about to tell her that I'm on the fizzy because my mind is fuzzy but with all the fuzz and the fizz, I forget.

She lands the Coke on the counter and just walks off. The barbeque consists, again, of these fatty beef sausages – that I suspect are also full of water – and pans of white, sliced bread. Oh, and there's ketchup too. The sausages are disgusting but naturally, we all eat them. Anyway, afterwards, it's back to the pumping music inside. The younger Canadian girls, Jena and Katia, are trying to organise a drinking game, which is pointless because of the "Intz, intz" blasting from the speakers.

I'm drinking these $4 vodka alcopops and free punch but I get two free drinks when I'm the first up to sing in the Karaoke. It's *Let Me Entertain You* by Robbie Williams. I'm as hoarse as a field full festivalgoers on the annual Laryngitis Sufferers' Association day out. Naked festival attendees standing around in the rain with sore throats, that is, while shouting at the top of their lungs in between swigs of beer and draws of cigars. You get the picture.

But I do, *do* my best so I do and, I even do throw in a few cheesy dance moves, I do. The southern hemisphere is known for its outdoor and active lifestyle. Backpackers largely spend nights (and often days) drinking, smoking, roaring and shouting in this part of the sphere, hence the hoarseness.

And this, my friends, is what happens on tour.

I help Maitena pick out a song – *500 Miles* by The Proclaimers – and we have a good laugh singing it. She's a bit shy, doesn't really understand my accent, but she follows me out to the beergarden anyway. She's wearing Ben's sunglasses and I take them from her, advising her that they "suit me much better", and so on. The gang are getting well tanked up now and there are about twenty five of us kicking it up at Element Bar. You could say that we're actually *in* our element. At one stage, when I'm well on from Kilkenny and Monteith's ale, punch, Heineken, vodka and the alcopop thingies, I need the toilet and find myself taking a piss in a urinal next to this huge Samoan. He comes in singing something like, "Be ma betch; suck ma deck..." or words to that effect. He sings it louder and louder – I'm sure in order to intimidate me – but I stand firm, as opposed to "hard" you understand. He goes into the cubicle to relieve himself so he's obviously a shy bully, man-rapist or whatever. I'm kind of wishing I was in a cubicle now because I'm nearly shitting myself. After a minute or so he comes out and I'm standing there washing my hands.

He's like, "Fack me brooo; ya' one big fackaaa'."

Like he can talk.

"Eh, thanks man," I reply.

He says something about me joining his rugby team and I'm having the banter with him; keeping him sweet, as you would a giant rugby-playing Samoan who, you suspect, wants you to be his sex slave. However, we both get out of the bathroom with our pride – and prejudices – intact so no harm done I suppose. Back in the beergarden-come-smoking area or whatever, things are reaching fever pitch and we're partying with some New Zealand Special Forces soldiers who are (mostly) these fucking huge Maoris. Things are getting messy and it's only afterwards when I discover that they're soldiers of the Kill-you-with-a-rolled-up-newspaper variety. This is just as well, really.

Some of the girls get their tops off and cajole Mike and I into doing likewise. We do so, for a laugh, until the Bouncer, a Samoan also, tells us to put them back on. I notice that he didn't tell the girls to do the same. I put mine back on but Mike, who's as pissed as...well, a beergarden full of trained Maori killers, doesn't seem to understand or, hear the instruction.

"GET YA TOP BACK UN," he repeats with his voice raised.

"I don't think he heard you," I tell him. "I TOLD HIM ABOUT SEX (SIX) TIMES," he adds, his demeanour getting ultra scary for a few seconds. You would not like to piss this man off: not on a rugby pitch; not anywhere. However, he's "as sweet as" thereafter. Later, we head inside and take to the dancefloor, to Rock, Indie and Hip Hop. It turns out that Kieran was kicked out for wearing flip flops when dancing. At closing time, it's just me, Mike, Emma and Alex left from our gang. Maitena is busy escaping the clutches of some idiot Kiwi guy and, at least two of the lads on our bus. Then again, she's young, she's French and she's HOT.

I rip my jeans in some ridiculous attempt to do the splits and outside, a kind Scottish women who's working in the hostel, *helps* me by finishing the job. She tears

191

at the seam and the jeans split all the way from the ankle up to the groin. We pose for pictures together.

She's tiny so Kieran tells her that she's like a Hobbit next to me. And that would, eh, make me an Ork?

Ahem.

DAY THIRTY FIVE

This morning, I sleep in until about 11am because the killer blister on my heel is preventing me from doing the twenty-six kilometre walk, while I'm too heavy to join the others in doing a parachute jump in Taupo. Also, I'm hungover and lazy. Sorry, "skydive", as they insist on calling it down here. Indeed, one must weigh less than 100 kilos to indulge.

So instead, I wander around town, scouting out some plasters and antiseptic ointment for said blister and a miracle dieting drug. I'm curious about the Taupo architecture and I notice that the tallest building around seems to be about the same height, or not much taller, than the average semi-detached home in Ireland. The buildings, low and flat-roofed, serve the city well, however. The views of the surrounding Taupo Mountains and indeed, Lake Taupo, are stunning. The streets are laid out in blocks so it is easy for me to find my way around. Though it's a bit too well planned and kind of depressing if you ask me – like some nuclear town in the US that I saw in a forgettable movie at some point in the past. It's similar to Bileola in Oz, though not as charming.

Taupo has restaurants in abundance and I finally settle for a place simply called, Delicatessen. It's a spacious joint for trendy foodies and New Age-ey types and it has Italian aspirations. I order a loin chop sandwich effort, an orange juice and a cappuccino. The fare is enjoyable but I feel that, at $26, it's expensive for New Zealand. While the food is good, the service – bordering on downright rude – is not. I pass on leaving a tip. An Internet café is a tad expensive because I get charged $2.50 for fifteen minutes. Here, a packet of Monster Munch is $3.50 and a Wispa bar is over

$3, more than double the price of the same goods back up in Ireland. Even though the stuff is imported, I'm still astounded at the price.

Afterwards, I go to this unassuming, kitschy cinema called Starlight at the Taupo Town Centre on Horomatangi St. and watch *Surrogates*, which is an awful, awful movie. I mean; it is ABSOLUTE kack, just in case I'm not clear enough. At McDonald's afterwards, I meet Alex, Emma-from-Essex and Emma-and-Vicky from Leeds. I'm there to consol myself, having missed out on the skydive. A burger will surely help the weight loss. They're talking about the dive and how it was disorientating, and so on. Outside in the adjoining playground, there sits a grounded aircraft. It's not real of course but it looks kind of cool. Alex, Emma and I go to Mulligans near our Base hostel and we sip on a couple of pints. There's two Irish girls working there, one of whom is from Waterford city, about two kilometres from my own home actually. Before leaving at about 7.30, I tell them that I'll meet them in Element Bar at 10pm or thereabouts.

However, it's after 11 when I get there because the Old Dog is slowing somewhat. There's not much point in saying otherwise to be honest. Down at Element, Chris – a dab hand with the pen or semi-permanent black marker in this instance – is drawing various tattoos on us. The girls have moustaches and slogans scrawled on the knuckles of those that want them. Kieran has a giant heart on his arm with "YOUR MOTHER" written on it. Tash says she will draw a "tash" on me and actually writes her name across my upper lip, which I think is very witty. Alex writes something on my lower back ("SLAG TAG", I discover). She does another one alongside it. I'm a bit disturbed to see a picture of said tattoo – a penis with the words "DICK SICK" accompanying it.

We seem to have split up into groups. I go to Finn McCuahal's with Kieran and the Welsh lads. Here, Kieran is disgusted with a frosted mirror that has a map of Ireland engraved on it. In fairness, I can see his point as Cork is situated where Kerry should be and whole inlets, bays and harbours, even cities, have apparently disappeared. I mean, how hard is it to get something like this right? If you bothered to find a map of Ireland to base it on, it would be actually hard to get it wrong, would it not? Was it made by one of Cromwell's minions, a blind minion who has no hands?

I get bored and leave, somehow ending up in Kazbar – there's a bar of the same name in Waterford too – with Chris, Nicola and her friend, Becky. I literally can't drink much tonight because my liver seems to be on a sanctioned strike. Hopefully, the brain and other vital organs won't come out in support. All the relevant parties are in talks.

These two crazy Dutch kids in their late teens from Amsterdam (Borris and Josh) who we've met....somewhere...are also at Kazbar. It's Saturday night and the place is full of Maoris – some of the women are STUNNING – and the music is, of course, Hip Hop. Various mean-looking dudes in hoods and low strung jeans slouch around the place and it's a bit intimidating to be honest. Chris, the two Dutch lads and I are outside in the smoking area. It's at the back of the venue and wouldn't be an ideal place to get cornered in a fire or a row, seeing as the only exit seemingly available to us is the front entrance.

Anyway, this rough-looking Maori chap with a black eye and missing teeth approaches. He points at the Dutchies one-by-one and goes: "I could have you – I could have you." Next he turns towards Chris and goes, "I could have you."

Then he turns to look up at me.

"I could –" he starts, and stares, mouth agog, "– nevermind."

He just walks off.

Honest.

DAY THIRTY SIX

We're on our way to River Valley, where some of us will go white water rafting on Grade Five rapids. Other activities on offer include fishing, horse riding and some class of a trek or other. We stop off somewhere – I couldn't tell you where because the stop off points are all starting to look the same and blur into each other at this stage but there is a town crier about the place if that helps. The Welshies get talking to Buzz about fishing and I haven't a clue. I'm interested though. Buzz tells us that there's a "feshing shop" of sorts around the corner so we go, chip in and buy a fishing rod, flights and a weight for $36 – so we can see if they're biting in River Valley later on. We buy stuff for lunch here and take to the roads again. But before lunch, we stop at a section of the Tongariro National Park.

We set off on a six-kilometre walk that should last less than two hours (well, I would certainly hope so!) and promises some "spectacular Lord of The Rings" scenery. The loop we're concerned with centres around Taranaki Falls at Tongariro, New Zealand's oldest national park and apparently, the fourth one created in the world.

Fourth? Wow! I mean, for fuck sake. Why bother? Is that even worthy of mention, really?

It also has world heritage status. The skyline is dominated by three volcanoes...Ruapehu, Ngauruhoe and Tongariro. In 1995, an angry Ruapehu belched out plumes of ash and dust about twelve kilometres into the atmosphere, emptying Crater Lake. So says my Kiwi Experience guidebook at any rate. Its brother, Ngauruhoe, has had a spot of indigestion also, leading to numerous rumbles, with the most recent occurring in 1975. The New Zealand's Department of Conservation states that Ruapehu is one of the world's most active volcanoes. It's the largest active volcano in New Zealand and the highest point in the North Island, reaching up to 2,800 metres. However, the more mature and placid Tongariro has been dormant since 1927.

Before we take to the trail, I apply some of the sticky and syrupy iodine-laced ointment to my heel, cover it with three plasters and put on a couple of thin socks. Hopefully, this will enable me to have a pain-free trek.

"What is that, iodine?" asks Ben.

I'm taken back to 1986: to Ray Daly's first year science class in a freezing, chemical-fumed prefab at De La Salle College in Waterford, to be precise. I remember painting potatoes and onions with the reddish brown substance, before placing them under a microscope and then viewing their cells.

I don my black hoodie and then my waterproof-less-jacket that looks the part, before throwing the Akruba on the bonze. The trek is a gentle one, the weather temperate. A smooth path leads us through some woods at rapidly-changing elevations, while a stream that is fed by the Taranaki Falls is below our path and to our left. We push on at varying paces (mine is moderate) and I don't stop to paddle in the steam like some of them do because I don't trust the plasters. Without them my heel kills. When we get to the falls, Antonio and Chris strip down to their shorts and bathe in the rocky pool under the lashing jets of water. The water pounds them, and any remnants of a hangover I imagine. Some of us stop here for our packed lunch, while others simply turn around and come from whence we came.

I don't see the point in doing that because pushing up around the head of the falls is very rewarding. I stop on top of it to take some phtos but I tell Antonio to keep on moving as he is soaking wet and he wants to dry off before getting on the bus. The scene from the falls is spectacular, apt reward for bothering really. Rolling hills, volcanic valleys and the overbearing presence of the volcanoes themselves gives great meaning to the words *Timeless* and *Unspoilt* that have sprung forth from my mind like the babbling streams I've seen en route. A well defined track cuts through low-laying vegetation and wild grass that looks suspiciously like heather to me. The walk takes me almost two hours to complete but to be fair, my break for lunch and my leisurely pace are the reasons. A quick pace with no stops and it could be done in little over an hour. But hey, where's the fun in that?

We leave for River Valley, stopping a couple of times to refuel and to take in the beautiful scenery. The hills surrounding River Valley need to be seen to be believed. Dramatic lushness fills the eyes and feeds the soul on the run in.

We arrive at the River Valley adventure lodge, a natural basin encircled by sharp, bush-clad hills with the moody Rangitikei River racing through it. The Welshies and I test out our new rod on the raging river but they aren't biting. The fish I mean. Mike is in stitches at my attempts to "scare the fish to the surface" by throwing rocks into the river. Country boyos like these have far more experience that I at this type of thing. There's this trolley on a rope-pulley system thing spanning the river and it looks very inviting. I decide to leave the fishermen to it and I try my luck at it. A young English couple, Peter and Hannah who are newbies on my bus, kindly offer to take pictures of me on my camera while I pull myself across by tugging on the overhead line. I suspect that they don't know what they're letting themselves in for. But it's fun and nothing dramatic happens, I'm pleased to report.

This is my second alcohol-free day on the tour and I'm looking forward to dinner. For $14, there's chicken, potatoes, vegetables and so on. Before dinner, Carly-on-crutches, Antonio, Buzz and I are panned out on the couches in the dining area-cum-common area. We have a disturbing conversation over the weirdest things we have eaten. Buzz hath tasted Man's best friend, it turns out.
I try to turn my mind to things different in nature.

At dinner, the chicken is actually pink inside and scares a few people. But not me, I'm famished. We used to eat chickens before they were plucked; before they were dead even, growing up back in Ireland. We used to eat them in one bite. Okay, okay, it's all untrue. Of course, the hungry Andrew defends the chicken to the last. An American girl, this gung-ho supervisor who's working for her lodgings and a spin down the river once a week or whatever, has a run-in with this fiery-locked Scot girl on our tour. Apparently, some chicken hits the floor and the American – possibly the most passive/aggressive person I have ever met – tells her that quiche will be her replacement.

Later, she explains: "When I told her that I did'nay like cheese, she said I should have told my drivaaa uv ma dietra' requirements...but I did'nay think I'd be gettin' chicken with mu cheese."

The Welshies, Leeds Emma and I jump into the hot tub and stay there for about an hour. Well, they do. I jump out after forty, feeling about fifty-years-of-age in light of the conversation. I dry off and make my way into the dorm that I'm sharing with four Germans. It's about 10ish and I'm on the top bunk. I have the light over my bed on as I write in my journal. There's a separate switch for each on the wall behind the bunks, while the switch near the door is the Master that turns them all off. The German bloke, with his girlfriend on the bunk below, jumps out suddenly and the next thing I know, the place is in total darkness. I lie there, in the blackness, half wondering what I'll do. The nerve of it. I can feel the blood rising but I hold back on saying anything. Then I find my torch and flick it on, muttering "Dickhead" in the loudest stage whisper I can manage. From here on in, the erstwhile gent will be known as, "Boring, Anti-Social Fuckwit!"

At least in my head.

DAY THIRTY SEVEN

The bloody alarm that I borrowed from Buzz last night didn't wake me. And this is mainly because I had it set for 7.30pm opposed to the intended time – twelve hours later. I'm in the dining area, it's 8am and thirty minutes before we're due to assemble for the rafting. I'm waiting on this bacon and cheese sandwich thing that I've ordered and paid $7 for but there's free tea and coffee. Tall Andre is there; we're sitting on the table facing the kitchen.

"Would you mind not sidding on the table – people have to ead (eat) off of that?"

"Really, have you run out of plates?" I return, but she just glares. We don't have a problem with the request as such, but with the way she has barked it at us. "There's a bench under there," she says, pointing at the table. "If you pull it out, you can sid on that."

Then, she looks at me and smiles – suddenly changing from sour to sweet. "Sorry, I didn' ged a cheeeance to talk wid you earlier." I look over both shoulders and then back at her again. Hang on, did I miss something? JESUS, this chick is just weird.

We're standing outside, kitted out in our gear which includes helmets, booties, wetsuits, fleeces and so on. Then, we pile into this Toyota Hiace van (I think) and we are being driven the twelve kilometres to our starting point. I start, not for the first time today, to sing an impromptu version of *Jessie*, by Joshua Kadison. I sing it in this cheesy, gravelly voice – in keeping with the spirit of the song. The song is

198

directed at young Canadian, Jesse, who's travelling with his girlfriend Jena and Katia. Everyone joins in and Jesse is laughing, out of embarrassment if nothing else. Tom, our guide on the rapids, is looking at me strangely, as if he doesn't know what's going on. However, his dog, Mini Mouse, a gorgeous little Jack Russell not completely dissimilar from my own pooch, Holly, seems to like it.

He's not howling anyway.

We're assigned to our paddles, lifejackets and rafts. On my vessel, there's Leeds lasses, Becky and Emma; fellow Ireland-ers Kieran and Nicola and trainee journalist, Rob, who's paired with Becky. And Tom is also there, busting our balls or whatever. He's an interesting dude. To me, he looks like James Hetfield, the lead singer and guitarist with Metallica. He's straightforward, has bags of attitude and seems to be a sound bloke. The raft has pairs at two along its length: Rob and Emma are at the front, Kieran and I are in the centre and Nicola and Becky are behind, while Tom brings up the rear. Kieran was also on the dry last night but looks like, and swears he's suffering from, a mild form of alcoholic poisoning – due to a massive vodka and Red Bull-fest in Taupo two nights ago.

Without warning, Tom just stands up and plunges into the freezing cold water. He gets back on board and then tells Kieran and I that we can do likewise if we so desire.

And we do! It is FU-FU-FU-FREEZING, even with the gear on.

So Taupo Tom, as I'm now calling him, puts us through our paces and gives us a crash course in handling oneself on "Grade Five" (or Class 5) rapids. I remember my friend Conor showing me a DVD of him and his wife Alison negotiating Class 5 rapids on the Zambezi River, where there were literally walls of black water. These rapids are as wild here but not as intense if you get me.

"Thoyse (these) ah technical groyde foives," Tom explains.

And we're ready to go...eh, we think. We're gently paddling and all is calm. Tom asks us about ourselves and whether I like Jessie or not.

"Yeah, he's a nice bloke. Why?"

He continues: "Well whoy weee' ya singin' thet song to 'im, eh?"

I don't feel like explaining my particular brand of humour to him but it turns out that he misunderstood me anyway. There are two Jessies on the river, it transpires. (Actually, there's one "Jessie" and one "Jesse".)

His Jessie is a guide in another raft, while *My* Jesse is the Canadian teenager who's on my Kiwi bus.

Tom goes on to ask Kieran about his drinking and tells us that he brews his own beer, stout and ale. And he asks me if I know of a good recipe for poitín. And I tell him that I know a man who does and will forward said recipe, if I can remember who the guy actually is. Tom tells us that he shears the arses of sheep when he's not a rafting guide.

"Hmmm, just their arses?" I ask, innocently of course?

"And why?" I continue cautiously, half afraid of the answer he will offer.

Oh...for lambing purposes...I see.

We manoeuvre along the river, easing our way down rapids under his watchful eye – paddling in the calm spots in between. "Paddle forwaaa'ds...paddle backwaaa'ds," he goes. "Hold on, one heeend...hold on two heeends...get down." There's three rafts going down the river over the twelve-kilometre stretch, which should take us three hours and costs us $135 without the accompanying DVD and pictures. So we brave rough, flecked foam interspersed with aqua blue and whole sections of white water. It is great fun, until he tells us that two people have drowned in recent years, while taking on an upcoming part of the course. One of them, we learn, was a hardened marine of some description. He says it without humour, probably because it turns out to be true. And to be honest, it's even more fun after that; partly because we are reaching the more challenging parts and partly because, well, you have to assume that people who do things like this are not adverse to a little bit of danger and risk at least. Eckhart Tolle explains this clearly in his incredible bestseller, *The Power of Now*. In it he says that "in life-threatening emergency situations, the shift in consciousness from time to presence happens naturally".

He goes on: "The reason why some people love to engage in dangerous activities such as mountain climbing, car racing, and so on, although they may not be aware of it, is that it forces them into the Now – that intensely alive state that is free of time, free of problems, free of thinking, free of burden of the personality."

We snack on Snickers bars to keep our energy levels raised. Tom stops numerous times to shake his head at this American guy who's helping out. This fella is staying at River Valley as he gets accredited to work as a guide in New Zealand, it turns out. He's not yet familiar with the river and flails about in this cataraft – a kind of catamaran-looking canoe with two paddles. Tom thinks he should have an easier time of it because he's strapped in and his backside is perched on a seat high above the water. I suspect there's a bit of machismo mixed with national pride underpinning all of this but hey, that's cool. After a couple of mishaps, the North American lad makes a good enough fist of things.

Disappointingly (for me anyway), we have to get out of the rafts at a couple of points and make our way down the rocks on the side. The river is too swollen and at high tide at these places for inexperienced rafters. When I'm thirsty, I drink the water and it is probably the purest I've ever tasted without exception.

We're near the end of the course, and we get a chance to jump off this rock – six metres above the water. Not too high but it's fun anyway. It's clear beneath us but the current here is extremely strong, capable of dragging us away and into a rapid that we would stand zero chance in, we're told.

I'm chomping at the bit, to be honest. I'm first off, and I'm studying the lie of the water as Tom is telling me to keep straight, keep my arms and legs tucked in and so on. However, the last thing I hear as I'm mid-air is him saying: "NO, NOT THERE, THERE'S ROCKS TH-"

I feel myself plunge deep. And the brawny current has other plans for me, though there are no rocks of course. Tom – that little arsehole. I can feel the lifejacket pushing me up again, my arms and legs doing star jumps underwater to assist this. I surface and swim to the rafts lined up at the side, some fifteen metres away. The pull is staggering; the current is not giving up easily. I don't know why but I'm determined to make it look effortless. It is not. I crawl hard against the current, feeling as if the lifejacket is slowing me down, pulling me back (conveniently forgetting that it's probably saving my life!). My limbs feel jaded but not so much so that I don't climb the rocks to do it again. Some go up to jump but think better of it when they reach the perch. One of the lads, who I'm not naming to spare him, gets into trouble. His efforts to swim are pointless and he remains swimming in the same spot. Then, he's exhausted.

"TUUU'N OVA' ON YA BECK," Tom yells down to him.

On his back now, he's kicking for all he is worth. He's red-faced and puffing, the current sucking him towards the rapid some twenty metres away. The gung-ho American goes to him in the cataraft and tells him to hold on while he tows him in to the side. You've got to love the Americans in these situations.

We continue down towards this waterfall. Under we go and it's a worthy end to the experience. Completely drained but exhilarated, we drag the rafts out of the water. Then we strip ourselves of our gear and hit the showers, where the banter continues. I'm singing *Jessie* again and when I come out, Tom asks me about the "whoite staff" in my hair.

"You should know; you put it there." When I look in the mirror, I can see that he was actually asking about the un-rinsed shampoo in my hair.

Doh!

We pack the van with our bags and say our goodbyes to Tom and Co.

Kieran is exhausted, partially hidden amongst the backpacks. Sneaky. I assure Tom that I'll look into the poitín matter for him and send an email on the subject and marked for his attention, to the lodge. On the steep walk up the incline up to the Kiwi Coach, I'm struck by how beautiful it is in this place. A real retreat. It's little wonder that many backpackers become ensconced here.

We push onto Wellington.

On the way down to Wellers, we stop at a little town called Bulls. Anyone who's been to this strange place needs no explanation. For the rest of you, would it help if I said the humble bull is actually the theme of the town? On my way to the

McDonald's, I just have to stop and take a photo of the local police station. Daubed on the walls and the garage doors here are bulls – dressed as policemen and policewomen. This burly cop is backing his patrol car into the drive and stops to wave at my open-mouthed stares. He smiles and seems friendly enough – obviously used to this sort of thing. The word "Consta-bull" is daubed as well as "Police".

Other amenities in the town are given the bull treatment also.

This is not just a load of bull, trust me.

Wellington....hmmm...there's not much I can say about the place because we get in late in the evening and leave early in the morning. I'm sharing my dorm at the Base hostel with Dutchie, Gus, and Matt. Both of these are newbies to the bus. The latter turns out to be from a Kilkenny townland that's about twenty kilometres from my home in Waterford city. Matt, the Welshies and I go to The Welshman, a Welsh-themed pub that we spotted in the run up to our lodgings. Here, I sup on an auspicious pint of black beer, though I couldn't drink too much of the stuff. We Celts sign our respective country's flags. I split from them because, the younger want to buy bread or pasta or something for their dinner but I fancy more sustenance than that. I stop off at a restaurant Hummingbird on Courtenay Place and order a "smalls", a plate of miniature proportions. I'm having an Angus Sirloin steak, medium-rare of course, something completely alien to me called Solarz potatoes (hey, I'm Irish!) and broccoli. It's just a taster really; there's not a lot of grub on offer. It costs me $19, while the bottle of Speights Old Dark is $7.50. That's expensive. I order some fries on the side, as recommended by the strong-accented French waiter. He's annoying; of the *too in-your-face* variety. I get the feeling that he wants to get me to the point where I (might!) leave a tip, and then just piss off and stop bothering him. It's better than being ignored though so I decide to leave about eight per cent in a tip. It all costs me $33 (or about €17).

Wandering up the main thoroughfare here, I check out some bars for later. A woman in a group of people stops to shake my hand as I pass them by. I pass on but turn on to see her whispering to the others. Aha, she clearly thinks I am former All-

Black rugby stalwart, Jonah Lomu. Or perhaps Ireland international, Paul O'Connell's brother. No, maybe it was my George Clooney looks or...maybe it's the Daniel Day Lewis thing or...

Back at the basement bar in the hostel, there's this really annoying quiz on the go. There's cheesy lighting, cheesy music and an annoying barman with a microphone that's dripping with cheese. We hate it. Tall Swede Andre (as opposed to his smaller friend who looks like Jude Law), the Welshies and I, leave for town. We end up in Establishment Bar on Courtenay, which is hopping. It's like how I imagine a late-night joint back in Waterford would look after my home county won a Senior All-Ireland Hurling title. If only. It's 10.20 and Wellington doesn't even have a hurling team.

Actually, it apparently has several of them tonight. I meet this Co Tipperary girl who's new in town and she tells me that she "thinks" there's some "GAA tournament" happening over the weekend in Wellers. (The GAA, or Gaelic Athletic Association, is the regulating body for the amateur games of hurling and Gaelic football back in Ireland.)

I'm guessing that the tournament was organised by the Wellington and Hutt Valley GAA Club. I've heard about them and the great work they do. The Tipperary woman says that Establishment is the sponsor. So, I wasn't a million miles out with my GAA description then. We go to El Horno's, also on the Courtenay strip, on her advice, but the place is booked out for a 21st Birthday celebration. Kitty O'Shea's is another recommended watering hole but we decide to skip it for this modern, trendy spot. We actually go back to Base then because Ben and Andre want to try and hook up with two of the girls from our group. I manage two bottles of Heineken and then slope off to check my emails, upstairs. I climb into bed, exhausted and kind of sick of all of this nonsense.

For now at any rate.

10. From Cuddles to Puddles - the South Island

DAY THIRTY EIGHT

Apparently, one of the younger girls got extremely drunk last night and jumped into one of the younger lad's bunks. Of course she had stripped off beforehand. Only then, she proceeded to vomit all over his bed, another chap's clothes and even another bloke's adaptor, rendering it useless. She was seen getting sick out of the window too. However, one of the other girls stopped her water fight in the corridor long enough to help her get cleaned up and to escort her back to (her own) room. And it's not that abnormal at this stage because this kind of thing is what happens on tour. Of course I was dead to the world at this stage so I, perhaps conveniently, can't for the life of me remember who it was.

A few hours after this, Dutchman Gus wakes me because it's time to head south. It's 7am. As the cloud lifts, I remember that, sometime in the twilight, Kilkenny lad Matt woke me as he came into the room. He had stayed up to watch *our* football team, Manchester Utd, get beaten by Liverpool FC in a premiership game. (BOOOOO! – my brother Tom, who lives in Liverpool and is a season ticket holder, will be ecstatic. Particularly seeing as there were dinosaurs walking the earth on the last occasion this happened. POW! Not strictly true, by the way.)

Matt has watched the game at Kitty O'Shea's and he doesn't look any the worse for it, fair play to him. Ah, the joys of youth; it's just days before his 22nd Birthday.

We make a burst for it and head down to the ferry for our three-hour journey across the Cook Strait, to the South Island. The trip costs $56, and it's a Government tax. On board, Kieran and I use our Irish radar to find the bar, even at this early hour. But we don't want alcohol – believe it or not. We just want a place to drop our bags, perhaps get a fried breakfast, and to watch the re-run of the "Man U v Liverpool" clash, as suggested by His Kieran-ess. On another screen here, New Zealand are playing Costa Rica in a soccer friendly and it's 1-1 (it ends the same way) and we're rooting for the All-Whites. This doesn't mean we're shagging for New Zealand or anything. The "rooting" I refer to above is used in a different context in Ireland.

The fried breakfast at the food court, which includes toast but not tea, costs $12.50 and tea is an extra $4. If I'm honest I'm thinking, *the robbing bastards!* I'm only half-watching the screens because I'm really tired and even though I only had four or five beers last night, I feel really hungover. I'm also hoarse and believe that I'm coming down with a cold. Nicola and Becca, along with Antonio and Carly-on-crutches, all missed the boat because they were kicking it hard last night.

Then, all of a sudden, Carly on Crutches and Antonio turn up at the bar. They rushed onto the street and hailed down a taxi when they realised that they had slept in ("out" in Ireland, remember?). Arsenal (The Gunners) are playing West Ham Utd (The Hammers) now so Naff, who's from Leeds, is glued to the screen because he is a huge Arsenal fan. He seems disappointed when it ends in a 2-2 draw after West Ham get a penalty, unjustified according to Naff but then he would say that.

We disembark and Buzz picks up another coach (we've left the other one in the North Island) in Picton. We leave here and make our way towards Nelson. The scenic vineyards of the Marlborough Valley on the way out of Picton acts as a welcome distraction for tired eyes. Later in the afternoon we arrive at Fern Lodge, a hostel built onto the Prince Albert Hotel for backpackers stopping off in Nelson. I'm in a dorm with Mike, Ben and Kieran and we decide to join our new tour buds, Will, Colin and Sarah for a walk to the *Centre* of New Zealand (I shit you not). I picture us setting up this giant drill in our attempts to get to its core with someone shouting, *Who knows, if we can get to the centre, perhaps we'll keep going until we reach the UK and Ireland?*

Colin and Will, friends who hail from some London suburb or another, are on a sabbatical from their jobs at World Bar in Queenstown. They met Sarah, also English and who's travelling alone, on their travels. Matt also joins us, as do the Swedish Andres. It's a grey day in Nelson and the sky, looming oppressively with swollen grey heaviness all afternoon, toys with us for a time with bouts of drizzle. And of course it pisses down when we're at our most exposed. The heaviest of this arrives after we've finished our steep climb to the country's centre. The peak lies at an elevation that gives us an impressive view of Nelson and around. The rain starts to batter us on the way down and while the others make their way back to the lodge, the Welshies and I push on into the town because we need to find a shop and an ATM.

We get a bit lost, however, and I get a bit worried as I remember Fern Lodge landlord Pete's tale about a lost "rather large Irishman" during check-in. Apparently this bloke ended up a bit worse for wear after a heavy night and it took him fifteen hours to return to the lodge from town, a twenty-minute walk at most. I'm wondering if he stopped for a drink every thirty minutes of thereabouts.

There seems to be a severe lack of ATMs in this town – outside of a couple on one or two streets in the centre of Nelson. About twenty minutes later, we are soaked and talking to an elderly man about finding Fern Lodge. He is fishing in the river. He seems to be panning of sorts for "whitebait", which is the first time I have ever heard these two words uttered together and in this order in my life. However, the Welshies seemed to know what he was at when they first laid eyes on him. The man gives us directions from this riverside fishing spot and then assures us that his catch, although looking sparse enough in his bucket, will make a meal once it's fried up with milk or butter later on.

Back at Fern Lodge we meet some other new tour mates and I join some of them for a beer-tasting session with Peter. We try ciders, ales, lagers and darks. Peter tells us about Max's Export Gold and Ben and Leeds Chris win prizes for a free binge in Queenstown. I'm sure there's a catch but they get to bring fifteen or twenty mates with them – at a twenty-five per cent *discount*. So two people get a free night, eh? As long as they bring twenty of their mates who will get the supposed discount.

Fair play to Peter though. It's a business drummer but he seems to be doing something that other landlords don't and you can tell he's genuinely interested in (and knowledgeable about) the beers he serves. Afterwards, we lash into a roast dinner (with Yorkshire Pudding) attached. The meat, vegetables and potatoes are smothered in gravy – whether you ask for it or not – and my earlier suspicions are confirmed when I discover that the hidden cuts largely consist of fat. Considering, however, that it comes with a pecan pie and ice-cream desert and it sets us back just $13, it's good deal. We devour the meal – it's actually not bad.

In our dorm now are Maaike, a talkative Dutch girl, and Chris, a decent English sort. Both of these – fit types – have just returned from some God awful two-day trek and are spent. I know how they feel...kind of.

DAY THIRTY NINE

We leave early this morning – though some of the gang are staying to trek about the Abel Tasman National Park. Some will stay an additional night and arrive in the today's destination tomorrow, if that makes any sense. We will meet most of these in places where we are set to stay two nights, such as Franz Josef and, more likely, Queenstown. Most of us will stay at least one week here, if not longer. The face of the bus has changed and I count just nine of over forty faces that have been with us since we left Auckland on October 16th.

The Abel Tasman National Park is named after Abel himself, a Dutch seafaring explorer chap whose expedition in the 17th Century was the first (European) to reach Tasmania and New Zealand. The park is one of the country's smallest national parks apparently, and is popular for hiking, tramping and the like. I'd better clarify here that "Tramping" is not wearing a filthy shell suit with shoes and sitting around an urban park drinking cans of Dutch Gold, while sniffing glue and smoking joints.

I'm reading *The Press*, which Buzz calls "the Christchurch paper". On page one is a yarn about how "Christchurch boy racers have again hit the headlines overseas, with a German magazine saying residents are afraid of car-based 'terrorism'." It goes on to say that Christchurch Mayor Bob Parker astonishingly "said the article was an accurate reflection of Christchurch." (The astonishment is mine, not that of the newspaper.) Of course, the Broadsheet backs this up with quotes in the copy – or rather, story, as you non-journalists might say. I don't like the headline that highlights "Chch's Streets of 'Fear'".

Dutch girl Maaike, who's not adverse to the odd polemic discussion, has asked for a look at my newspaper so I duly oblige. However, she tells me that a story entitled, "Survivor wades through 'streams of blood'", about a bombing in Iraq and clearly a (news) colour story, should not appear on the front page of the world section as "that page is for news".

"Is that story not news?"

"No, it's a feature," she tells me. "News is about facts."

"It is, but it's also about more," I go on. "It is a news story; it's a colour piece that accompanies a factual news report about what happened."

But she's having none of it.

I'm wondering what she's really arguing about; she only had the paper in her hands for, literally, seconds before she came up with that.

Anyway, it passes the time until we get to the Nelson Lakes National Park.

It's a bright day for sure but strong winds are churning up beautiful Lake Rotoiti and from Kerr Bay it looks glorious in its natural wildness. Mountains, dusted in snow and looking like some delicious cake that only your grandmother knew how to make, appear from behind pulled curtains of lush green Honeydew beech forest on both flanks. The show is entertaining and arresting. The light has that blue tinge that you only get on spring mornings.

When I pose for a picture, with the lake as a natural backdrop, my Akruba gets blown straight off my bonze. I run after it, imagining that I look like Charlie Chaplin, Larry, Curly or Moe; or indeed Stan Laurel himself. Everybody seems to be having a good laugh at me chasing my hat across the foreground near the trail. I'm surprised that I don't hear some jangly piano music. Of course, my hat doesn't stop until it reaches a mucky puddle and it's destroyed with water. It is not, however; Akruba type hats are hardy and resilient. The wet and muddy patches add character to the thing so I'm not bothered. Plucky ducks teach their chicks how to walk or how to be real ducks or whatever. Mammy leads them up to us to say hello: they're clearly used to being fed by tourists. They actually peck at you if they don't get it, as if to say, *Come on, what's keeping you...hungry duck here you ugly fuck!*

The lake itself is a common spot for yachting, water skiing and fishing, while groups of Maori also stopped to fish here for years and years. Geologists believe that the lake was basically a basin dug out by a glacier. But I prefer the legend according to the local literature, stating that the lake was created when Chief Rakaihaitu dug holes in the ground with his *Ko* or Digging Stick. Lake Rotoiti (small waters) was thus formed, as was Lake Rotorua (large waters). I break away from the others and try the gentle *Honey Dew* trail through the forest, which takes about forty minutes according to the signpost. It only takes me about twenty minutes though and trust me when I say that I'm not running here. *Did the park's rangers, or whoever, walk it backwards on their hands?* I'm left wondering.

This afternoon we're spinning along the road that clings to the Buller River. We're on our way to Wesport (Yes, there's also one in Co. Mayo in Ireland). We stop at a picnic spot of sorts called the Kilkenny Lookout. Ben has found this small piece of black rubber so I get it from him and tear it into a couple of smaller strips. Kieran is chewing some gum. I hand the rubber to him as he takes out the gum, attaches it to the rubber and sticks it to the sign between "Kilkenny" and "Lookout". Kieran (from Cork) and I (a Waterford man) get Matt, a Co. Kilkenny dude, to stand in front of the sign with us. Our fists, in turn, raised against him in a pugilistic pose. For those of you who are going, "WTF?" allow me to explain: the [Co.] Kilkenny hurling team is at this point in time the best in Ireland, while [Co.] Cork and [Co.] Waterford are among the contenders, though trailing considerably in terms of skill and recent success. Do you know how hard it is for me to admit that?

The pictures have turned out well anyway.

We hit the road again and arrive at Buller Adventure Tours some kilometres away and some of us prepare for our Jetboat ride with the centre's proprietor, Doc. He turns out to be a hoot; if crudeness, sexism and a bit of racism are your thing, that is. Anything said is in jest with no real offence meant, though it would probably be fair for you to tell me that it's "easy for me to say that".

We're kitted out with oilskins, wetsuits, yellow beanie hats and these tinted glasses/goggles. We look like attendees at an Ali-G convention. Or penguins. In case you're wondering, a Jetboat is propelled by a jet of water blown out of the back of the boat. A kind of "Waterjet" prototype was designed by Sir William Hamilton in 1954, the whole point being that the boat could manoeuvre shallow and fast-moving rivers without a propeller striking rocks. This happens because, while a powerboat uses a propeller below or at the stern (the back of the boat) to push the boat forwards, the Jetboat sucks up the water into a pump, which then blows it out through a nozzle at stern.

The Jetboat is on a trailer and Doc hitches it up to a tractor. We all hop into the boat and are taken across the road and through a field. Kieran and I get a great kick out of this because the scene reminds us of something that would happen in Ireland. You could picture it in an episode of *Father Ted*. I tell him to imagine this to be the actual tour – in a boat on a trailer being dragged through fields by a feckin' tractor because the vessel is actually broken.

We reach the Buller River, the largest free-flowing river in the South Island apparently, and Doc backs the trailer into it. The river flows for about 170 kilometres – from Lake Rotoiti on through Buller Gorge and into the Tasman near Westport. Doc gets into the boat and backs the thing out of the trailer. Then we're powering down the river and weaving in and out of the rocks at the banks. Water is spraying up on us on both sides of the boat, depending on how he turns it. The deal is this: he drives you at speed towards some rocks but then turns at the last minute. It's great fun. All of us get soaked when Doc stops suddenly does a 360° turn. When we stop, Andre points out that the terrain is familiar. He's right, we're in the water, looking up at the Kilkenny Lookout. Doc tells us how Kiwi Experience "kids" used to be allowed to jump off the bridge above, which has got to be at least fifteen metres up (in this tide). He tells us that this all ended, however, after a mishap with "Hong Kong Fuey!" Hang on, did he actually say that? The tale involves a Korean tourist who knocked himself out by hitting the water incorrectly during his jump. We look at each other in disbelief

211

when he uses the cartoon reference. After this, he tells us a very funny story about a tour guide who used to go by the name, Cuddles. The guide was, apparently, always giving out that he had done it all and couldn't get enough "hoighs and thrells". So, his kind mates down in Queenstown organised an electrifying treat for him. The friends (foes, I would say) grabbed him at a bungee station (I think he said it was the 134-metre Nevis canyon bungee jump) when he was not expecting it, covered his head and strapped him to a chair. They apparently sent a charge through him with a cattle prod and told him that they would get the chord to attach to him – but they had already done so, according to Doc. Then, they pushed him promptly, resulting in him wetting himself. "So thet's how he got the noooyme Puddles."

Erm, well wouldn't you? Wet yourself I mean!

During this discourse, Doc starts sentences with statements such as, "Whin I'm a retaaa'd..." and "He'll be uff quicka' than a Jew's foooo'skin". He doesn't flinch as he says these things, though I'm quite sure that no actual offence is meant.

We reach Westport and get ourselves checked into Basil's Hostel. I go into the common area/TV room or whatever, and start talking to the new English girls on our bus. There's a stove with a chimney leading up through the ceiling. I absent-mindedly put my hand out and lean my weight against it. About six nanoseconds later, I jump about five feet into the air. My hand is in agony and I have it under the cold tap for the next thirty minutes or so. I recount the story again and again as my fellow travellers peer at my hand with curiosity and obvious humour. I know what you're thinking but it's warm outside (I didn't think they'd have lit the fucking thing!). A kind of trellis pattern actually burned into my hand. Ouch! There's only one cure for it...drink.

Some of us go to the supermarket in town and I half expect to see tumbleweeds blow across our path, the occasional sleeveless farmer-tanned arm hanging out of the rolled down window of a pick-up truck and country music blaring, as manic eyes follow us; dancing crazily atop a toothless grin.

We won't be disappointed later on, I can assure you.

One of these things did not happen. Actually, I'm not entirely sure that New Zealand has tumbleweeds. After buying our drink in the supermarket, the Swedish Andres and I stop off at this bar/restaurant place that has as many TVs as it does pool tables. We are waiting for some time, looking at a mullet-sporting couple who are clearly regulars. She's wearing short-shorts and is shoeless; he has his remarkably clean overalls and boots on. However, these mullets aren't the ones you will see worn with awkward faux coolness on heads up in Ireland, the UK or wherever. These are worn without any sense of irony or throwback; trust me on this one. There are fat, older guys in string vests and baseball hats. This place rocks. On the TV screen nearest us are Ken and Deirdre Barlow – characters from UK soap opera, *Coronation Street* – who seem to be having a fight. But there's no sound. A closer look and I educe that it's an old episode. It's over a year old. We're getting pissed off waiting for our pizzas and tall Andre's (OTT) imitations of me are awful but hilarious.

"Where's my FOCKING pizza, you focking focker," he goes to me in his best Irish accent.

"Focking Oirish," he repeats.

The pizza's worth the wait though. Back we go to the hostel and sink a few cold ones before heading into town again. Maaike, along with German girl, Karmen and Scot, Kim, pester us until we agree to go. At a local sports bar, I try a Mac's Black – a locally-brewed beer that the owner casually refers to as "chinkey darkie". Meanwhile, these girls, who are as uptight as some gang of ageing, right-wing nuns at a rave, are not impressed with us. To be more precise, they are not impressed with me. Imitating Fr. Jack, I ask them again and again, "Who are you supposed to be?" It's a catchphrase I've borrowed on this tour and most of the others don't seem to mind. Au contraire: there have been talks among some of them about getting it printed on a tee-shirt to commemorate our tour. These girls are missing the point of the question and are taking it all literally. So I'm probably being an annoying git but there you go, none of us are perfect so they'll have to live with it.

The English folks including Will, Dave, Sarah and Colin; join us in the bar. The Welsh lads and I end up drinking these weird tequila-laden shots with this bloke – a miner who goes by the name, "Gary the Maori". He has these chilling mineral green eyes that look straight through to your black heart, a goatee beard and a dark ponytail hanging out from the back of his beanie hat. And he's as rough as be damned but he's alright. Gary the Maori, who I guess is in his early forties, tells us that he has fathered eighteen children in various New Zealand locations in his career. He has got to be at the mine in about five hours' time. I need to flex my diplomatic muscles and intervene when he insults one of the girls – though he definitely doesn't mean it.

GARY: "Ya nod a bed-lookin' check; ya've god a big noise (nose) bud otha'woise, yu' beaudiful."

ME: "Would go away outta that, Sarah is beautiful; I love her nose and everything about her."

By the way, I'm not lying here...said girl is stunning. I basically just keep talking over him until he gets bored and changes the subject. Some local kids at the bar, who seem to be aping LA gangsters, show us their battle scars such as dislocated fingers, cut and bruised knuckles and so on. One of these has cut his knuckles on someone's head just before talking to us. Two of them take on Ben and Mike in bouts of arm-wrestling and lose. They lose badly, for these Welsh country lads are made of alloyed steel. The local delinquents are not best pleased so we make our excuses and leave them to it. The US isn't the only country that has a Deep South, if you follow me, but I'd put money on there being no tumbleweeds here.

DAY FORTY

We're on our way to Lake Mahinapua – or the nearby "Poo Pub" – about ten kilometres south of Hokitika and quite close to the town of Ruatapu. A short drive from Westport is Cape Foulwind and Tauranga Bay, near to where we disembark our Green Goddess. After walking some distance we arrive at New Zealand's largest seal colony, the country's closest point to Australia, apparently, and the home of the New Zealand Fur Seal. No sooner has Buzz cleared the bus when he drives away.

Of course the rain comes.

Most of us are wildly under dressed for such a party. I'm wearing Aussie surf shorts and flip flops but I do have my hoodie. I'm annoyed that Buzz has pissed off on us but the rain stops as soon as it has started and the walk is definitely worth it. Showers starting and stopping shortly thereafter seems to be a feature of the Kiwi weather, as it sort of (totally) is in Ireland. Of course in both countries it also can continue for days on end. We're walking along the trail, which has farmland to the left of us and dramatic coastline to our right, west. Ahead, horses stand perfectly still on the hills while sheep get nervous and run away from the fence as we approach. Our reputation precedes us then. Ha.

To our right are horses of a different variety. Large white galloping waves rise up and crash down immediately. Limestone cliffs, sheer and pancake in formation, are showy then shy in almost equal measure. It's quite dramatic, as is the vegetation lining the fence on the coastal side. This is a gorgeous part of New Zealand, reminding me of parts of my home county of Waterford. However, it's more like the coastlines of Co. Kerry and especially Co. Clare, which can boast of the Cliffs of Moher – whose awesome natural wonder has resulted in it being shortlisted for voting in the search for the Seven Natural Wonders of the World. Surely this shoreline would have acted as comforter for the Irish who settled around here in search of gold from the 1860s onwards. Figures show that the Irish and their descendents made up one-quarter of the population of the west coast from the middle of the 1860s up to the 1920s. Most of those that emigrated from Ireland to the west coast were males. Mining was dangerous work, with many miners dying when tunnels collapsed, if they managed not to fall down mineshafts that was. Drowning while trying to cross the region's rivers was also common.

We're coasting down Highway 6, the longest single national highway of the country's eight, and I'm engrossed by the scenery. It's diverse in that it encapsulates rainforest, green farmland, isolated towns and golden fields. The sun commands all below this land and the rivers that cut through it. Suddenly, the Southern Alps dominate the skyline. This beautiful horizon, from some distance at any rate, looks like the bottom

215

of a blue page. A page that has been ripped randomly across the bottom and reveals a jagged section of blank white page underneath.

It's late in the afternoon when we stop at Greymouth, the main commercial hub of the west coast. It's been raining intermittently but it stops just as we hit town. When we're getting off the bus, Maaike tells Buzz that "Little Kieran is sleeping at the back of the bus". Little Kieran? That would make me...never mind. I laugh because he's not exactly a small bloke. Later, it will emerge that only for Maaike, Kieran, who doesn't have our mobile phone numbers, could have been locked on the bus for ninety minutes or so because Buzz was walking away when she stopped him. None of the rest of us had noticed.

Here in Greymouth, we pay a visit to various ATMs and then a supermarket. Buzz is shopping for our barbeque at the pub later on and we are fishing for materials to use in the production of our costumes. Tonight we will take part in a fancy dress party; the theme being, "The Beach". I'm walking idly around the place – my Mitch Buchannon idea ebbing away from me like an outgoing tide.

"Fuck it, Transformers it is," I tell Kieran.

He looks at me as if I have two heads and tonight, I will have. After seeking advice from a helpful lady at the helpdesk, I scout around for cardboard boxes of varying sizes. I also buy: a) a large tin of bright chrome spray paint b) a ruler c) a black marker d) an architect's scalpel e) a packet of honey roasted peanuts and f) a bottle of chocolate milk.

"Megatron on his holidays," I tell my stunned fellow backpackers with pride time after time again as I board the coach and walk down the aisle to my seat with the materials in my arms.

"Who are you supposed to be?" Andre enquires. Smartarse.

Weird choice of costume? Perhaps so, but the other Irish lunatic who shares my Christian name is going to the party as...a deck chair. His turns out to be a very simple and clever costume. It's a long rubber camping mat that doubles as a deckchair when he cuts a hole for his head to fit through as he half sits on the floor, resting on his elbows with knees bent.

216

We arrive at the Poo Pub, where we will be entertained by proprietor, Les, who is aged 84 at present and reminds me of the now-deceased legendary Irish folk singer, Ronnie Drew. At least he reminds me of how Ronnie looked about twenty years ago, Bed of Heaven to him. To those of you not familiar with The Dubliners' former singer, imagine a stout-drinking Santa Claus with an edge, a big heart and a speaking voice like a *lump of coal being dragged under a closing door*, as it was once described. However, his New Zealand doppelganger is a bit of a grumpy git, as I suppose anyone of his age is probably entitled to be. Les has never left New Zealand, it transpires. Furthermore, he has never even been to the North Island.

You can start playing the duelling banjos now.

Les gets on the coach and gives us a rundown of What's-What, including a fairly sick tale about threatening a poor Canadian with putting his antics – behind a door with a young lady – on the Internet. Nice. He tells us that every part of the place is covered with CCTV. For fuck sake!

"What in the noyme a' God aaa' yew goin' ez?" he asks me as I'm leaving the coach with my boxes.

"A Transformer; I'm going to spray paint the boxes," I answer.

"No fackin' waaay," he goes. "Ah (I) hev' it up ta heee' with you goys usin' sproys an' paints abaaat the place. "Ah'll heve a fackin' bluey if enyone uses sproy paint araaa'n the place."

I'm gutted. We're taking this fancy dress very seriously. But I must press ahead. I mark out the face and cut out the eyes and the mouth on one of the boxes and I colour it black in reference to Megatron's Evil nature, putting a larger box over my torso. Two longer and narrower ones go over my shins. Costume-less, I go to dinner in the dining area with the others and eat an outstanding meal including steak, corn-on-the-cob and salad. I decline the venison but the corn is by far the tastiest that I have ever eaten. Good job Buzz. The dinner plus our lodgings is costing us just $30. That's €15.

217

I'm stumbling out of my dorm and the lads are doubled up in laughter as I bump into various railings, walls and so on. Attempts to light and smoke a cigarette through the mouth are met with more giggles, even though I'm risking life and limb for my addiction. At the pub, I get one of the girls to tape the head to the torso so the eyes will remain in one place. And I'm mingling with beach bums, lifeguards, Miami "beach gangsters", pirates, a shark, a mermaid, beach superheroes, drunken sailors and blokes sporting grass skirts. I can't hear, be heard, drink, see or be seen sufficiently in the costume. Me at my best, you say? However, after some time, I un-tape the head and it flips down at the front, conveniently.

There are drinking games, there's dancing and there is a jukebox. It's Matt's 22nd Birthday so we draw slogans all over him with a marker. It turns out to be a good night, though I spend the later hours of the party literally running away from a mad Brummie, the colloquial name for someone from Birmingham in the UK. I christened her Marlene. The Marlene reference is given in honour of the wife of Boycie, a character in UK hit comedy, *Only Fools and Horses*. She actually sounds more like Boycie than Marlene. Marlene buys me a drink and tells me that I will owe her "a favour later". So far, so good. However, as the night wears on she starts following me around and telling me to "get back here immediately". Sorry love, I'm not that easily bought. She's as hammered as a freshly made house and starts calling me names when I don't obey like a good little puppy. Some of the lads, including Dave, Colin and Matt, go swimming in the lake (Mahinapua) after the party.

Meanwhile, Ben, Mike and I take about ten of the partygoers back to our tiny dorm and with Ben's huge inflatable gay Blue Whale present, there's not much room. Kieran is trying to sleep, and there's no drink so we clear the room. Except Marlene doesn't want to go to bed yet (not alone at any rate) and she starts getting incoherently abusive again. I look at Kieran, rolling my eyes as I struggle to talk her out of the room. I walk her back to her dorm – to her mates – and knock at the door before leaving quickly. The door is opened. After a stint of teeth scrubbing in the men's bathroom, I walk outside and see her again. She's walking around and mumbling to herself so I wait until she slopes off again. I can hear the Welsh lads in Maaike,

218

Karmen and Kim's dorm so I join them there. But when I get back to my own dorm, Marlene's asleep in one of the beds there.

And I can't sleep, probably out of fear!

DAY FORTY ONE

It's a short drive to the Bushman's Centre at Pukekura, where we're greeted by the proprietor, Pete. He gets onto the coach and tells us that we can take a look around the centre for $4 before breakfast. Inside the weird centre, we're taken to watch this weird 'movie' about deer hunting in New Zealand. He goes on to tell us that the movie was made "when Bembi wuz a terrorist". There are about twelve faces from my tour at the screening. Pete is decked out in his bush boots, khaki shorts and shirt. He's sporting a short beard. Pete reminds me of Bill Oddie circa 1982. He tells us that the soundtrack, one very popular hit song from the 1980s that I can't for the life of me remember, was written by a friend of his.

"But it wuz repped awf by some loo-za' in Hollywood," he goes on.

Eh, no.

The screen looks like, and probably is; some A1-sized sheets of paper taped together and hung on the wall. We see shots of some hunters shooting deer from a helicopter before the famous "Kiwi ingenuity" leads to some genius starting a craze of jumping out of a helicopter onto the poor deer and wrestling the beast to the ground. According to the God-awful documentary, the hunters then used net guns which did exactly what they said on the tin. This involved a large folded package being shot from the end of the barrel of the gun in the hope that it could trap the terrified animal. At best, I'm at some carnival of the surreal and at worst; I'm caught in a time warp – back in Ms. McDonald's third year Religion classes watching some video (remember VCR?) with a message. I remember that Ms McDonald herself, quite the hottie and probably only about nine-or-ten years older than us, was the focus of our hormone-fuelled imaginations and not the terrible movies.

However, there's no message in this car-crash documentary that I'm interested in so when it ends, we stroll around the centre and I'm in awe at the number of chainsaws and axes on display. There are possums in a cage and a Homer Simpson-esque button with a sign attached warning tourists not to press it. So of course some of us do and get squirted in the eye with water or Possum Piss for our trouble.

End of tour. I'm afraid.

We head into the restaurant at the front and get served by a Bushwoman and her younger version. The tension between them both is palpable. They get Kieran and mine own orders mixed up and tell us that they "nooo'mally doyal (deal) wi' du Koiwi Experience payple sep'rotloy". Just give us the food already. They're advertising "Pete's Possum Pie" and I think it's all a joke – expecting that it's actually made with pork, beef or whatever. I'm about to order it for the craic but I check with Buzz just to be on the safe side. He swears that it is indeed made from Possum. Call me a wuss if you want to but eh, fuck that.

On the way out, I notice a picture of Bushman and Bushwoman (Justine) flanking comedian, Billy Connolly. On the front door, there's a sign that says, *Woman required...must send a photo of rifle and knife.*

It's then that I hear duelling banjos and everything goes swimmy again.

Oookaaaay, let's get out of here.

The scenery on the way south to Franz Josef, in the Westland National Park, is dazzling. Snow-tipped peaks, dunes and beaches are dotted along the lush green landscape. The area, which has heritage status, is the northern gateway to Te Wahinpounamu – a World Heritage Site park.

Then, Franz Josef appears suddenly. The affluent and well-planned town, although sparsely populated at present, contrasts boldly with the isolated wildness leading down to it.

The majority of us are brought to an office to pay for our various excursions up the glacier tomorrow. Some of us will choose the half-day option, while the lads and I pay $150 for the day-long hike. We grab some food and find an ATM. We check into the Rainforest Retreat Hostel and we're met by a chirpy Liverpuddlian (I think) bloke and two girls at the desk. There's a pint of lager and a glass of Vino Blanco on the counter. He makes one of the girls, perhaps aptly a Mancunian lass, chug the pint in one go once she admits to drinking the occasional lager shandy or whatever. German girl Anna gets the wine, which I suspect is goon, and she cleverly sips on it. The Welsh lads, Kieran and I, drink cans of beer each as we watch *The Life of Brian* on Kieran's laptop.

All of us crash, waking up when it's well over.

I make some spaghetti bolognaise for the lads and myself while they head to the hot tub. Afterwards, we skip the local watering hole and hang out in the dorm. The Swedish Andres, Maaike and Karmen – a right pain in the arse at this stage – watch *Taken* starring Liam Neeson. And, we're not drinking. Andre and I take the piss out of Maaike as time-and-time again she lifts her hands to her mouth and eyes during the more violent scenes. Our visitors leave us to it afterwards and Kieran puts on T*he Big Lebowski* on my request.

And it happens again. Tonight I get to the part where the Big L asks The Dude to assist him in rescuing his kidnapped wife. It's the fifth time now that I've tried to watch the movie. But every single time, I crash. Perhaps it's because I've never tried to watch it without being in an altered state of some description or, extremely exhausted. It's just as well really, as the mighty Franz Josef looms large. Tomorrow we will hike up the glacier.

Nobody better tell me how *The Big Lebowski* ends – I am going to watch that movie in its entirety. At some stage. Dude.

DAY FORTY TWO

As I've already mentioned, Abel Tasman was the first Pakeha, or European, to see Franz Josef Glacier. He saw it as he sailed along the coast in 1642, according to my Kiwi Experience guidebook. However, it would be another 222 years before Austrian explorer Julian Von Haast named the glacier in honour of his Emperor. The Westland (or "Tai Poutini") National Park contains sixty named glaciers and Franz Josef and Fox Glacier are just two of these. The glaciers flow down from snowfields in the

Southern Alps and Franz and Fox are actually the only ones on the planet to flow down onto temperate rainforest. They flow into the Tasman.

According to Maori Legend, a beautiful girl, Hinehukatere asked her lover, Tawe, to ascend the mountains around Westland with her. But he fell and died, while Hinehukatere's tears formed the glaciers. The area is actually known as "Ka Roimata o Hinehukatere", meaning "Tears of the Avalanche Girl" or thereabouts. The peaks about the park can reach up to 3,000 metres and Franz and Fox can move up to four metres per day.

Standing outside the office – from where we will be bussed out to the base of the glacier –, I stare up at the white wonder. Scores of tourists pile into the office as I'm left wondering if Von Haast or Tasman felt as small as I do now. The sun is high in the sky, brightly illuminating the icy Giant, and the air is cold and fresh, almost like sucking in air through a menthol lozenge in your gob. We go inside, grab our jackets, our "spikes" (or crampons), gloves, boots and backpacks and wait outside for the bus. It arrives and I'm the first to board so when the others come along, I sit in the driver's seat and ask them for their tickets. The passengers who don't know me from Adam fall for it and it's only when the bus is full that I get up and join my tour buds at the rear. It gets a good few laughs.

It's a short drive to the carpark and then a two-kilometre walk to the base of the glacier. One of the guides tells us that the rocky mound – about halfway up to where the summit meets the sky – is to be our destination. It looks deceptively closer than it is, approximately four kilometres above us.

We will hike about six kilometres on our route to it, however, as I am in the "advanced" group. There are twenty two in my group, while this will be split in two; subsets "one and two" apparently. I'm in one. A further twenty two hikers follow us (the intermediate group, "two") and about ten or so people (group three or "The Losers"...joking) bring up the rear. This Chinese woman – she's actually Danish, it turns out – from our bus who's been travelling alone and has got to be approaching sixty, kicks up a bit of stink because she wants to join the first group and there are objections. Karmen starts complaining the loudest to anybody who'll listen and I get annoyed with her. I tell her that the woman can "join whatever bloody group she wants to" and to "stop being a control freak" – adding that I will stay back with her, should she lag behind.

The lady finally agrees to go in the Intermediate group and she does brilliantly. I can't for the life of me pronounce this woman's name but Buzz later tells us that she has actually made three Kiwi Experience tour guides cry in recent weeks. So perhaps she didn't need my help after all.

The first thirty minutes are the hardest for most of us. We grip the guide ropes as we trek over the rocks and then the ice steps that are cut out by the various guides on a daily basis. Our guide, Brendan, is hacking at the steps with a pickaxe and I'm behind him. Occasionally he stops to check the terrain and to wind a steel rod into the ice. Ropes are run through carrabunkels – allowing us to grip them on the incline, "palms facing upwards".

There's a chance for me to jump over some crevices and I'm loving it. I'm wearing my boardies because jeans or trousers, when wet, stick to the legs, do you see? The shorts also dry much more quickly. I'm wearing this light grey hoodie that I've borrowed from Ben: it's too small for me but it stretches. I have a tee-shirt underneath and it's enough clothing to be wearing. We're generating our own heat as we move up the icy lump. I have the blue weatherproof jacket, the ones they give you to wear, tied about my waist. I'm also wearing my hat, which is made from Merino wool, and I'm wearing shades.

As we go up, we dig our crampons into the ice, occasionally sloping down into the crevices thanks to the cut-out steps and ropes. My group stops for lunch and Mike, Ben, Kieran and the others in the second group catch up with us. Mike and I are taking snaps of each other when my camera suddenly powers off. I'm miffed to be honest; all of the power bars were showing this morning. The cliffs to our right are cut with icy waterfalls and clumps of vegetation cling to the rock face. Kea Birds, or "Alpine Parrots" as Brendan tells us, scale these for berries, spiders and so on. One of the cleverest and most inquisitive birds on the planet, they will drift down for a nosey – and even follow us for a bit. Brendan tells us that, should we to leave our bags

223

unattended, the mischievous birds will be "en it an' on et". If the bags contain both chocolate bar and camera/phone, the cheeky little shits will actually attack the devices first, pecking at and breaking them out of curiosity and I suspect, devilment.

To our left is a mass of elevated woodland with occasional footbridges that are barely-visible to the human eye from this distance. Behind us, a few kilometres to our backs, is the valley from whence we came. It looks like the most beautiful of paintings and apart from our breaths and occasional chats, the silence is deafening in the best possible sense. It's a majestic place – a halfway point where I imagine God and Darwin might meet.

As we near our summit, the bunch of rocks I've already mentioned, we come across these smooth, wet tunnels of ice that are so white they're actually blue if you get me. And they are stunning. Again and again, we crouch as we enter the slippery and cool tunnels. When entering a smaller one, I forget to take off my backpack and nearly get stuck inside. However, when we enter one of the narrower crevices, I actually do get stuck. The crevices have gotten deeper, bluer and more beautiful. Not to mention narrower. With backpack slung over one shoulder, we ease ourselves down into these, our feet shuffling sideways at a 90° angle to the left of our squeezed torsos.

We're in the deepest and narrowest one now. And of course my torso, which turns out to be the broadest in our particular group, gets wedged in between the walls of ice. I'm in the middle of the line of trekkers. I yell up to Brendan, who assures me that he'll get me through. So, under his instruction, I dig like a dog with my front boot, creating a mound of ice that I will then stand on in the hope of creating leverage and pushing on. It helps me a bit but my chest is still wedged in. I finally tell our instructor that it's not happening and apologising to those I'm holding up, I back the hell out of there. But I don't care, enjoying instead the jumps over the actual crevices several metres above the others. From here on, it's easy because we're going back down.

Fairly spent after the day-long hike, we take off the crampons and walk back to the bus.

I'm thrilled to have done it.

I make some noodles for dinner and I'm surprised I've even got the energy for that. We go for a few quiet drinks at the hostel bar this evening – catching up on some of the others (such as Rob, Essex Emma and the Leeds lot) we've left behind in Nelson. Colin finds this ancient and cheesy smoke machine behind a door leading into another area so of course Ben and I activate the thing into deactivation. The place is smoke-filled to the point of invisibility. I listen to small Andre prattle on about how much he misses his girlfriend before I slope off to bed – in the fog so he won't notice until I'm long gone.

I'm like some shadowy fugitive from an episode of *The Twilight Zone*. Du-Du, Dudu...

11. Hooter's or Shooters?

DAY FORTY THREE

I sipped on less than a handful of beers last night, yet I'm as hungover as a Helsinki barman. The days are starting to blur into one another and, if the nights be heavenly, the mornings be nightmarish. The fact that the mornings are arriving about four hours after the aforementioned 'nights', would go on to explain this in part.

We have left for Wanaka this morning, and we're stopping off at a couple of beauty spots en route. One of these, Knight's Point, is an expanse of bay on both sides of the jutting platform that we're stood on. Ladies and Gentlemen, to our left a thick column of hazy mist shrouds the horizon – I have never seen anything quite like it. It's so intoxicating that I don't get around to what's on the right.

When I'm done snapping, I head up to the public toilets there. There's a queue and when it's (tall) Andre's turn to go, I run in front of him, pretending to cut into the line as it were. However, I skip on a mucky puddle (of water I pray) outside. My legs go out in front of me and I go down on my arse. Luckily I manage to get my hands down on either side of me. My toes smash into the wooden door. Ouch! Thankfully I'm wearing my trainers and not my flip flops. The lads are bursting WITH laughing...and who could blame them?

We get back on the bus and I fall asleep, waking up a short while later at some waterfall or other. I use the rocks there as stepping stones of sorts. However, I misjudge my footing and I end up soaked up to my left knee.

Putting it mildly, I'm not having the best of luck today.

Then, as Ben is posing for a picture on an isolated rock, I decide to reach down and splash him a bit. "You fucker," he says, laughing.

And another frigging thing happens. On the way back up to the coach, I'm messing about with tall Andre and I slip on a rock, ending up on my arse. What the HELL is going on? My camera is in my back pocket and it takes the brunt of the fall, so now there's a dent on the housing but thankfully it's still working.

"That's Karma," Will reminds me, obviously referring to my splashing of Ben.

Fair enough but this time it's more imminent than a cup of Maxwell House. I do seem to be falling for this country. See what I did there, huh, huh?

Nevermind.

We arrive at Wanaka, stunning Lake Wanaka, in the mid-afternoon. After checking in at the Base Hostel here, I head out to look for a barber of hairdresser to trim my hedge. I do find two salons and then a barber's place but it's Saturday and in true Kiwi entrepreneurial spirit, all of them have closed at 3pm. It's just before 5pm.

Otherwise, I'm suitably impressed by the place, which has low-lying buildings with handsome snow-capped mountains as a backdrop to the town. The mountains are known as the headquarters of the Mount Aspiring National Park and we're only staying overnight so I'm not going to get a chance to explore them. It's another World Heritage Area of the South Island. People use the area, including Lake Wanaka and Lake Hawea (about ten minutes from Wanaka), to fish, swim, camp and water-ski. And naturally, in the winter, the place is a haven for skiers and especially, snowboarders. Queenstown is 120 kilometres to the south west of here.

I'm sitting on a jetty facing onto the town front – my aching feet soaking in the freezing waters Lake Wanaka. It's weird, the place has no smell. None. My mind gets to sky thinking as I look up at the dominating mountain range and also to what I suspect is Roy's Bay. I fill my lungs with possibly the cleanest air I've ever inhaled in a town anywhere. I look under the water and can see my feet almost as clearly as they would look without the presence of the water. My feet have been cut badly by my flip flops and after wearing them for ONE month, I still haven't broken them in.

Nearby, on the gravelly sand, a duck teaches her babies how to swim. I watch for about twenty minutes until my feet are red and thankfully numb, a relief from the itchiness and swelling brought on by the numerous mosquito bites and, I suspect, dehydration. Apparently, Lake Wanaka enjoys a continental climate with four distinct seasons. The weather's quite dry, while the annual rainfall is 682 millimetres – about half the national average. Winter highs are about 10℃, while summers are dry and sometimes have temperatures in the 30℃ though the average is 24℃.

After some time, I stroll up to the bars across from the tourist information shop that is now closed. Thankfully, the bars aren't but strangely, some of them soon will be. I choose this chilled little place and order a Brewski Beer. I've never before seen so many tattoos, hoodies, dreadlocks etc. After this I go for a meal – some poppadoms, a vindaloo and Nan bread – and with a bottle of Heineken, it comes to $30, which seems reasonable. It's more than I can say for the service. It's unfriendly so I don't leave much of a tip.

Back in the dorm that the Danish girls are sharing with Kieran, the Welshies and I, Ida Maria and Signe are busy wrapping themselves up in toilet paper. Tonight is Halloween and they are going out dressed as (Yummy) Mummies.

"Kiwi" – that's what they've taken to calling me as they can't pronounce my name – "ore you dressing up for Hollo-ween?" Ida Maria asks me.

I haven't planned to but it gets me thinking. The lads and Buzz have gone down to Mint Bar at the bottom of the hostel. They're watching Australia taking on New Zealand in the Bledisloe Cup (named after ye olde Governor General of New Zealand, Lord Bledisloe, who donated the trophy back in 1931 apparently). The game is being played in Japan.

I arrive at the bar about twenty minutes into the game. But the commentary is muted and the beats are pumping through the speakers. So we leave at halftime and make our way to the Bullock Bar, which has been recommended to us earlier. We find the place and go inside to find about twenty screens, betting slips, cashier desks and so on. The place is clearly one of those bars that incorporates a TAB.

Oh by the way, lest I forget, I'm looking like my version of a Bedouin tribesman. Or an Arabic oil tycoon at any rate. This is all thanks to a hostel bed-sheet, my shades and a PLO Scarf procured from one of the crew.

Kieran looks like a cross between a Gypsy and an effeminate Thai boxer, while the Welsh lads have donned red horns and boas. We get the strangest of looks from the locals. Outside, in the smoking area at the front of the bar, I tell a man that I will offer him "ten camels for your womans", which I don't think he fully appreciates. It's a joke that my brother-in-law, Samy – who's from Syria and is wed to my sister, Sharon – used to make with me.

Anyway, inside, a huge, bald shithouse-of-a-man with no neck comes up to us in an aggressive manner. It turns out that the woman outside was actually HIS wife.

Oh. Dear.

I'm sitting on a highstool, watching the rugger – the All Blacks beat Australia 32-19 – and this Monster is asking us if we're Aussies. Now, even if I were, I'd be putting on the un-Aussie-est accent that you could possibly imagine here. He's telling us that the Irish and the Welsh are "faggots" and that we'll both be crushed on the Kiwi team's European tour. (Not us, we'll be playing, AND BEATING, Australia. So, ha! I don't tell him this though: I'm not psychic and, I don't have a death wish. Though the Aussies and Kiwis are arch rivals in rugger and seemingly, everything else.)

Anyway, this guy's fingers are nearly the same width as my wrists, I shit you not. His nose is flat and it turns out that he's a former Central Otago rugby player so, the very best of luck to you, Sir. Either way, he's just sussing us out and we don't rise to his bait while trying to show that we're not intimidated by him. But his arms are like tree trunks and he's at least six-foot-five inches tall. His name is like, get this; SPIKE! When I discover this, I'm actually imagining my journalist colleagues back home writing reports on my murder/disappearance.

Spike's friend, Hooter apparently, comes along and joins in the banter. They seem to start respecting us, as we look them straight in the eye and regale them with our Celtic charm or whatever. We must do something right because at this stage Spike's telling us that he wishes he'd met us earlier. He says that we "cudda stoyed et" his house and "god all facked ap". He could have meant anything by that, seeing as Hooter, at this stage, tells me to move my knee because "he'll steck his crotch en et". The Giant does seem to be swaying a lot more and getting closer.

I took all this as them having a bit of fun with us until, at the local Shooters Bar, he actually starts rubbing little Kieran's back. Holy Shit! Shooters Bar is actually situated on Ardmore St., while Ardmore is a town in Co. Waterford so, wherever you go, there you are it seems. Anyway, I hope Spike doesn't have ancestors from Waterford. I'm imagining him turning up on my doorstep with his bags and the creepiest smirk on his mug. At about 1.30am, we go back to Base and try to get into Mint. It's shut but there's about thirty of us. After a bit of negotiation with the bartenders and bouncers, it's, "Dum, dum, dum; hey girl...dum, dum, dum; hey boy; superstar DJ, here we go".

And it is on...we tear up the dancefloor.

DAY FORTY FOUR

It's a short enough drive down to Queenstown – the real adventure capital of The World or New Zealand if you're feeling less charitable. We stop at a place called Puzzling World, a centre designed to melt the brains of the most-together visitor. The centre, which has been in operation for over thirty five years, attracts more than 160,000 visitors annually. However, upon arrival here I discover that my camera doesn't appear to be working. I try in vain to take various pictures of the sloped buildings from outside but alas, to no avail. It's only then that I remember having left my SD (memory) card stuck in one of the computer's ports back at the Base Hostel in Wanaka.

Feck!

I sheepishly approach Buzz and I can tell that the big man is hungry; keen for breakfast. However, he's obliging enough. Will has left his camera in some girl's room there also. So Buzz and I go back in the Green Goddess and I'm having a nightmare because all of my snaps of Australia and New Zealand are on it.

Luckily, it's still wedged in the machine I was using to upload some images onto Facebook last night. I don't think Will fared as well though, and Buzz leaves a message for said girl to hand it in. I profusely thank the helpful Spanish girl working at reception and get back on board and within fifteen minutes, we're back at Puzzling World. I buy a bacon butty (€3 to Kiwi Experience visitors) and plan to check out the mind-bending mazes, holograms and illusion rooms.

230

Before I do, however, I get told by a woman (I guess in her 60s) working there that she "was married to en Oirishmen fo' thurty-four yee-ors". Then, one day she woke up and found out that she was bored. She says it all in this awful put-on Scottish accent. Her poor (ex?) husband.

"You were obviously with the wrong Irishman," I joke with her. "Besides, I'm not Scottish, I'm Irish," I add.

"Ya' roight," she replies, relaxing back into her native speak. "I know ya' Oirish."

"Whut koinda brekfist is thet?" she asks me, going into mother-mode while eyeing up my sandwich, crisps and coke.

The centre is weird. I get pissed off walking around the maze so I cheat – climbing over and crawling under the wooden fences in a path-of-least-resistance escape of sorts. Don't judge me, I'm not alone in doing this.

Inside, I wreck my head with optical illusions: there's this strange Illusion Room that has its contents at weird angles to the perpendicular. Billiard balls, stairs and a kind of sliding chair, deceive us into thinking that gravity is working in reverse order. Watching balls rolling UP a pool table on a downward slope while hungover, is not a good idea if you're worried about mental fragility. There's a weird Hollogram Hall and a Hall of Following Faces. Not a good place to be with a dose of *The Fear* – trust me on this one. There's even a Leaning Tower of Wanaka outside, tipping at an angle of 53° to the Pisa tower's measly 3°.

We leave and about an hour later, arrive at AJ Hackett's bungee station over the Kawaru River. At forty three metres (142 ft), it's less daunting than the 134-metre Nevis jump. However, seven of us book the Nevis jump from the station and only one of us, Scottish girl, Kim, does the baby jump here. Like me, she didn't intend on doing any jump but she responded to a lethal sales technique from this extremely hungover worker there. This involves getting all of us to apply peer pressure on her – primary school style. I stupidly told someone that if Kim agreed to do it here at Kawaru, then I would agree to do Nevis. Me and my big mouth! As mentioned, I've ordered the jump here but I didn't have enough cash on me and...don't get me started on the Laser issue. I booked it and will have to pay for it ($216 with a discount) at the office on Shotover St., when I arrive in Queenstown.

We roll into Queenstown in the afternoon and Buzz drives us to a scenic spot where we will get a group photograph done (this will be flogged to us if we want it!). We check into (yet another) Base Hostel (costing yet again $27 per person in a dorm) on Shotover St. I'm sharing an eight-bed dorm with my country folk Kieran, Matt and Angela, Welshmen Ben and Mike, Englanders Dave and Sarah. It looks like it's going to be a tri-nation cup of sorts in outdoor and adventure pursuits. Or perhaps drinking.

A number of us go over to Fergburgers – these massive and gorgeous burgers from an outlet of the same name. They start at about $5 and are a meal in themselves. We go back for a snooze, except it's not happening for Ben and I, who are both light sleepers. I use these hours to catch up on my journaling.

By the way, the town of Queens has developed over/around a long, thin Z-shaped lake. Explorers William Gilbert Rees and Nicholas Von Tunzelman were the first Europeans to settle here. Rees settled a farm where the town centre is now, in 1860. Meanwhile, gold was discovered in Arrowtown a couple of years later. Queenstown is the largest town in Central Otago and has an estimated resident population of about 28,000. It has been flagged to me and my cohorts as being "a party town" and has been coined "The Adventure Capital of the World". It is popular among snowboarders and skiers, mountain bikers, skateboarders, hikers, fishers of fish, bungee jumpers, paragliders and skydivers.

And other lunatics.

Local bar workers, Will and Colin (who, as I've mentioned, have joined us on our tour) arrange a "specials night" for us. This will involve two-for-one Jäger Bombs, house drinks and so on at bars such as Altitude (at the bottom of our hostel), The Thirsty Ram (next door), Winnies, and of course at World Bar where they work. Here, we will get teapot after teapot filled with unknown concoctions, while a pint of ale will cost about $4 (€2), apparently. Not too shabby, eh?

At the Thirsty Ram, a tall and fairly cute woman asks me for "sex" when I order two-for-one vodkas with lemonade from her. Allow me to explain: the drinks come to €5, so I hand it over.

"SEX," she yells at me.

She's not mean or anything, the music is just too bloody loud for granddad.

"SORRY?"

"SEX; I NEED SEX," she then shouts.

"JESUS – DON'T WE ALL?" I shout back.

Wow, these Kiwi girls are really forward, I'm thinking to myself – wondering how I'm going to handle this one.

"RIGHT NOW?" I continue.

"WHAT? I SAID I NEED SEX DOLLA'S."

Shit. The penny hath dropped. It's the bloody Kiwi accent. What is it with them and their "e" for "i" (and "i" for "e") pronunciations?

DAY FORTY FIVE

Death has become us. At least that's how it feels to me. I look around the dorm from my bottom bunk and all I see are the casualties strewn about the place – spat out by Queenstown after last night's drinkathon. I'm sicker than a virgin sailor on the High Seas and I'm not the only one. Two hours later we're sitting in the beergarden at Red Rock Bar & Cafè on Camp St., adjacent to Shotover St.

However, I can explain. Some of the group – about nine or ten of them – are going to walk up the sharp incline to Bob's Peak, known locally as "The Ledge". They will luge down it. Then they'll go walk up The Ledge only to luge down it again.

Do what?

Eh, fuck that and to Hell with you too, BOB! There are only four of us (Kieran, Ben, Mike, me) but the rest of them come and go in ones and twos. I'm sipping on a cappuccino, Colin is eating a breakfast and Kieran and the two Welshies are drinking pints. After a while, I decide that a 'cure' might work so I get myself a Monteith's Ale.

233

This afternoon, I'm calling down to the see a friend from home, Marianne. She works in the Pig & Whistle, an English-themed pub on Ballarat St. I turn the corner onto Ballarat St. and climb the steps into the pub.

She's not behind the bar. I ask the barman there, who turns out to be the manager, if Marianne is working today. "She's heee' olright," he says, adding: "but Oi'm not shuuu' she's wooo'kin'." It's a joke of course, seeing as it turns out that she's the best asset the place has got.

I order a coke and the sausages and mash, which are a lunchtime special dish. Then, she walks down the stairs, goes in behind the bar and she spots me. We catch up and I have a beer and then a water followed by a beer again. We chat up in the moments that she's not busy. However, when I go for another glass of water, I mustn't have been clear because she gives me another beer. At this rate, I will be falling out of the place.

I go outside for a smoke as I sit down at a table and chill. There's a KFC opposite, below the impressive Ledge. Numerous gondolas, like white beetles from this distance, crawl up and down the undulating alpine mass. At one stage when I'm inside ordering at the bar, I feel a pair of eyes burning into the back of my skull. I look around and see a tall, greying mass of long curly hair and a beard of the same colour. The shape that's staring at me still is wearing a leather jacket, which seems crazy to me because of the heat.

Ross and I get chatting in the beergarden and it transpires that he's a Queenstown native who claims to be "fray (free) of oll choyns (chains)". He tells me that he has lived in a cave some distance up the peak (The Ledge, Bob's Peak) across and dined on scraps from the KFC in the bins across the road. He seems to be proud of all of this. I look at his glass suspiciously. He's drinking water.

CHAINS, CHAINS...WE NEED MORE FECKIN' CHAINS OVER HERE GODDAMNIT!!!

"Oftin, Oi steeend heee' lookin' et the cabbige troys (trees) wavin' en the wind...I see the inigy (energy) camin' awf et, an' Oi wrap muself araan' it."

234

Inside, there are a group of people talking and laughing – oblivious to us. Making my excuses, I edge nervously towards the door. Towards perceived safety. I'm joking of course; it's obvious that Ross wouldn't harm a fly.

Marianne has a meeting and when she finishes, she gives me her number and we make arrangements to go for a trek up Queenstown Hill for tomorrow – her day off. I make my way down Queenstown Mall to a store called Jay Jay's to buy some new and cheap clobber. Often, backpackers throw away clothes and buy new ones; more than likely cheap ones that are easily replaceable. It turns out that the sales assistant, a youngish girl-woman with layered pink hair, knew an old teacher at my secondary school, De La Salle College on Water St. in Waterford city. It's a small world: it turns out that Cork girl Jane's mother is a friend of Martin Verling's wife. Martin, *Mr Verling*, was a biology teacher and while I studied the subject, I was in Ms. Hewson's class. He did, however, put us through our paces on the rugby field (if I'm not mistaken, ours was the first rugby squad in the school) in 1990 or 1991. Sadly, Jane tells me that Martin has passed on.

Kieran and I go for a Mexican (meal, not a person) at Sombrero's on Beach St. near our hostel and we're both suffering from dodgy stomachs afterwards – though we're not food poisoned or anything. The bloated stomach-grumbling and flatulence keep us from the cheers and the beers tonight, possibly pushing our dorm mates out of the door, however. When Sarah and Dave come back early, we lie in our beds and list our top five tragic bungee accident theme songs for the funerals following tomorrow's jump. Songs such as *Freefalling* by Tom Petty and *Jump* by Van Halen are among them.

It actually helps us to relax.

DAY FORTY SIX

I'm sitting at breakfast – it's one of those awful buffet things with cold, rubbery toast that you can get with the voucher thing they give you at the reception upon check-in at Base in Queenstown. I'm pondering the wisdom of eating even a light breakfast such as this, considering that in a couple of hours time I will be hurtling through the air at 130 kilometres per hour, for about eight seconds and 134 metres before springing back up again. Hopefully! I've put on a few pounds since I left Ireland and I was never a small bloke exactly: I imagine what will go through my mind when the chord snaps. I have a feeling that it will be my arse. The jump is held in high esteem in the world of extreme sports and activities apparently. So safety is obviously paramount. I keep telling myself this.

We get ourselves organised and stroll to the AJ Hackett bungee station further up Shotover St. and we get checked in and, more importantly, weighed in once again. I'm waiting, nervously – imagining the assistant punching in the wrong weight resulting in the chord snapping instead of bouncing. I'm a positive sod at times.

Eventually, we're taken up to Nevis Canyon by minibus, and the journey takes about thirty minutes. We eventually hit – oops, unfortunate choice of word there – Nevis and slowly climb the incline to the diving station of whatever. We get processed and the staff strap our harnesses onto us. The jumpmaster talks to me about my previous back injury; I've already been told at the station that the final call as to whether I can jump or not will be his decision and his alone. This man, a laid back sort who always has a cup of coffee in his hand, asks me a few questions but seems happy when I tell him about my surgeon advising me that nonsense of this variety would actually cause my back no further harm. He in turn advises me to make a dramatic dive; high and far. A better dive will cause less strain to my back I'm told and at least I'll look good as I hurtle towards imminent death.

Seriously though, some actually believe that bungee jumps can be good for the back. I know what you're thinking: they're the ones *without* back problems. Still, it's not as mad a theory as you would think.

We're led, like lambs to the slaughter, to this trolley on a cable pulley system thingy. And we're taken out to the jumping platform (actually known as a pod), which looks like a stationary cable car with no front. For all intent purposes, it is. So there's the two Swedish Andres, Welsh Mike, Canadian girl Katia, Danish girl Ida Maria and English chap Dave, all staring down into the abyss. Other bungee jumpers there do likewise. Well, we stare through the glass strip in the bottom of the platform anyway. Angela and Sarah are with us also because they'll be doing the canyon swing afterwards. The bright green river cuts through the sun drenched valley that is lit up like a U2 concert about 200 metres below us. As far as last sights on this planet go, it's not a bad one. It's a cold comfort on such a warm morning.

I'm told that I'm up first, as I knew I would be because I'm the heaviest in the group. (Later, my mother will tell me that they "probably make the heaviest fella go first to show the others that it's safe"...thanks for that Lily!) Of course, the chord chosen is proportional to the particular jumper's weight. The others are cheering me on, obviously curious as to how it all works and surely glad not to be first up to take the plunge. One of the warders leads me to a Lazy Boy chair of sorts and checks my harness one final time – telling me to smile for the camera above as he attaches these velcro pads around my ankles. Smile? Is this guy for real? Still, I manage a nervous grimace as the Officer of Death attaches the chord and there are straps everywhere. About fifteen concerned faces stare on intensely and solemnly from the gallery opposite. The guard gives me instructions about what to do in the air and I have to ask him to repeat it. He says "not ta wurry" about a certain kind of snapping noise that I'll hear as it's just the winch.

WHOA! SNAP – what's that now?

I'm now prepared for my final journey; surely there's no way back. The Executioner leads me – legs bound together like a man on death row – shuffling, to the edge. I scan the place, looking for a man with a white collar to read me my last rights. I've not been offered a last meal. However, standing on the edge, and with not an insignificant quantity of irony, I finally become resigned to my fate.

The fate of a condemned man.

I feel a bit numb, actually. Perhaps the fear has been so overwhelming that I've actually realised that it's pointless, and I'm left to enjoy my final moments. In fact, Tolle, in *The Power of Now* writes, that for the majority of the population "only a critical limit situation has the potential to crack the hard shell of the ego and force them into surrender and so into the awakened state". I've already touched on this stuff but the theory is that largely, parts of the "ego shell break(s) off, and this allows small amounts of the radiance and peace that lie beyond the mind to shine through".

Speaking of condemnation, Tolle says that there have been cases of murderers on death row who, "in the last few hours of their lives, experienced the egoless state and the deep joy and peace that come with it".

Hmmm. Perhaps that's what's happening to me.

The Officer of Death counts me down...

"FIVE."

...the water snakes gently around the rocks and bushes below me as I stand alone and first before all...

"FOUR."

...literally trembling on the brink of life...

"THREE."

...the only thing I can hear is the soft wind rustling about us...

"TWO."

...and perhaps aptly, the gunshot sounds from the song *Paper Planes* by female artist M.I.A pumping out of the speakers.

All I wanna do is click, click, click, click – kerching...

"ONE."

... and take yo' money.

"AAAAAAAAAARGH"- and I'm gone: hurtling through the air, I can hear my executioner say that I've done a nice dive as the others cheer and a second later I can hear nothing except the wind rush though my ears and opened, silent-screaming mouth as I plummet further still, wondering what the hell it is that I think I'm doing while the river is getting ever closer and it's a strange sensation; probably because the blood has rushed straight to my head and the adrenaline is coursing through my veins and it's not something I can explain exactly but there's no turning back now because I can see my shadow on the banks of the river below me turn from a mere dot into a human shape and suddenly; there's a jolt...I hold my breath as I realise that the chord hasn't snapped and I'm disorientated as I fly in the opposite direction; suddenly falling into

238

the sky before stopping at the peak of the first bounce for a moment, then falling to earth again, except the bounce this time is not as pronounced so I look up and I'm falling into clear blue sky again and I'm staring at my feet when I hear the snapping sound but a millisecond later I remember what I've been told so I pull the red chord running down the side of my left leg and then...I'm sitting upright.

I punch the air and shout repeatedly for, maybe a minute, while I'm bouncing up and down and half-not believing what it is that I've just done. My shouts are swallowed up by the canyon. I can see and hear the excited screams of the others, who have come here for the canyon swing and to lend their support and are waving at me from a viewing platform in the distance. The bouncing stops and I'm winched back up to the other jumpers. I'm still shouting as I'm helped back in, 'high-fiving' anyone in sight, as generally happens after these types of activities. As I've said, free-falling for almost 140 metres in this way is a strange experience and my head feels blocked, a bit heavy afterwards. Andre's next up after me and his eyes look bloodshot when he's winched up. As I guess mine are.

After the seven of us have completed our dives, along with two Irish blokes and a girl, we're taken back to the bungee centre at the top of the canyon to pick up our photos. Before we do, however, Dave and I accompany Sarah and Angela for their canyon swing. To be fair, it looks awesome: they're sitting side by side on a swing and facing us – poised for dropping into the canyon in a huge backwards-sweeping arc. Following some nervy false starts, they're dropped into the void and within a second or so, I can see them about one hundred metres below us. They disappear into apparent oblivion, only reappearing as a dot against a sun-soaked backdrop that is the canyon floor. I've being recording it on Sarah's Blackberry for her and it's been near-impossible to track. Upon returning, the girls are ecstatic, though in the excitement, we can't seem to find the file on Sarah's phone.

We collect our packages (including photos and DVDs) and we're on a high in the van on the way back, calling into Fergburger again to celebrate.

I'm meeting meet Marianne this afternoon for a hike up Queenstown Hill. We're to meet at 'her' bar, The Pig & Whistle, and then we'll head for the hills. Perhaps laughably, we start by exercising counter productivity, stopping after about five minutes for a cigarette. But then we're off at a good clip and, fair play to her, she's able to keep up with my lanky stride. We stop for a few minutes at a large rock about halfway up for a rest. I'm carrying my manbag so I'm glad to ditch that and my broad rimmed wool hat – excellent for keeping the sun of the head and neck, though it's made of wool so it's bloody hot. During the rest of the hike up the beautiful hill, we talk only at moments where we can manage it through gasps. A few hundred metres further up, we stop again for a minute at these signs. I quickly realise that I've forgotten my bag.

FUCK!

Marianne finds it hilarious – she kindly offers to trek back with me to get it but I tell her not to bother. No point in both of us dying of exhaustion. On the way down, I meet two Krazy Kiwi girls who ask me if I've seen a bag of crayfish that they've lost.

WTF??

"Sorry, I didn't."

At least I only lost my bag. I give the thing a right good kick when I get there. Finally, we reach the summit of Queenstown Hill and it's definitely worth the effort. We climb into this Giant stainless steel basket placed at a natural viewing spot and we jump into it. In between catching up and so on, we scan the panorama in front of us. I'm blown away by Cecil's Peak, Coronet's Peak and The Remarkables in front of us; the double cone of the latter is the highest point of these at 2,319 metres. The mountains are stately in their presence – sparkling amid Lake Wakatipu in the November afternoon sun like the jewels of the Southern Alps that they are.

It's only while here that we realise what day it is...the Melbourne Cup is on, though I couldn't really care less. I'm not much of a betting man. After about forty minutes, we head back down again for a pint in Monty's, a really cool bar with a view of Lake Wakatipu and the Remarks'. I'm getting worried now because my Laser card doesn't seem to be working...in ANY of the ATM machines. Aha, it's Melbourne

Cup day. Little wonder that the cashpoints are devoid of notes. However, when I call the offices attached to some of these, they tell me that there shouldn't be a problem. The banks down under DO NOT have a can-do attitude. If I've learned anything here and in Aussie, it is this: the attitude seems to be, *Can't help you, now piss off!*

Slumping back to Base, I'm basically shitting myself and wondering what I'm going to do. I have enough money for a packet of crisps and a coke and I spend my last $5 in cash on a Global Gossip calling card. I'll need to use the internet, plus call my bank and my mother at home to see if I can get some money wired through. So I get through to my old dear and the bank and, long-story-short, I give the bank permission to hand over €1,500 to Western Union via Lily so she can wire it through to me. This will surely keep me going until I can get back to the small dog in a week's time. I've made plans to meet Marianne at Surreal Bar, this funky little spot on Rees St., where her friend John – a fellow Waterfordian who I know from home – currently works. It's just midnight, so I'm thirty minutes late. On the way down, I try an ATM on the 'off-chance' and manage to withdraw $200. Spare me! My instincts were right; it was the Melbourne Cup situation. So the 'nice' ladies in the BNZ outlet were obviously mistaken then. Grrr.

Finally, I make it to Surreal and there's an Open Mike night of sorts going on. I've not even ordered a drink and there's this psychotic Maori drinking there who basically tries to start a fight with me and I'm in NO mood for him. He'd better get out of my face, like yesterday! He's standing there alone, arguing with himself aggressively and waving his arms about the place so he's clearly not a well bloke. However, I must keep an eye out for a sneaky attack. When I ask John, a laid back bloke, what the deal is, he at first looks confused but then just goes, "Aw yeah, him!" So is this normal behaviour in Queenstown? I hope not.

I go for a smoke and when I'm coming in, he's on the way out, thankfully. Marianne and her pal Edwina (Eddie) sort-of goad me into playing a couple of songs. Another friend of hers, Dev, also a friend of hers from home and who's living with her and a couple in Queenstown, is playing guitar and singing onstage. I'm quite impressed. Despite my own reservations – I haven't played in months – I myself give

241

into the peer pressure and take to the stage. I fluff a few bits but the crowd seem to enjoy it. Marianne's co-workers Edwina from England, South African Mark and Andy from Manchester (who also lives with her), are here too and Tuesday is obviously a popular night. Afterwards, Marianne and I go to Bardeaux, a plush bar with a large open fireplace at Eureka Arcade off the Mall that stays open until 5am – God help us. We're drinking bourbon and coke now so I tell the Canadian barman working there to hit my horns with a wooden mallet, should they appear.

I spy the drinks menu and tell him that we'll have one of the $3,400 bottles of wine, though of course I'm not serious. Shortly before 5am, I buy a bottle of Heineken and I'm surprised to return from the bathroom a few minutes later to find that one of the bouncers has taken it. And it's not on, so I tell him so and retrieve it. However, he's being a smartarse; so I'm a smartarse back – calling him an arsehole on the way out. Perhaps I've had enough anyway. It was the bourbon he should have taken from me.

You should never touch a man's drink.

DAY FORTY SEVEN

* The next few days in Queenstown go by in a blur. I'm still enjoying myself but there's just a few days of my tour left so I feel as if I might as well just push on with it and enjoy the rest of my time away. However, my liver will thank me for getting back into a routine that doesn't involve getting hammered most nights, while getting up at an unconscionable hour – only to do it all again. We've been warned that Queenstown would go by at a ferocious speed and it indeed is. I regret to say that the numerous activities on offer to us are largely ignored by my bus (the eight of us staying in my dorm anyway), along with the Leeds and the Swedes. We're drinking late into the night (early morning) now, every single night. Who am I kidding? I don't regret it at all. It's what we've been doing all along but at least now we have the option of chilling out all day if we want. We want – it's a relief to an old(er) codger like yours truly after all the late-night-early-mornings-then-travelling by coach. I had lofty ideals of hiring out a car and doing a little tour of the sights down here, but...!*

I've just grabbed a couple of bottles of Vino Blanco and I'm heading up to Marianne's place to watch a DVD. I meet her at The Pig' at about nine o'clock and we pick up a movie at the rental store nearby and get a lift up – from one of her housemates, Darragh from Co. Cork – to their place. Finally. We were both indecisive but we decided upon *My Best Friend's Girl*. I've seen it before but I assure Marianne that it's more of an edgy comedy than predictable, limp-wristed Rom Com (despite the title!)

The others, meanwhile, have been living it up every night, caught deep in the clutches of the Queenstown nightlife, largely laid on for the backpacking masses. Dark and evil potions – often mixed with caffeine-and-taurine-loaded drinks – and teapots containing unlabelled, mixed alcoholic drinks are largely the drugs of choice. Apart from going on short walks around The Ledge, the (Queenstown) hill, getting food and so on, the days now seem to involve laying around the dorm watching movies on Kieran's laptop until it's time to go out and do it all over again. Buzz is still around Queenstown (he's heading north again with another tour any day now) and some of us sometimes meet him in bars such as The Thirsty Ram next door to Base. I'm not too enamoured with the hostel but I may as well remain here until we go our separate ways.

DAY FORTY EIGHT

This evening, I meet Marianne again – along with some of her friends – at Surreal. A girl called Catherine, who's also from Waterford, is in town. It gets messy here for sure, and I'm talking to the drunkest Kiwi I've met so far (there have been a few). We're talking about swimming and above the music and general noise, I can't understand a word he's saying and he seems to be frustrated, as he's getting more and more aggressive, though with himself and not me exactly if you get me. At one stage he knocks over my drink with his wildly waving hand but he buys me another Tui Ale, fair play to him.

243

Meanwhile, Mike and Leeds Emma stumble into Surreal and they are as locked as the door on Scrooge's safe, as hammered as an Auctioneer's gavel. You get the picture. Emma's got a thin moustache pencilled on above her top lip and she can barely speak. Mike manages to communicate somehow, telling me that they've just been thrown out of World Bar. They've apparently protested but I can't see why, exactly. It turns out that Mike and Ben had Emma held aloft, holding one leg each in front of the bar. The moustached Yorkshire lass has only reached over to the bank of beer taps and turned them all on. So yes, it's rather unfair that they got thrown out on their collective ear. Hmmm.

They disappear as soon as again and before long, Mike pops up again but with Ben this time. It's past 3am at this stage, however, and the bar is closed. Marianne and I, along with some names that I can't even remember, make our way to Bardeux again. And I'm blaming my recent fondness for bourbon and coke on her alone. I'm not, under any circumstances, allowed to have whiskey – no matter what it is or where it hails from. However, Jack Daniels is not "whisky" or "whiskey" and is therefore a horse of a different colour. So I tell myself, convincing myself that I can indulge without turning into an *actual* pirate.

"It's strange; this drink tastes like cola," I tell Marianne, as I lash back yet another of the Devil's drinks.

DAY FORTY NINE

It's after 3pm, following yet another sluggish day in my smelly dorm with the others, when I call into the Pig & Whistle again. The plan, my intention, is to have a coffee. However, Eddie and Brad, a solid Kiwi bloke who's a regular at the bar, are drinking. I join them and sip on a Monteith's Original Ale. And then I have another one. And one after that. You can see where this is headed, can't you? Eddie tells me that two of her extended family are published authors. So I'm obviously interested in talking about that. She works in the bar also but she's off today and tells me that it's her fourth day on the rip. I can hardly talk, seeing as I've being doing so for seven weeks now. I teach her some Irish words, or rather get her to say some phrases "as Gaeilge" that she doesn't understand. Well how could she? When she's going in to get a drink or go to the bathroom or whatever, she's acting as the opposite of an Interpreter if you will, to Marianne and fellow Waterford woman (and Pig' worker) Una. So I get her to work on her pronunciation before she asks them ridiculous questions in my native tongue and it's a good laugh.

Eddie leaves but Dev from Waterford and some others come along so I'm hanging out with them. I know what you're thinking...have all of Waterford's inhabitants actually moved over to Queenstown? Marianne finishes work at 9pm and joins us. I'm well on now. This wasn't part of the plan.

DAY FIFTY

My mind is telling me that I need to get moving, though my body is telling me otherwise. I appear to have developed a cough-cold type of chest infection that's been coming on for the past couple of weeks. There's loads of coughing, nose-running; I've got a croaky voice and I'm sweating. Although I'm very run down, I feel as if I have to keep going because standing, sitting or even staying in bed are not options – regardless of how I feel physically. Not today.

Wandering around alone, I'm trying to make sense of some of the stuff that's running through my head. Perhaps I've been caning it with the drink too much but this will surely end in a few days because I'm due to fly back to Dublin from Christchurch via Sydney and Frankfurt on Monday. I want to leave Queenstown, yet I want to remain here. I'm all over the place. In my miserable state of mind today, I imagine that she wants to entice me with pleasure only so she can watch with cool detached amusement as I perish following the brief union.

Post session depression, as we'd call it back in the small dog.

Yes, that's it. I feel numb, though I take the gondola up to The Ledge. I'm glancing down at the town of the Queen. Yesterday, I planned to come up here to see beauty yet today, all my subjugated self can see is one grey eye staring up at me with indifference, tainted with faint glee, the reasons for the onslaught almost forgotten but not entirely.

245

Again I'm looking at Cecil's and Coronet's Peak(s), Deer Park Heights and Queenstown Gardens, but now with jaded eyes.

It's five o'clock and I'm meeting the others at the Red Rock watering hole. I'm not allowed to remain too miserable as the others tell me to get my arse over to Jay Jays to buy some gear for a neon party later that evening. I join Andre and Kieran and we head over and scavenge through the special offers for tops and, eh, leggings. This should sort the men from the...from the...women? After digging deep, both literally and figuratively I can assure you, I eventually find a large pair of leggings and a floral top – because it's the only one I can find that even comes close to fitting me.

At Base, I don my Speedos (shorts, not briefs) and struggle into the tight leggings. I've also bought a pair of pink disc earrings for the craic and slip one of them in though the piercing in my left ear, which has been there for all of my adult life. We meet down in Altitude (the cheesy bar underneath the hostel) where designs are painted on our skin in various shades of neon paint (there are stripes, dots, smiley faces and so on). Nu-metal I could just about live with but Nu Rave? It's not really me.

We do a "Jäger Train", which sets us back $5 each. Numerous Slim Jim glasses, about one-quarter filled with Red Bull, are laid out in an "S" shape on a table. Shot glasses filled with Jägermeister, a spicy German herbal digestif, are perched carefully atop and in-between two glasses. I'm way too old for this type of behaviour and my doctor would probably get palpitations at the sight of it, but there's not much of the energy drink involved and I'm only having the one. The shot glass on the far end of the table is pushed into the glass below, after tipping the next shot glass on the way down and, to the sound of about one hundred bright "clunking noises"; they all end up in the bottom of the glasses as a result of a domino effect. We slam the shots and *rave* into the early hours.

That's right: we are Raving Lunatics.

It's the last night that we're due to drink together as a group. We leave Altitude to go on a Colin-and-Will-organised drinking tour of the town. Unfortunately, I bump into Brad, who's a rugby-playing Crane Driver.

"WHAT DA FAAACK?" he goes, laughing and shaking his head.

We take in Winnies on The Mall, do a mass pose for the customers on the veranda of Surreal Bar and then hoof it down to Buffalo Bar on Brecon St. The bouncer warns us to "take caaa' wid ya goiii'llfrinds" because there's a rowdy rugby team inside but they turn out to be utter gents (unlike some of the goons we will meet at World Bar later on!).

At one stage, most of us are outside World Bar smoking but when we climb the steps to get back in, the bouncers won't let us because we're apparently "not clearing the area". I try to reason with them – two Irish guys and a Kiwi – but to no avail. The cops are standing yards away, watching it all, so it's obviously all for their benefit. The Police in this town are scrupulous about checking up on the doors but this is just ridiculous. All we did was go out for a bloody smoke: we have stamps from the club on our hands, for God's sake. Most of us slope off but after a while, Welsh Ben, Leeds Chris and I are left back in so we're the only ones from our gang who are left at World Bar.

I don't remember getting back to Base. Memo to self: floral and neon parties are dangerous.

DAY FIFTY ONE

I wake to find myself in a bed. I'm in a dorm with Irish Nicola, Chris, Becky, Natt, Emma and Vicky and I'm not entirely (at all) sure how I got there. I have to throw the pocket-less neon garb back on before heading down to my own room two floors below and even though I search my bag, I can't find my bloody wallet. Nightmare. I comb the recesses of my brain, and it doesn't appear to be in the room. It's not down in the Internet cafe, where I apparently was last night, either. I report the missing wallet at Reception and it hasn't been handed in. I go back to my own room again and it's not there. I have one last search of my bag before showering and, lo-and-behold, there it is – hidden out of sight in the large pocket at the back of my bloody manbag.

Ben, Mike Kieran and I go to the Ministry of Sport to watch Wales try their best against New Zealand at rugby. I try to order something to eat that won't stop my heart dead in its tracks but the only bar food that seems to be on offer there are large baskets of deep fried chips with battered onion rings. I indulge but get nowhere near finishing it. The game has been played at the Millennium Stadium in Cardiff about eight hours previously and of course the Welsh are beaten, much to the disappointment of Ben and Mike, naturally.

It turns out that Ben "had to" punch the English chap who was pestering us last night, as he started picking a fight (with Ben) outside World Bar. But let's get it straight: he punched the guy because of his actions, not his nationality. I don't like violence but I do ask him why he only punched the bloke just once. I meet Marianne at the Pig & Whistle at five o'clock, when she finishes work and we have a drink there before meeting Dev, Brad and some others at Monty's for a few. I take out my camera and show Brad the shots from last night and I should have kept my big gob shut because he was well on and can't remember meeting me. I say a normal goodbye – not letting on that I'll be leaving at first light. No point in creating a fuss.

12. Leaving the Town of Queens

DAY FIFTY TWO

The Welsh lads, the Canadian sisters, along with Vicky and Becky, are among those from *my* bus who are also leaving for Christchurch today on the Kiwi Experience. We've been in Queenstown for one week and, as I've said, it's gone by in a blur. The only real adrenaline activity I've indulged in during this time was the Bungee Jump. And liver roulette.

I'm not joking.

We leave at 8.30am and the scenery on the way north is spectacular in fairness. This is particularly the case when we zip through the Karawau Gorge and on up through the Lindis Pass. We're moving through McKenzie country – named after mysterious Scottish character, James McKenzie who was blamed for stealing sheep in the middle of the 19th Century. Mckenzie – along with his dog and pack bullock – became a known figure in Cantebury and Otago, especially when in 1855, 1,000 sheep were stolen from the Two Levels station. The likely suspect(s) were McKenzie and his crew because the footprints of a man and his animals led *them* to him. McKenzie couldn't speak English, at least until he cried and protested in that language after learning that his dog Friday was to be put to death, with the judge calling her a witch. Some reports suggest that she was actually shot, while others said that she was banished from Canterbury and sent back to Otago, where she spent the rest of her long days in peace. The doggie farm, eh?

Sorry, but that's just bollocks.

McKenzie himself spent five years in penal servitude but escaped. He escaped three times so as usual, he failed in his endeavours. He was apparently pardoned after just one year, so perhaps not. Some reports say that he took a ship to South America or Australia, where he just vanished.

Stopping off for views of Aoraki, or "Cloud Piercer" Mount Cook, is definitely worth it. Cook, of course named after you-know-who, stands at 3,754 metres and can boast of the country's (and indeed Australasia's) highest natural peak. Meanwhile the Tasman Glacier, at twenty seven kilometres in length, makes its own presence felt. Lake Tekapo sparkles in the foreground like a turquoise jewel: its beauty seems to mock our hurting heads and sick stomachs. Queenstown has chewed up and spat out its latest victims, so it seems. I even skip lunch so I must be coming down with something.

Another stop in the Canterbury region that's worthwhile, but only in a banal and surreal way, is Geraldine. It's 140 kilometres south of Christchurch and therefore, acts as a stop-off that's useful for coach passengers hoping to use the toilet and buy some ice-cream. Our guide tells us that Geraldine is the place where retired farmers are put out to pasture. Enough said. He's not lying: the place seems to be largely populated with the silver-headed folk. I'm a fan of the older generation but balance is important. Geraldine has been populated with European settlers since 1840 and I imagine that most of them are still walking the streets here.

Perhaps we've been a bit spoiled by Buzz but at one of the stops I ask the driver, whose name I didn't get, if he can open up the undercarriage so I can get something from my bag. He tells me that I'm "ez useful ez en eshtroy on a moda'boike (ashtray on a mtotrbike)" so I ask him if he has a problem with me and he apologises, saying he was joking, which he clearly wasn't but no harm done I suppose.

Shortly after four, we arrive at Cathedral Square in Christchurch – the biggest city on the South Island. These names are of passing interest to me because, as I've said much earlier, there's a Church of Ireland church of the same name on a square (of the same name) back home in Waterford city. The square here stays true to its British/Anglican heritage and attracts various preachers, evangelists and other nuts. The God Squad pound the square – spouting Scripture in the vain hope of leading us sheep to Salvation or whatever.

After checking in at (two guesses...) Base on Cathedral Square, I do a mad thing. I decide that I'm not yet done with New Zealand and indeed the Southern Hemisphere so I decide to extend my flights by a few weeks.

On the way up here, I've been having a silent debate – go home as planned or stay and explore the South Island some more. Of course I tell Ben and Mike, who'll be staying in Christchurch for a couple of days, and they think it's a good idea.

The well-meaning folk at Reception in Base, however, send me on a bit of a wild goose chase. I'm told that the Qantas office is on Armagh St., basically a block over. I rush to get there before six but when I arrive at the Price Waterhouse Cooper building – where it's supposed to be –, Qantas doesn't appear to be there. Great! I'm due to fly home in thirteen hours time. A nearby flight centre is closed.

I'm screwed.

But then I get a brainwave, something I'm surprised that I didn't think of sooner. I decide that I'll ring my travel agent at home. However, I must wait until nine o'clock (Ireland is thirteen hours behind us here) to ring Caroline at Travel Creations in Waterford city. Surely I can re-book another flight at a future date by using my Laser card.

In the meantime, I have to wait.

Sometime after ten, as Ben, Mike and I are smoking outside the front of our Hostel; we see a taxi pull up on the road, about thirty metres away. There's a rather large, hairy-faced Maori gent sitting in the front passenger seat.

"You Welsh caaants," he shouts over.

Our heads turn in unison, and it takes us about ten seconds of fear before we realise who it is.

"BUZZ!"

We almost say it all at once.

The big tour guide struts over and hugs us – laughing at our shocked reactions. He jots off after a while as another tour north beckons apparently. After speaking to Caroline shortly before midnight – seven hours before I'm due to fly home – I discoved that I can have a flight in three weeks time. It costs me $200. So my love affair with New Zealand is not over. Not quite yet anyway.

251

DAY FIFTY THREE

The Canadian sisters, Kayla and Chantelle, have gone at first light. They've taken a coach back down to the bright lights of Queenstown. Mike's ex-girlfriend Josie, who is living in Ashburton with her uncle, has come to visit him here in Christchurch. He and Ben will go to stay with her in a few days time, it turns out. We have some breakfast in some joint and then go and watch the Brainiacs try and outwit each other on this Giant chess board on Cathedral Square. The Preachers pace about the place, continuing to spread the good word and make themselves hoarse in the process – even when nobody is listening. After a while we pop into Christchurch Cathedral for a look around. It's worth a look but after we get a bit bored we take it upon ourselves to snap each other with our cameras, as we strike Devilish poses.

In the afternoon we stroll down to the Christchurch Art Gallery and Canterbury Museum at Roleston Avenue near the Botanic Gardens but we don't make the gardens at all. The highlight of the afternoon is undoubtedly the Fred and Myrtle Flutey Paua Shell House at the Canterbury Museum. Before we can enter the zanily re-enacted house, we must sit through a six-minute film about them. We learn that the crazy couple collected hundreds (if not thousands) of Paua Shells over the years at their home in Bluff and that Fred polished them with his grinder before he hung them on these nails driven into their bare living room walls of their home.

Apparently, "No shill is loike enothaaa'," explains Fred on the screen.

Well, did you have to go and prove it ye big eejit? I'm wondering.

Anyway, when the terrible mini-documentary ends, to an awful organ-soundtrack, we go next door to the reconstructed living room. It incorporates all the weird little artefacts from the original house. Exactly, it's insanely obsessive, creepy and surreal, if not entirely harmless.

We head back towards the square and I go into this Vodaphone shop on one of the surrounding streets and buy a pretty basic Nokia mobile phone. It can make phone calls and send texts and it costs $120 so, great. I've been without a phone now for some weeks because the other thing finally packed in. I haven't missed it at all if I'm honest.

As we head back across Cathedral Square to our hostel, we're stopped by some preacher, a nice enough, well-meaning man who's wearing a hat not unlike an Akruba.

"Would ya loike ta take du Good Piii'son Tist?" he asks us.

We look at each other and shrug our shoulders in resignation as he shows us various laughable cards of people in a variety of scenarios. One bloke is yelling out of a car window and shaking his fist and another of a fist pointing a gun at somebody. He asks us what we think each one represents.

"Have eny of ya eva' loid?" he asks us.

Have eny of ya eva' stole enythin'?"

Mike, Josie and I answer "Yes" to each but Ben says "No" to all the questions.

"Well, ya sed ya never loid whin Oi asked ya so I know ya've loid," he tells Ben.

"En, ef ya've loid ta me wance (once), whoy should Oi believe that ya nod a thoif eitha'?" he says.

So he tells us all to repent and to ask God for forgiveness and, out of politeness really, we tell him that we will.

Though Ben's not too convinced.

It's later in the evening, as Ben and I go for a walk. He has already eaten but I haven't so he sits with me at a food court in a shopping Mall a couple of streets over from the hostel. It's after seven so the food has obviously been sitting there for some time. As a result, the beef in black bean sauce and fried rice I get is quite dried up but it only costs $7. This chest infection has me in its grip but nonetheless, my horns start poking through my head and I (stupidly, it has to be said) suggest going for a pint.

"Just the one mind," I add.

So we decide upon going to Mickey Finn's, this HUGE pool hall-come Irish themed bar-come music venue on Hereford St. We get a couple of pints and head down to the smoking area, talking to some arrogant – and not so subtly racist South Africans. There are four guys and one girl in their mid-twenties. One of them, Simon, who has a long floppy fringe and is wearing a black polo neck top, is a bit over zealous with the put-downs. So I feel it incumbent on myself to turn them back on him. (He later tells me that he was a "problem teen", sent here by his mother to an uncle because of his wild ways.)

I'm not feeling the Mae West (*The Best*) so after one pint I tell Ben that I'm ready to go home. I'm sick, mostly from eating crap, drinking too much and sleeping too little. Ben has a chest infection too; his is actually worse than mine. However, his interest in staying out heightens when two perky, hot little Kiwi girls arrive and sit at the table next to ours. It's not long before they join us. It turns out that one of them, Jodi, clearly has plans for Ben, who she keeps calling "Colen Faaa'll" (Colin Farrell).

The little Welsh fucker.

The other girl, Lorna, is a cute, short-haired blond with a killer figure and big brown eyes. After a while, we all end up going to some late night bar and then go on to Boogie Nights – a retro disco bar effort on Manchester St. And it's clear that the girls fancy our company over the South Africans. The girls are young, however. They're probably too young for me at any rate, though not for Ben I guess, who is ten years my junior. Jodi, who's celebrating her 21st Birthday, keeps asking Ben to move over to New Zealand and he's kind of playing along with her but the girl must be dreaming. The four of us break away from the others and head for brighter lights of "The Strep (strip)", thanks to Jodi, who goes on to tell us that she's originally from Essex in the UK. She says us that she needs to find an ATM but warns us that her wages might not be in situ just yet because it's just past midnight. It's now Friday. I'm starting to suspect that we're being taken for a ride here and, unfortunately, I don't mean that in any literal sense. I tell Ben, when I get a chance, and he's in agreement. These suspicions more-or-less turn out to be true when Lorna can't access her own funds because her Landlord has apparently taken out his rent. We go to a KFC and then Ben and I make our excuses and leave. I've already been carrying Ben, and I can't keep the bloody four of us going.

Jodi gives Ben her number and asks him to meet her at 3.30pm tomorrow.

"What finishes at 3.30?" Ben asks me, as we walk back to the hostel.

It takes me a few seconds to figure out where he's going with this.

Aha.

"SCHOOL...OH SHIT."

Narrow escape.

DAY FIFTY FOUR

I must change from my double room to a dorm this morning because it's already been booked. When I get to the room on the second floor, I find a double bed on a bottom bunk there so...SA-WEET! We go to the Botanic Gardens and then cross the road to a series of flat and perfectly kept green pastures in the huge park there. The pupils of Christ's College, an independent, Anglican secondary day and boarding school for boys. Many play rugby and cricket on the unending green nearby. Others not playing games slouch about; sporting their pristine school blazers and crisp white shirts. It's all very upper-middle class, quaint and a serious nod towards England's traditional public (meaning private) school system.

We choose a spot and crash in the afternoon sunshine for about forty minutes. Ben and I are feeling the effects of our respective ailments now and are still smoking the occasional cigarette in between bouts of coughing our lungs up. Idiots for sure but it's a dreadful addiction, isn't it?

It's early evening at Cathedral Square when we see our Preacher from yesterday. He's standing at the same spot outside Christchurch with his easel, obviously trying to get others to take his little "Good Piii'son Tist". We're trying to find the cinema and we can't look him in the eye because we're going to watch an evil movie. The lads want to go see *Saw VI*, and who would I be to stand in their way? We're trying to find a Hoyts Cinema and after searching for what seems like an Age, we see one of the Yellow Buses that will take us there for free.

However, when we finally get in the place, wherever it is, we're amazed at the particular brand of Kiwi ingenuity on offer. I tell the attendant that I want to see the movie: so far so good. I also want a large popcorn and coke – check. The lads are watching the moola so don't order any rubbish. I tell the guy "No" when he asks if we're all together. Of course we are all together but we're not *together* in any sense other than the fact that we're actually going to see it together. Unless it's cheaper to pretend that we're in a gay relationship.

Moving swiftly along...it's clearly not cheaper this way, so we're all paying separately. But he insists on charging us all-together and then deducting the relevant amounts that we must all hand over. Give me. STRENGTH! This country can be a bit backward in certain ways and this is a perfect example of what I mean.

Inside the theatre, it's all blood and gore and it's great stuff altogether. Crap movie, naturally, but as good as *crap* gets in a *Snakes on a Plane* kind of way. At one stage, Mike knocks my popcorn out of my hand (there was really no need, I'm sharing it out). He did it accidentally of course but the stuff is ALL over the floor. So the two lads start scooping the stuff up and eating it from their hands. It's hilarious, the boys reminding me of the Hobbits, Merry and what's-his-face (?) from the *Lord of The Rings* movies.

At the Base Hostel bar, I get talking to a girl I met in the lift (escalator) at our hostel in Queenstown a week ago. She comes up to me at midnight and wraps her arms around me so she's obviously keen then. Meanwhile, the lads meet English Colin, who was on our South Island bus. He's just back from a week's holidays in Sydney. I say my goodbyes to the Welsh lads, wishing them well for the rest of their travels in New Zealand and Oz. Said girl is English and her name is Marianne, as it happens. It's the last night that her group will be together and she asks me to meet her in one hour at the bar and "we'll go for a shag" in her room.

Well I never: the cheek of some people.

DAY FIFTY FIVE

Colin, who works at World Bar, is on my bus south back to Queenstown this morning. I was supposed to make sure he was up and indeed I did. However, I forgot that I didn't have his mobile number so I had to ring Ben (they we sharing the same dorm), and apologise for doing so. We're on a Newman's (Intercity) bus and this grey-haired driver with glasses as strong as – and I'm not joking here – a NASA telescope ticks our names off the sheet on his little clipboard. Colin and I have just bought our tickets inside the office and not on the Internet so our names are not on his little list and he appears thrown further than a javelin at the Olympics. The fact that we're clutching tickets (for God's sake) means little to him. He insists on putting everyone's bags on the coach for them so we must queue. Wouldn't want to upset his routine now would we? The order all seems...unnecessary, to Colin and I anyway (work practice study Numan's please!).

Our driver, Bob, is certainly a talker – a lot of these drivers are so, probably out of boredom if nothing else. He drones on about every little thing...in minutiae. Less than three hours after we've started, he tells us that he must stop at a nearby garage (somewhere), as he thinks "the wheels aaa' fawlin uff".

Say what now?

We exchange wide-eyed stares and then we think it's a joke. But he's not joking. This is how he actually delivered the news. He goes on to explain, after some time mind you, that the wheels were only fitted this morning and needed to be checked after so many miles. Yeah, right Bob, we believe you. After a while, we leave again and then stop at Lake Tekapo about forty-five minutes later – my second visit in four days. Here, I go into this restaurant, McKenzie's, and order a bowl of homemade soup. There are only about ten people here and all of them are already seated. I'm left waiting for thirty of your earth minutes for a bowl of bloody soup! FOR A BOWL OF SOUP? I'm sitting there and I'm annoyed, left wondering if they went to McKenzie's Scottish homestead to gather the ingredients for the homemade soup. I've only got another ten minutes before I'm due back on the bus. I can hear at least three voices coming from the kitchen, which begs the question as to, *What the hell are they doing in there?*

Back on-board, I don't want to hear Colin's theory that it's "probably made from scratch". Anyway, we're on the road again but with a different driver. So, Bob obviously just does the Christchurch to Lake Tekapo leg of the journey then. Our

257

Lake Tekapo to Queenstown driver tells us about his peanut allergy. Apparently, it's so strong that he would go into anaphylactic shock just from the odour. So we're curious as to why he drops us off at the fruit centre in Cromwell (I think) that, aside from fruit obviously, largely sells nougat and fucking nuts including fucking peanuts for fucksakes. Of course he doesn't go near the place but he lets us go 'nuts' (ba dum tssss!). I know Kiwis are known to be the adventure-loving sort but this is just sheer lunacy.

I come out with a bag of chilli nuts (flavoured with lime, allegedly) and climb on-board. I can't wait to open them to see what happens to the driver. Joking?? Of course I'm, eh, joking. I immediately tell him that I've bought the nuts and he tells me that it's fine once I don't open the bag. He's a very trusting man. So we're once again hurtling towards Queenstown.

We've just left the centre. I check the pockets in my shorts and realise that I've lost my phone, just as I remember taking it with me when I went in there.

The driver is understanding enough and tells the others through his headset. Maybe he's playing along because he knows that I have the nuts. Jaysus, it's like that movie with yer man, Keanu Reeves....*Speed,* that's it! *If you don't do an immediate U-Turn and take me back to the fruit centre, I WILL open the bag of nuts!!!*

I make my way back to my seat, apologising to the other passengers quietly. Damn it, forgot more stuff! This passenger, a Dublin girl, gives me her phone to call mine while I'm in there. But the staff have not seen it, it's not in the bathroom. Neither is it on the patch of slanted pavement that I sat on for a few minutes.

So I ring it. It rings a few times before someone answers.

"It's on the bus," the voice says. I embark and Colin is shaking his head as he hands it over. "Where was it?" I ask him.

"Under your hat, where you already looked for it," he goes – shaking his head.

"Bloody Irish," he adds.

There's little I can offer in my defence.

I'm back in Queenstown – at the Base hostel on Shotover St to be precise. I'm here because the Canadians, the Swedes and the Leeds lot are here.

DAY FIFTY SIX

I've arranged it for myself to stay in the dorm that the two Andres are bunked down in. Also, in this room, is this zany kid from New York City (Manhattan) and this English bloke who doesn't get out of bed for two days because he's sick. I'm not too ecstatic to be back at Base and as soon as the others move on, I'm out of here (providing that I'm still in Queenstown myself). This decision was made easier because of the carry-on just hours earlier. Fully grown men and women were chasing each other up and down the hall outside my room, even banging on my door. This only stopped when I went out and told them to.

Anyway, true to our Queenstown form, we spend today arsing about really. The most productive thing I do is to
wash my clothes, along with beating Leeds Chris at pool.

This evening, World Bar is celebrating its 13th Birthday by having a Nerds' Ball or something and I'm not too enthused. In fact, I'm as unimpressed about it as an old fart can be but I keep my mouth shut because Chris, Emma and the Canadian girls are eager and they go all out with their costumes, fair play to them. There is bet-down hair with single spikes of hair shooting straight up, checked shirts buttoned all the way up to the neck; there are braces and black-rimmed glasses and shorts that are worn with knee-high socks.

Chris, in particular, is very enthusiastic about the $1,500 bar tab on offer to the Nerd Herd. We have a couple of drinks at Altitude Bar and while the others remain, I join Carly on Crutches and Antonio in Buffalo Bar. I discover that two-for-one drinks are on offer here for residents of Southern Laughter, a nearby hostel on Isle St. This pair will stay here in this hostel for one month in total and we take turns producing their key at the bar to get drinks. Some follow us up here while others have gone to World Bar, with everybody coming home early enough because they're leaving for

Christchurch at 8.30am. Tonight, Chris #2 and the Canadian sisters are staying in my room because of some other loud, drunken idiots: two Norwegian guys who insisted on playing pumping techno at 4am and then challenging a complaining Chris when he asks them to stop.

Anyway, when I get back to Base, there are all these fire fighters outside the place and a few cops inside. The American Kid from my dorm is sitting on a sofa at Reception and he's got his head in his hands. He's flanked by two cops. He looks absolutely out of it.

Next to him is a plastic bag filled, literally, with the former contents of his stomach. He is also being read his rights. A short while later, the cops escort him back to our room to pick up his gear. The female officer tells me that he has set off a fire alarm there – though The Kid tells me that he has "no recollection of it". I tell them that "he's not a bad kid really but he's just a little messed up from the drinking" (shock, horror!) and though they seem sympathetic; they're escorting him out of Base and he's being arrested and charged (with some public order offence I imagine).

It's been a strange night of celebration. It's the last time I'll be seeing most of my fellow travellers, I expect. Can't sleep.

Oh yeah, it's after midnight; meaning that it's my Birthday!

13. To the End of the World...or Close Enough Anyway

DAY FIFTY SEVEN

I'm normally on top of these things but I can't, for the life of me, remember how old I've just turned. Perhaps the dementia has finally kicked in but the only thing I can remember is that if the two digits are added together, they make up the figure nine – apparently *my* number in numerological terms. So, I'm either 18, 45, 81 or 63 years-of-age. I'm sure that I haven't reached 90 yet. WAIT...of course. I'm 36, that's it. I'm sweaty and drained, and I'm coughing.

I'm still in bed, noting that it's a nice day outside when the door is suddenly flung open.

"CIARAN, yu'r always late coming down tu us; are yu staying another naight?"

The penny drops as soon as I recognise the whiny, faux-American accented female voice of the girl working at Reception.

"Actually, I'm not," I answer. "Well if yu'r nod down soon wu'll have tu charge you fur another naight."

But before I can utter my triumphantly-witty retort, she's gone.

"That told ya," offers the sick English lad.

It's like something out of a POW movie. I'd forgotten that the poor guy was even in the room until he just peeled back the duvet there for a second.

"Yeah well, she has my deposit," I go.

Of course if it had been such a movie, I'd have been saying, *Get some rest Jim, our boys are coming...it won't be too long now and we'll be back in Blighty...you, running through a glen with your lassie in your bonnie homestead...and me, lost in the arms of my precious Cassandra. You just have to hold on Jim...must...hold...on...Jim. JIM.*

(Shakes Jim's shoulders vigorously).

JIIIIIIIIIIIIIIIIIIIIIIIIIIIIIIIIIIIIIIIIIIIIIIM!!!

261

I get my stuff together and check out, before heading up to a smaller and much more laid back hostel, Southern Laughter. I book into this double room that shares a common area incorporating shared bathroom, kitchen and TV area. There's a dorm next door. The room costs me $52 and the dorm costs $27; the same as Base really.

This afternoon, I go to the Pig & Whistle, as agreed with Marianne in a text last night. I have a cappuccino, then a Steinlager, before Marianne comes out with these weird shots she's apparently invented or something. It's Southern Comfort, mixed with some butterscotch liqueur and Captain Morgan's rum. After this, it's another lager. There's about seven or eight of us (mostly locals) sitting outside in the beergarden, soaking up the sun, the beer and the laughter – even if the banter mimics that of Saturday last.

Millionaire Mike, a local builder who runs The Show itself – or so he would tell you anyway – shows us some of the scars he received on the way home last night. Apparently he was attacked from behind by a few muggers. He was struck with some implement or other and the gang only scattered when a girl started screaming, he tells us.

Then, Marianne tells me that she has to go and buy a Birthday present for her friend, Rosa.

I go and get this really rancid (yet effective) cough mixture called Buckley's in a local pharmacy. The menthol and ammonia vapours are enough to cure you, if they don't choke you first. Talk about going for the burn. Then, I go back to the Pig' to see New Zealand beat Bahrain 1- 0 to qualify for the World Cup. The Kiwis are delighted and I'm delighted for them. Yes, that was a soccer match!

Monty's is next on the cards and local musician, Kane, is playing fantastically as per usual. I meet this Kiwi woman at the bar and it turns out that she's celebrating her 37th Birthday tomorrow. She tells me that she lived and worked in Dublin "for years" (though I actually thought she was Irish because of her flawless accent). We have a joint celebration with her two friends and a couple of nice English blokes and things liven up after a couple of rounds of shots. One of Birthday Girl's friends – who says her name is Georgie – tells me how she split up with her husband two weeks ago.

She actually complains like this: "Kiwi wimmen don' wunt eny uf that soft-cock staff loike flowaaa's en' chocs but, I oftin hear abaaa't my frinds' husbinds runnin' baths for 'um whin they cam' home frum wuuu'k." This lot are well messy and don't seem to know whether they're coming or going so I leave them to their confusion, in exchange for the company of three younger American girls. We all go to Buffalo Bar for *my* Birthday drinks, though I buy the vodka and Red Bulls. Here, one of the girls asks me for my passport and hands it to the barman as proof of my Birthday and scores us a free round of Jäger Bombs. It was her round so it's kind of sneaky (or at least enterprising) but sure you'd have to laugh it off really. Another of the girls then buys more 'bombs before we go to World Bar. While here, we score some teapots filled with Devil Juice and the rest as they say, is @~#%"$(o.

DAY FIFTY EIGHT

It's a Sick Sunday and that's for sure. I really should be taking better care of myself. I have a bottle of antibiotics in my bag that I've brought from home but there's only half left as I gave some to Alex when we were touring southwards because she was sick. Then, I gave Ben a few more. I start taking the things though I'm sceptical about them working, not that they'll be any good to anybody when the superbugs get a grip on the world and the zombies rule All. Either way, I need to clear the cobwebs so a walk followed by a pint should do it. I walk down Shotover St. towards the harbour, circling Lake Wakatipu as I pass on by towards Queenstown Gardens. It's a bit blustery today with an occasional few drops of rain. The Remarkables look...well...remarkable in the background while to the fore, the *TSS Earnslaw* (a steamer used for ferrying tourists about the lake) chugs confidently along the icy-blue glistening sheet. I stare at the foam on the peaks of the Earnslaw's wake. It's a clear day, which contrasts starkly with my heavy head this morning. The water laps the shore in endless, broken, confused waves.

The wind is picking up as I stop at the car park on the side of the road. Various vehicles – mostly campervans and coaches – pass me by. Most of these are heading towards Glenorchy, about forty four kilometres north-west of here. The sky looks threatening so I decide to head back towards town. I stop at Pub on Wharf when I hear some fine ballads wafting out of the place.

Inside, a friendly barmaid agrees to give me a hot chocolate. Brad, from the Pig & Whistle, is here. He's sipping a pint with a guy and a girl. We exchange pleasantries as I take a seat at the bar. An Irish guy with fiery red hair who's standing there waiting to be served, watches Brad put on his jacket. It's black with pink lining.

"Love de colour," he tells him. "It REALLY brings out yer eyes."

I offer: "If you'd seen how many fuckin' pints he had last night, you'd know why his eyes are pink."

It gets a brief spike of laughter and sure it warrants that at least.

I look at my watch. Funnily enough, it's beer o'clock. I order a pint of Sassy Red, which costs me $7 and is a bitter but I suspect it's quite high in terms of alcohol content. After some mild flirtations with the female bartender I see Marianne's friend from home, John, coming in through the door.

I buy him a drink. He's leaving for Oz in a few days and even though he invites me for goodbye drinks with them all tomorrow night at Surreal Bar; I already know that I won't be there.

I go to Monty's, read over excerpts from my diary and spend my time writing out the names of bands and books for Scottish barmaid, Holly (my dog's name, actually). She has asked me to do this and I find it a bit strange but at least it helps me to re-focus my mind.

Kane is playing this afternoon. I get talking to a Californian couple, Maybeth and Casey, who have just arrived. I'm relaxed now. And I'm drinking again, but slowly. I'm just sipping.

It's early evening when I head for Fergburger and buy one of the huge, legendary cow sandwiches and onion rings. I enjoy the grub but I have to enlist a bottle of Gaviscon in an intense heartburn battle afterwards.

DAY FIFTY NINE

I'm having a lazy morning, as is fast becoming the habit and in the afternoon – following a lunch of tomato soup and a pork loin sandwich at Pub on Wharf costing me $20 – I go for a walk along the same stretch as yesterday. However, instead of heading over to the gardens, I stay on the town side and opt for a walk up Fernhill. I actually intend on going up the challenging Ben Lomand trail but I'm sweating like an orange on a radiator, short of breath and my heart is going ten-to-the-dozen, as we'd say back home. It's the chest infection: I should be taking much better care of myself but I'd rather be out-and-about than stuck in bed. Sickness or not. I stop at a bench to rest a few hundred metres up and take the opportunity to get some scribing done. I spend over ninety minutes here, lifting my head only when walkers pass by.

I leave when I get cold.

I go to Alpine supermarket on Shotover St. and procure some provisions. Back at Southern Laughter I throw together a salad and have some pasta. All manner of nationalities (mostly English though) are good-naturedly manoeuvring the small space as they attempt to prepare dinner, which is made from various ingredients taken from these cotton storage bags they give you to store your food away in the kitchen. There's a large pot of potato soup simmering on the hob for the poor backpackers so I indulge in this also. At the table, I meet a couple of Swedish girls and a Polish guy whose name I can't, for the life of me, pronounce.

Everything's going okay until he finds out that I'm Irish. "The problem is that Engleesh people arun't educated about Aireland," he just goes, obviously referring to the northern question.

Here we feckin' go.

There are a couple of English people sitting around the large table with us and there's about eight more in the TV/Movie room – just metres away. I tell him that I

265

don't want to discuss the issue. However, he continues on so I repeat myself, probably a bit too forcibly. I mean, the guy means well and I largely agree with what he's saying but, as I've just told him, "I do not want to talk about this."

There are a few Germans about the place too but you don't hear me banging on about the occupation and subsequent persecution of Poland.

DAY SIXTY

I get the public bus out to Frankton and spend about ninety minutes here, waiting for my connecting bus to beautiful Arrowtown. I had intended to browse around Remarkables Park – one of the stop-off points on the way – but the concrete Mall looked unremarkable to me.

Frankton is a strange little place a hub of Queenstown really. There are two Franktons in New Zealand. There's one in Waikato, near Hamilton on the North Island and the other is here in Otago, near Queenstown. That is all. Seriously though, there doesn't appear to be much to do here. Anyway, I'm still under the weather and want to keep what energy I do have for Arrowtown. So, what better way to burn off some frustration than to whack some balls about the place?

Of course I meant Golf balls. Baddabing!

I pad over to the driving range near the bus shelter and though I'm not much of a golfer, I rent out fifty balls for just $5, which seems like a bargain to me. I've chosen a couple of Drivers; a 1-wood and a 3-wood, to be precise. I've taken a 5-iron and an 8-iron for good measure. It is literally hit-or-miss with the clubs though. I slice them and I hook them with the Drivers, though occasionally I hit them straight up the range – over 200 metres in distance on a few occasions.

It is more *miss* than *hit*, however, with the 5-iron. My first five attempts with the club are fruitless, the iron striking the ground instead of the ball. I'm starting to feel like Adam Sandler's character, *Happy Gilmore*, from the movie of the same name. I'm the only one there at the moment and I imagine that I can feel the stares and hear the laughter from the conversation between the members and the guy working in the shop, just metres behind the glass-panelled door behind me. I'm more successful with the 8-iron though and I lob most of these over 100 metres along before they even hit the grass. To my mind, I feel as if I'm single-handedly undoing the good reputation that has been built up by Irish golfers such as Padraig Harrington, Darren Clarke, Graeme McDowell and Rory McIlroy in recent years. However, I do enjoy myself.

The last bus back into Queenstown is at four, the driver tells us as we disembark at Arrowtown. So that gives me two hours and thirty earthling minutes, which I'm okay with. I haven't the energy for any hikes or such. The place is inundated with tourists, little wonder really because the place is beautiful. The majority of these seem to be couples of the retired variety. With large, broad-brimmed hats (and other headwear) and sunglasses on, they stroll about the place – eating ice creams and looking for some of the numerous trails on offer or something to aim their cameras at. Both are fairly accessible.

And there are plenty of families.

I go looking for a decent eatery, and I settle for a smart-looking place called Saffron on Buckingham St. The owner (I suspect) is sitting at this wooden bench outside with her children and they appear to be planning some party or event for the weekend. They don't seem to spot me eyeing up the specials menu. There's a choice of two courses from the starter, main and desert (menu). This is probably expensive by New Zealand standards but good enough value considering the type of restaurant that it seems to be. I'm fed up waiting for someone to notice me so I go over to them and have to ask them for a table. Not impressed-dotcom. In fact, as I'm sitting in the shade under a large sun-brella (as I call them) and waiting for my food, quite a few tourists stop to look at the menu board but then push on when they're left standing. Generalisations aside, New Zealanders can be so bloody lazy – or laid back if I'm very generous – in my experience.

I choose this gorgeous omelette with salad for starters and shoulder of lamb with potatoes for the main course. I pass on desert. Well who wouldn't, at about $15 a pop. I've been a good boy and opted for water over wine. The sun is baking these old, white-washed wooden houses that look as if they belong in the Wild West, way back when. Indeed, it gives the place a very quaint feel in obvious homage to the

1860s – when the town was born out of its gold mining activities. One of the highly recommended attractions on offer here is the Chinese settlement, though I don't have enough time to check this out properly. Instead, I go on part of one of the walks; along the Arrow River towards Macetown, which is fourteen kilometres north of here. The clear and cool water shines on the flat stones on the bottom of the shallow stream. The slow-moving water is framed by rocky inclines that lead up to pancake-type cliffs, while the snowy peaks of the Remarkables provide the perfect backdrop to this masterpiece. "Unspoilt" does not do the scene justice. To me, the place looks as if human eyes have never landed on this: I actually don't believe the natural beauty before my own eyes. I've said this a few times now, haven't I? New Zealand is that visually attractive.

As I've said, you're not meant to remove stones from here and I don't but I pick up a stone from the bed of the steam and look at it closely. Its mineral composites, whatever they are, give particles of the stone a shiny appearance, rendering it like some curious jewel to the naked eye. Little wonder they don't want you taking their stones from their natural habitat and so on. Of course, Arrowtown is a mining town. During its gold rush heyday, the population of Arrowtown grew to above 7,000 people and towns such as Macetown and Skippers took the overflow. However, fast forward one hundred years to the 1960s and at one point there's less than 200 people living here, while Macetown, Skippers and Bullendale are ghost towns.

Today, Arrowtown seems to be buzzing.

There were over 3,500 Chinese people living in Otago in 1874, according to the Census figures at that time. The overwhelming majority of these were men and the first Chinese women did not arrive in New Zealand until a year earlier. But get this...twenty two years later, in 1896, there were only eleven Chinese females living throughout the whole country.

Most of the Chinese would have lived here on the periphery of the European settlements and around their mining spots.

I get the bus back in and have a coffee in Monty's followed by a pint in Pub on Wharf. Back at Southern Laughter I again eat some of the free soup before finishing off the Tortellini from yesterday.

Back in my dorm I meet an English man in his 60s who's wearing round glasses, a long silver ponytail and looks like he's been sponsored by Low Alpine, such is his evident love of their clothing. Kevin, clearly an old school hippy, has lived in both Sweden and South Africa for most of his adult life. We get talking and he turns out be an interesting man. It turns out that he's cycled most of the way down here from Cape Reinga (at the tip of the North Island, if you remember) and he's due to take a two-day trip to Milford Sound in the morning.

Quite a bloke.

During our conversation, he takes out something from under his bottom bunk opposite that he calls "a backpacker's guitar" and just starts playing and singing. Haha...this is just class. If you can imagine that a regular acoustic guitar as a Volkswagen Beetle, well then this would be a three-wheeled Reliant Robin. (If you don't know what this is, go look at the Trotters' T.I.T. mobile in some episodes of the classic British comedy, *Only Fools and Horses*.) Anyway, Kevin asks me if I can play guitar and when I tell him that "I can", he just hands the thing to me. It's a long and narrow instrument and very, very weird.

He takes it back after a while and goes off to have some sort of jam session with some Swedish people and I go to bed to try and sleep off my sickness. I've never been to a *Swedish* jam session. I imagine them laying on the ground: all of them zonked, their faces smattered with sticky jam; some of them rolling, groaning, sweating and puking, while others writhe about the room in ecstasy.

Sometime in the early hours, I'm woken by a drunken English couple who come trundling into the room and start stripping off. Loudly. I am NOT impressed when they jump into the bunk on top of me. Actually, when I left the room at the previous lunchtime, the bed was vacant so I took the duvet and pillow from it because it gets bloody cold at night here. I'm dazed when I'm woken and Kevin is in the bunk opposite and he's shining his torch on them.

269

"The Waila's was wicked man," the guy says to Kevin in thick Cockney.

Bob Marley's old band, The Wailers, earlier played at Memorial Hall nearby, while Akil from Jurassic 5 performed at Revolver on Shotover St. afterwards.

"They was so well rehearsed," the guy continues.

I get up and ask them if they want their duvet and pillow back but they decline – probably because they have those belonging to her bed. When they've finished talking with Kevin, they start kissing and he's basically trying to shag the girl. The bed sounds like a trampoline with rusty springs at some fat camp during an exercise session.

But she obviously won't let him. And thank God for that. I would never begrudge a man his way, unless, of course, I'm not having mine.

DAY SIXTY ONE

I'm feeling awful this morning; the antibiotics don't seem to be up to much. I've thrown on my boardies and a tee-shirt and I'm heading up to the kitchen before this pair wake up. Kevin is gone but the noisy couple are crashed out in the bunk over mine.

"Sorry mate," says the clown on the top bunk. "Do ya 'ave moy phowne?"

I stop at the door and look over at him – all I can see is his stupid head sticking up at the top of the duvet that's thrown over them and four feet protruding from the end.

"Sorry?" I ask him, the blood rising a bit. "How do you mean; 'Do I have your phone?' What would I be doing with your phone?"

"Oh, I hurd ya mamble somthin' about a phone an' then gettin' oudda bed jurin' (during) de noigh'."

I'm trying to stay calm but I can't believe the cheek of the guy. He's clearly not the brightest tool in the shed.

"Yeah, MY phone was charging and then I got out of bed to use it," I tell him. It has a handy torch feature on it and I needed it to go to the bathroom, quietly...pity he wasn't as courteous at about 3am.

I add: "Is that alright with you?"

"Ow, 'c-course; sorry."

"I'll be back in about half-an-hour," I tell the idiot before leaving the room. Well, I'd rather give them space than have to deal with their crap. So I chill out in the TV room after breakfast and watch some God-awful movie with a cool Norwegian guy. Then, I go and move into the Love Shack, which is a twin room downstairs with sliding patio doors as an entrance. It has a TV boasting of fifty fuzzy channels along with tea and coffee-making facilities. If I'm to rest and recover from my malaise, I need some quietness. The Love Shack costs over $50 but it's a quiet spot, even though I feel as if I'm living in someone's garage extension.

I empty my backpack and manbag of their contents and decide to wash everything, including the receptacles themselves. This will be the first time that the bags have been washed since I left the Small Dog. The backpack smells – not of anything putrid as such but of these herbal vitamins (yes, they're just vitamins) that I've brought with me from Ireland. I've dropped some of them into it and they render the bag smelly in a strange way. And oh yeah, there's probably the reek of about eight weeks of washing hanging around also. I do wash clothes about twice every week and place the dirty stuff in a large cellophane laundry bag but you know what I mean.

I get my house in order, as it were, and I just chill. I go for a short walk in the glorious afternoon sunshine but I'm feeling weak enough. Carly-on-Crutches and Antonio are down by the lake and I stop to talk to them briefly. Then, Will from World Bar comes up to me and he's in great form. It's exhausting, so I grab a McDonald's and head back to the hostel. After remaining in my room for a few hours, I'm bored out of my wits and feel tempted to go see The Wailers, who are playing at Memorial Hall, which is just down the road and around the corner really. I text Holly, who was at both gigs last night and she says that "Akil was only okay", though "it was flattering to get a Shout Out from him". Marianne got a free ticket for last night's gig and texts me to say that The Wailers were "class" and that a dub reggae band from Invercargill who supported them, were "deadly", meaning good back home, as opposed to *lethal* or *dangerous*.

271

It's 8pm, and I'm at Memorial Hall. I'm feeling pretty shook and sweaty but guess what? I'm going to see and hear The Wailers. The venue is a sports hall or gymnasium that you'd see at a decent-sized school or sports hall. And that's what the hall seems to be. The smoking area outside overlooks the immaculate and spacious Wakatipu Rugby Club grounds. The place has balconies, cool balconies that flank each side of the dancefloor and run down to the stage at the front, beneath.

Cans of Max Gold and Speights beers are on sale for $5, while soft drinks are $3 each. But I'm not drinking so I stick to Sprite. The place is slow to fill up but by the time the support band, Rhythmonyx take to the stage, the place is jointed. The band, I count nine of them though I could be seeing double because of my malaise, are very tight. A soulful and funky sound emanates from the collective – though I feel an overhaul in image and something to finish off the sound wouldn't go amiss. God knows there are enough of them to do so. They are a really good band, however. They kind of remind me of The Kelly Bell Blues Band, who I used to go see play in Baltimore, Maryland, when I was living in the US in 2000.

Rhythmonyx have a wild crew following them. One Wall of a man, a Maori, the singer's cousin I hear someone say, is bouncing about indiscriminately in front of the stage. He's got a baseball hat on backwards and fancies a bit of moshing. But he's the kind of guy who would flatten everyone – not necessarily out of meanness but simply because you got in his way.

Two modes: flatten, stop flattening.

Then, The Wailers take to the stage and by now, I'm fit to drop. Although, the first song they play is *Stir it Up*, which is actually one of my favourite songs of all time. Most of the more popular songs are played and some new ones also. The band is awesome, tighter than Joan River's face, and it's a great performance.

Meanwhile, Marianne has text me to ask me what I think of Rhythmonyx and I we end up making arrangements to have dinner with her on Friday night. It's Wednesday, isn't it?

Anyway, the lights in the venue are very strong and they don't seem to be too well operated. I'm blinded by a green light, then I'm bathing in blue before I'm stuck on an orange light as I work my way to the front. I'm following the potent and unmistakeable smell of weed, though I don't actually want any. The smell lingers at the steps – to the side of the hall, leading up to the balcony – and the Bouncers standing there don't seem bothered at all. Perhaps they're resigned to it because they don't bat an eyelid or twitch a nostril.

After a couple of hours, including an encore; the band leaves the stage. I'm as sick as a doctor's waiting room in January now, so I leave and head for a Fergburger – though I actually get some of their gorgeous onion rings. However, while I'm waiting for my number to be called (from the hatch opening on Shotover St.), this Maori woman starts randomly talking to me and telling me that her grandmother "is Muuu'phy from Oi'land".

"Here we go," I tell myself, laughing. Another Irish-Maori hybrid. Of course I play along with her. When I'm crossing the road and up the awesome, well-lit *Steps to Heaven* (as I have been calling them) on Brecon St., she's shouting, "G'NOIGHT MUUU'PHY!" across to me.

Strange day.

DAY SIXTY TWO

Last night I asked my mother to text me the result of the Rep. of Ireland v France World Cup 2010 qualifier at Stade de France in Paris because nowhere here appears to be showing it and it's happening in the morning. Morning time here, that is! She texts me and tells me that "Ireland have won the game 1-0" and I'm over the moon because our hopes of qualifying for the finals in South Africa next summer are still very much Alive-Alive-O'. (Apparently, Lily has been watching the game with her sister, Peggy, at her house in Waterford city.) I should mention that the game is the second leg in the qualifiers and that Ireland faced them on the back of a 1-0 defeat in Croke Park, Dublin.

Oh, there's another phone call.

SHIIIIIT! It turns out that she called me at full time. However, France came back in extra time and scored – in the 103rd minute. Lily thought it was all over, but it wasn't. Thierry Henry handed down a ball to Gallas in the box and he scored with his head. And, Henry (the little shit) was apparently offside anyway. I need to see this so I rush over to the Ministry of Sport in the vain hope that they will now show it. But alas, Non. Down I go to the bungee centre on Shotover St., and I get to one of the Macs (Internet access is free to Jumpers). I hate bloody Macs but this is no time for pedantics. On Facebook, somebody's already set up a group called "Thierry Henry is a Cheat" so I immediately join it to see footage of the controversial goal. And there it is: a clearly-offside Henry palms the ball across the goal line into open space with Gallas unmarked. He heads it down and past our goalkeeper, Shay Given. Even Henry admits that it wasn't a goal after the event. The Football Association of Ireland (FAI) has made calls for the match to be replayed.

I'm gutted.

I've been moved from the Love Shack into another dorm on the other side of the complex, because the shack has already been booked for this evening. It's on the upper deck on the outer building, if you will.

I go out for a few hours and when I return, there's an English girl in the four-bed dorm. Kim, from Oxford, has been working in a hostel in Christchurch and is on a "mini tour" of the South Island before she moves to Oz for another year. She's glued to the TV. *Home and Away* is followed by *Who Wants to be a Millionaire* (both British and New Zealand versions), then bloody *Wife Swap*. I make a stir fry in the kitchen unit and give her some of it. We have a chat and then I decide to pop down for a bottle of wine.

We're having a drink when the door flings open suddenly and in walk these two guys. They introduce themselves and I can't pronounce their names. Though I think that I can place the accents.

Time stands still.

"Where are you from?" I ask the taller, blond one.

"FR-

No.

"-AN

NO.

"-CE.

NOOOOOOOOOOOOOOOOOOOOOOO!

(That's FRANCE in case you didn't get it.)

JESUS!

"YOU FUCKERS," I spit, as they double up in laughter. So I warn the lads to "sleep with one eye open" and later, when I'm smoking with Kim on the decking outside; the taller, blond one comes out singing, "Zere's ownly one Thierry Hen-reeey; one Thier-ey Hen-reeey..."

"There'll be no fuckin' Thierry Henry if I get my hands on him," I tell them. We do have a good laugh about it though and in the main, we hit it off. The French lads head out to Buffalo Bar where, as I've mentioned, there's two-for-one drinks for Southern Laughter residents. They ask me if I want to join them but I'm wrecked and need a quiet night.

They come back shortly before 3am. It's not long since I've drifted off and they wake me when they stumble into the dorm. But just as I'm nodding off again, the building suddenly shakes me from my pending slumber. Violently. The vibration seems to be moving from *my* end of the building to *theirs*. Kim, also on the other end, doesn't budge but the lads raise their heads.

"It's an earthquake," I tell them. "Fucking cool eh?" (I realise that since this has happened, those in Haiti and in Christchurch wouldn't agree and who would blame them, considering what they've gone through as a result of the earthquakes there. However, this was our reaction at this time.)

As for Kim, an earthquake couldn't wake her. Like, literally.

DAY SIXTY THREE

The earthquake was over in about thirty seconds and this morning on the TV news, I find out that there were two – one in South Queenstown and one in Amberley, Canterbury, measuring 3.6 and 4.2 respectively on the Richter Scale. Apparently the

275

Queenstown 'quake was about half of the intensity of the earthquake that occurred in the country earlier in the year. In a weird coincidence, Kim and I had spoken about this just hours before it happened.

It's a scorcher. It's late afternoon when I meet Colin for a drink at Monty's. We also go for one in Pub on Wharf before they go to play Frisbee Golf or some other nonsensical game (on a course, by the way) in Queenstown Gardens on the other side of Lake Wakatipu.

This evening, I'm meeting Marianne for dinner at Luciano's, a decent enough Italian job on Steamer Wharf whose walls are splashed with various Italian notorieties and Hollywood gangsters from previous decades – cheesy slogans spouting from their mouths. I wonder if somewhere, sometime in the future; similar words of so-called wisdom from Limerick or Dublin gangsters' mouths, or from those of the National Front for example, will appear as murals in various eateries around the world. Somehow, I doubt it. We know better than to glorify mindless thuggery these days, don't we? Don't answer that. Anyway, I'm waiting in Atlas Beer Cafè – a funky little bar that also serves food – next to the restaurant. I order an Emerson's Red and chill.

This bloke sitting next to me pipes up. "Sew, wheee'y ya frum?"

I tell him that I'm from Ireland and he says he's from Melbourne, though he hates the Aussies and thinks of himself as a Kiwi. *Traitor*. This is something I've seen down here (more an Aussie problem than a New Zealand one, I'm noticing) and It's my opinion that anyone who betrays his country without good reason (and it better be good) should be shot! That's right, shot! So the guy tells me that he's a former rugby player and yada-yada-yada and he nearly has a meltdown when I tell him that I used to play second row forward or "lock forward" as we used to call it. His whole demeanour changes; he thought I'd have been a wing forward or "flanker". Better not tell him that I also played as a winger when I started or he might just throw himself (or me) in the lake.

There are these pane-less windows in the joint. We are sitting, drinks and elbows resting along this ledge facing onto the lake. We get talking to these girls (one of whom is from Cork) who are sitting outside smoking and some European chap there joins in. We talk about the ridiculous referring decision in the Rep. of Ireland v France game, if that's what you'd call it. They ask the Irish girl and I if we can speak Irish so she asks me, "An bhfuil cead agam dul go dtí an leithreas?" and I start laughing. Every child has asked a teacher this in primary school back in the Small Dog.

It basically means, "Can I go to the toilet?"

Marianne turns up during this to-and-fro and gets herself a glass of white wine before I can reach the bar. It's gone 9pm, we go next door for dinner. I have a pumpkin salad and steak and she has broth followed by sole and she declines desert, while I have apple crumble. Of course, there's a couple of bottles of the local pino gris. One cappuccino and latte later and I'm asked to pay $182 (or about €90) and that's not cheap by New Zealand standards but the food, the service, the company and the surroundings were all very nice so I'm happy enough.

We go to the Pig & Whistle, where she assures me that "they are all on it". *It* meaning "The Piss". Una is working here tonight while Catherine (also on tour) and Eileen (living with Una here in QT), are also at the 'Pig.

There seems to be more Waterfordians here than even Kiwis, tongught. I get talking to Eileen and although I don't know her from home, I learn that I went to school with her brother Matt – a genuinely nice bloke – at De La Salle College in Waterford. It's a small world and all that. She calls him on her phone while he's at work back home – where, at 13 hours behind, it is not yet *today* meaning Saturday there, if you will. We chat briefly, though I can barely hear him because of the noise here.

Marianne has to work (later) in the morning so she goes home early, after midnight, while I go to Surreal with the Waterford lasses. Brad is supposed to come with us but he's more twisted than a thing that got very twisted indeed so he can't join us.

We mosey on to World Bar, where I secure a (gratis) teapot with Jägermeister, vodka and Red Bull in it, courtesy of the Hospitality Bar.

Ding-Ding-Ding. Time for *Tea*.

DAY SIXTY FOUR

The man with the little hammer is certainly earning his bacon today. I do little with the day, except go to Alpine supermarket for provisions and feed the hangover with a litre of orange juice, a large bacon and cheese Ciabatta, a large tub of Pringles and numerous cups of tea. It's gluttony of huge proportions but I don't care. I need to soak it up and hydrate. In the shared living (dead) area at our lodgings, I meet a sound Japanese guy called Yohei who's staying in the dorm there.

I'm at Cow – a pizza joint on Cow Lane. It's busier than the proverbial hive and they don't seem to have a free table. But they offer me a space at the bar when I ask them for directions to Winnies, their arch-enemy. I get talking to a girl and two guys from Cork who have stopped off here for a few months apparently. We get chatting and finally get seated together. The pizza is fairly good but it's expensive. An eleven-inch pizza with one extra topping of pineapple, a coke and a bottle of ale, costs me nearly $35.

After a beer at Monty's Bar, I go back to the hostel and I watch *Clerks 2* on TV with this Spanish guy. I've seen it before but it's hilarious. I love the *Clerks* series. I'm sipping a glass of this Jacob's Creek sparkling white wine that I've purchased in a bottle shop yesterday. I text my sisters (Lorraine and Liz) before I crash out. I'm woken when one of the chaps from the dorm makes his way past me en route to the bathroom at stupid o'clock.

The TV is buzzy. I get up, turn it off and stumble into bed.

DAY SIXTY FIVE

It's Sunday so that means one thing. I go to the Ministry of Sport to watch the mighty All-Blacks take on England as part of their European tour. And I drink a pint of Coca

Cola (coke if you will) so I do, so I do. Then I order lasagne, chips and another coke and – all of this – costs, like, $16 or about €8. An unbelievable bargain, so it, so it is. In case you're wondering what the "so I do(s)" and "so it is(s)" are about; why they're a nod towards how some of the older or rural people in Ireland *spake*.

Anyway, the place looks kind of like an arcade or cheesy bowling alley except, instead of pinball machines, bowling lanes and video games; there are both massive screens and small(er) screens. And of course there's a bar, tables and seating. It's not the kind of place you'd bring a girl on a date, which makes it perfect for viewing sports. The "Oll-Blecks" take down England handily, while on a big screen in the centre, Scotland defeat Australia 9-8 at Murrayfield – for the first time in 27 years, apparently. Good on them.

New Zealand beat England 19-6 in an unremarkable game. Meanwhile, Manchester United is taking on Everton (in a Premiership clash) on another big screen nearby so I have one eye on the rugger and one on the football. That's soccer to you Americans. Actually, some American Football game is being shown on another big screen and there's a family of American tourists watching it. I should mention that all of these games are of course, NOT live but are being shown several hours later.

I'm a massive Man. Utd fan and so is my friend Leonard so I text him to tell him I'm watching the match and when I ask him how our friend Conor's stag night went, he just texts me back the result of the game, "3-0".

The little shit.

"Ye little fucker," I send in reply.

"Haws," he goes, meaning "Haw Haw!"

I then watch Ireland give Fiji a second-half masterclass in the sport of rugby, hammering them by 41-6. I go for the now (almost)-daily walk around Queenstown Gardens, followed with a coffee in Monty's.

At the Pig & Whistle I order possibly the spiciest (virgin) Bloody Mary that I've ever tasted. Is Marianne trying to poison me? Ha. Over dinner on Friday, when I said that I'm going to go Mad Dog River Boarding she told me that she wanted to go.

However, now she says that she can't do it. Either way, I'm chomping at the bit, though it turns out that the thing is far more hardcore than I'd imagined. Even when Damo, an English chap who drinks in the 'Pig, told us that "people have died" doing it, I wasn't deterred. Hmmm, that's unlike me!

Andrew, Rosa, Neil, the boys' parents, Pat and Barbara; Brad, Darragh and some others, are all here. Everywhere is drenched in sun and some chilled sounds wash over us, as we sit in the beergarden outside.

This means one thing: cider! Monteith's with ice on the side, in fact. It's a heavenly drink. A group of about fifteen Irish and Australian folk come along and we have some banter with them. They are on a tour down to Milford Sound and are being led by a couple from Co. Wexford, my neighbouring county back home. The couple been living in Sydney for twenty years and there's no sign of them having lost their accents. I joke with the group about them being a brave bunch to let a Wexford man lead the way.

I'm a bit sunburnt and well, shook from the drink. And the slightly-improved chest infection lingers yet so, after a couple of ciders, I bid my farewells and hit the trail. Onion rings from Fergburger, a glass of vino roja from Yohei and some bread with cheese on it, make up my nutritious (not) yet delicious meal. A Polish guy whose name I don't get has moved into my dorm. He tells me that he's hitchhiking around New Zealand and the nutter has forsaken a $30 fare for a Christchurch-Queenstown bus journey, to hitchhike his way down here.

"De monay is butter (better) in moy pockit," he says in his thick and charming Polish accent.

Butter? *Well spread it around then, man.* Of course, I don't actually say this.

14. A Few Tunes, Mad Dogs and an Irishman

DAY SIXTY SIX

This morning, I go down to the office/shop on Shotover St. and book my Mad Dog' for tomorrow. It costs $149, which is not cheap by the country's standards but then again, this is Queenstown so that's to be expected.

It's Queenstown Gardens again, and the aim today is to take some photos – though, my camera is acting up, being temperamental. Sometimes it will work, other times, not. I take the trail around Lake Wakatipu and it's fairly blustery. The wind churns up the water before me and around me, while the trees behind me sway heavily in the breeze.

I'm journaling.

I'm there for over an hour and the view of Queenstown across the lake opposite is a good one. Various tourists pass by and suddenly, the beacon to attract the attentions of the local (apparently voluntary) fire-fighters goes off...AGAIN! It's like, the third day in a row and it has gone off now several times while I've been here. It sounds like some WWII air raid siren which I've obviously only heard in movies and documentaries. I'm not *that* old, thanks. My mother's father, Thomas Russell, did, however. He worked in London during the blitzkrieg bombings and also served as an ARP (*Air Raid Precautions*, which became known as the *Civil Defence*).

The alarm consists of three shrill winding sounds – you know the one – and it makes me laugh as it sounds so old-fashioned. I mean, has this town not heard of pagers and mobile phones. Am I missing something here; is there a good explanation? It's strange but not for the first time here, I think of the place as a trap. A kind of haven for those who seem to be running away from something. That's my tuppence worth, anyway.

I stop at Monty's for a cider on the way home, before going to Alpine and getting the ingredients to make spaghetti bolognaise. However, as usual, I make enough for two and glutton that I am, I eat all of it. Then, I get the meat sweats and I have to lie down.

I'm awake and it's 9pm – so two hours have passed – and about an hour after this I decide to go use the Internet at the Base Hostel and perhaps have a nightcap (just the one mind) in The Thirsty Ram next door. So that's what I do. Except, as I'm walking up the steps I'm met with about one hundred blind folk being led by an equal number of sighted people. A sea of them is working their way down and it is indeed a bizarre sight. Of course I realise that my tour-buds Colin and Will must be somehow involved and I'm not wrong. It's a bar crawl organised by the YHA Hostel and Will is at the centre of it all – dressed as...looking like...he basically looks like a cross between Björn Borg and a Rapper from Welsh Hip Hop outfit, Goldie Lookin' Chain.

We make plans to meet for a beer tomorrow night but there's no way I'm turning up looking like some faux-gangsta', chav version of John McEnroe.

DAY SIXTY SEVEN

I'm running a bit late today, it's hard getting out of the scratcher. After wolfing down a bowl of cornflakes and a cup of tea, I leg it down to the Mad Dogs on Shotover, our pickup point. There are nine in our group and there are also five guides and a photographer. There are nine blokes, while two of the guides are girls (or ladies if you prefer). So, we board onto this minibus effort and we're whisked out to the Kawaru Gorge – this dis-used mining shed or whatever – where we're kitted out with helmets, wetsuits, lifejackets, bootees and flippers. We are each supplied with body boards that have these plastic wires (similar to those attaching your receiver to your handset on your phone at home). These wires are basically made into handles at the top of the boards. Then, we're taken to a quieter spot in the river, don the flippers etc. and are told to get into the river where we'll be put through our paces. We're told to lay our torsos on the boards, grip the handles with our weaker hands, while the stronger hand must grip the end of the board. Of course my board is a biggie – "Titanic" is scribed on it. The water is freezing and takes our breaths away at first; the currents are oh, so strong. They show us how to turn into the current by lifting the front of the board vertically out of the water and by kicking hard with our flippers, then turning the board and ourselves around $360°$. The guides make us dive down until our flippers are...well, flipping at the surface and they make us race each other to these rocks, about ten metres away, and then back again. I'm first back, along with this gung-ho Californian type a near second.

Not good. I'm absolutely knackered out and recovering from a chest infection. I'm feeling as weak as a six-minute-old kitten and we haven't even started down the rapids yet. We have to climb back up this rocky incline to our minibus and I'm worried that I may actually have to wuss out, I'm that tired. Fair enough if I'm sick but it's not something that I plan on doing.

I don't. But I'm hoping that I can last the six-kilometre course. We're taken to another spot and we're let loose. We float down; the icy, rapidly-flowing water taking us where it will. Our leader, a large and bald German man named Arnal – at least that's how it sounds to me – is leading from the front, while Jen, a bossy Kiwi girl, takes up the rear. The need for the instruction earlier, and indeed the way she's barking at us now, is quickly becoming apparent though. I'm in the middle of the group and I'm kicking away, seemingly holding my own. However, the water suddenly gets choppier than a Butcher's cleaver and before we know it, the Roaring Megs are on top of us, above us, all around us. Severe currents pull us towards the rocks to the side and walls of waves arrive in quick succession. The guides tell us to dive under the wave (much in the same way as one does when surfing against a wave) with the boards. But I feel that when I do, I'm met with another wall of water just as I re-surface. Water is swallowed and inhaled (by surely all of us). At one point it gets very scary, so much so that I'm wondering again why idiots like me choose to do these things. After a while, though, I somehow learn the secret: to kick just enough to offer ample resistance against the current and therefore, keep me away from the rocks; though not to kick too much that I exhaust myself completely. It's only when I start to learn how to do this and actually enjoy the experience, when we're nearly through the Megs.

The struggle ends quicker than I thought it would and from here on in, we're simply drifting down the Kawaru. Suddenly, one of the guides comes ripping past us on this big jet-ski with a large board attached to the back and I'm left wondering where exactly he got the thing out of. Just minutes earlier, he was in front of me on a body board. In pairs, we drag our torsos onto the board and we're dragged up and down the Kawaru – at an awesome speed. It's one of those experiences that has one laughing and shouting at the top of one's voice – though the sound is swallowed up by the deafening sound of engine and blades on water.

Water splashing in our faces literally blocks out our vision, as the smell of diesel is almost overwhelming. When our number, sorry, *time* is up, we're dropped off near this jetty where the Shotover Jetboats are moored. Exhausted and exhilarated, we drag ourselves out of the river and up to this large rock several metres away. The rock is apparently seven metres high and the jump is great fun altogether, though there's a strong drag in the river. I lose concentration for a split second and nearly get pulled away as I swim about twenty metres back to the jetty. I do another jump and when we're all done (for), we're taken to this massive, manmade slide that's lubricated with water.

We take our boards and slide down on them thrice or so each – once the jetboats have safely passed by. We go down the slide in the following ways: belly down, head first with back down and kneeling down, before standing up once the board hits the water. The last option allows the slider to skim along the water for a good twenty yards or so, while the jet-ski drags us back to the bank for more. It's all great fun but exhausting, so I don't feel too guilty about the KFC meal and pint of Guinness that I treat myself to back in Queenstown.

I've made some loose plans to meet Will for a pint tonight but he hasn't text me so I decide to go it alone. Actually, yesterday afternoon I agreed to play a "few tunes" at the open mike night in Surreal Bar on Rees St. – with fellow Southern Laughter resident, John. He's from somewhere in England. Dr. John I call him because he's some kind of gastric specialist up in Wellington. Carly on Crutches and Antonio said they'll come along. However, it's just 10pm and things don't really get going at Surreal until midnight so I go for a pizza in a joint called Hell up some alleyway. I meet the crazy American Kid who set off the alarm at Base and he tells me that he's due to go to court in the morning regarding same. I wish him well with it.

It's still early so I pop into Póg Mahone's across the road for some Dutch courage. I have a couple of pints of Kilkenny as I listen to the singer in local covers band, Cartel, play acoustic guitar and sing with some girl. Cartel are awesome and so are these two performers.

There's this Kiwi girl who's trying to get every guy in the place to dance with her. She's pissed and everybody seems to be interested in laughing at her, but not with her. She eventually succeeds in getting a young American bloke on his feet – much to his embarrassment and to the amusement of his friends. It's quite funny really.

I go outside for a cigarette and spot Essex couple, Carly and Antonio, on the balcony at Surreal across.

"Oi, Ciaran yew prick," says Antonio in his strong Essex accent. "We come to see you and you wasn't here."

Huh? I cross over and tell them that I'll be over "after I've finished my pint". But when I go back in there's two Aussie girls in my place.

"Would you take my grave as fast," I ask them.

They don't seem to understand me but I get talking to Jasmine ("Jezmen") and Amber ("Embaaa'), who are actually Kiwis whose family moved to Aussie when they were younger. Two guys from San Francisco amble up and buy a round of what they think are Jäger Bombs, except they're not really because they've ordered Lucozade instead of Red Bull. I'd call them Faker Bombs myself.

I tell the girls to come see me play in Surreal if they want, and then I leave. I meet Dr. John and his hippie friend whose name I don't get. It turns out she's playing a few songs with him afterwards, as well. A talented guitarist, he's a tad nervous because he's never played "live" as such before this. John plays guitar (excellently it has to be said) for me as I sing Damien Rice song, *Cannonball*. He plays Djembe drum for me while I play guitar and sing *Ain't no Sunshine* by Bill Withers and my own song entitled *Legend Never Dies*. My own song is a faster version of the song I recorded on my own EP, *Power of One*, back in 2000 with Andrew Strong. Andrew was the singer in the Alan Parker movie, *The Commitments* and I met him through his father Rob, who's also an awesome singer and had become a friend of mine.

However, apart from my effort here three weeks ago, it's the first time I've performed live in almost a year and it goes quite well if I may say and Dr. John gets a real kick out of it.

I join Carly, Antonio and some others from the hostel for a drink but then get distracted when Amber and Jasmine come in. They have the two American dudes with them but Amber makes a beeline for me and before I know it, she has somehow wriggled her way under my arm, the cheeky little thing. We grab a couch and get to know each other over a few Vodka and Red Bulls on the couch. Amber has gone back to their hotel with one of the blokes.

A couple of hours later, I head back there with her sister, as the Yank is leaving. On the way back to Southern Laughter I meet Will and his ex-girlfriend from back home (*his* UK home, obviously), who I've met already. She lives here now.

I five him a hard time for flaking out on me because of his "better offer".

DAY SIXTY EIGHT

This friendly London chap has moved into my dorm. Dave is in his mid-40s and, in a story that I've heard quite a few times already on this tour, has decided to come on tour when he was made redundant. He was working with the same company in the UK for about twenty years and, finding himself suddenly jobless and with a wedge of redundancy money, opted to go on the trip he'd always wanted to take.

And why not?

Dr. John has apparently gone back to Wellington, I learn from his hippie friend. We spend the afternoon jamming with her guitar and singing cover versions.

Marianne texts and asks if I want to meet for a coffee before she goes to work at 6pm so I meet her in Vesta, a quirky little cafe and souvenir shop on Marine Parade by the lake. She asks me why I'm being quiet and I tell her I'm not aware that I'm being so but that like everyone else, I do have my quiet times.

This evening, Dave and I are having a couple of Tui Reds at Buffalo Bar on Brecon St. Dave is a real Gent; a genuinely nice bloke who comes across as a bit conservative and timid at first but who's actually extreme in the extreme. He's already done skydives and has done the Bungee jump in Bloukrans, South Africa, which is a mother of a jump at well over 216 metres, easily *one* of the highest commercial jumps in the world.

However, his attitudes are also extremely extreme. Dave is as intense as a man can be when it comes to the opposite sex and he analyses every single aspect of his interactions with women in miniscule detail. He heads home before midnight because he's doing the Milford Sound day-long trip in the morning.

Eileen has texted me, asking if I want to meet her and Una, their housemate, Fiona, and Catherine at Winnies Bar on The Mall. So I do that. Scottish girl, Jane, and South African Mark who both also work at the Pig & Whistle, are also there. Marianne and Andy come in after work and then we all go to Surreal. We have a good laugh, fuelled with vodka and Red Bull and shots of Jägermeister. Fiona's giving me sums to do and I'm jumping from the steps onto the footpath – imagining that I'm landing on the buttons of a giant calculator. Enough said.

Later on, we go back to the girls' house in Enright Lane and the drinking continues. We're met with spectacular views of The Remarks', Lake Wakatipu and Queenstown from the decking out the back.

We try to make out various shapes from the mountain opposite. Homer Simpson, Jabba the Hut and a piranha are just some of these. Dusk brings a lighter shade of blue to the scene, as beams of red light shoot up at sharp and obtuse angles straight from behind The Remarkables for hundreds of metres. It is dawn in Mordor – eh, I mean, Queenstown.

I call a taxi, then stumble into it at 7am. After a session of Irish proportions.

287

DAY SIXTY NINE

Today's buzz word is "Chill": I hang out during the day, watching TV, going down to the Bungee shop to check email and so on.

This evening, Dave and I are going to the Reading Cinema on The Mall to watch *The Invention of Lying* starring Ricky Gervais. The cinema is a kitschy little joint and when we are directed to the screen upstairs, I imagine that we're walking into someone's Living Room. We're talking carpet, stained doors, banisters and unsterile toilets. It's kind of cool. I keep expecting to bump into a friend or relative.

The movie, to be fair, is not too bad. There are some laughs in the absurd flick – even though it wanes and sags a bit in the middle, probably not unlike Mr Gervais's waistline. Afterwards, Dave is meeting Nadine – this German girl who works for Google at their Headquarters in Dublin. She's staying in the room next to us in Southern Laughter apparently, and he met her while touring the North Island or something.

And he won't shut up talking about her. He asks me if I'll join them and I'm reluctant until he tells me there will be another couple of blokes from her dorm with her. Hmmm, I smell a rat. The way Dave has been talking you'd think that he was due to meet Nadine for a date. But here we are, at Buffalo Bar with her and two other blokes. There's a wet tee-shirt competition starting here shortly, and my own shirt will probably be as wet by the time it starts because the place is heaving and there's this giant, circular stone stove near the entrance. I get talking to these two Aussie girls in their 20s who are here for a few days on holidays. I tease them about only coming to the bar to take part in the competition. The louder of them strenuously denies this, while the quieter one says nothing. I'm talking with two lads from Newcastle who I met while doing the Mad Dog, as Carly-who's-no-longer-on-Crutches and Antonio – who seems a little too enthusiastic about his girlfriend being ogled by a group of raucous men, and who knows, maybe women. Perhaps it's the $200 prize money that has perked his interest.

"Caaa'ly will win this hands down," he tells us.

288

"She'll onla' win it ef she gets hur tits oot," says Stephen, one of the Newcastle boys.

So it's not long before there's five girls prancing about and gyrating on the bar, being as suggestive as they can be considering their inexperience, the width of the bar and the fact that buckets of water are being heaped over onto them by one of the *in-house* dancers. And would you guess it? The quieter of the two Aussies is up there, strutting her stuff. It's always the quiet ones, eh? This girl is rocking it out. She's like a character from the movie, *Coyote Ugly* or something.

It's a knockout (pun intended) and the girls are eliminated one-by-one – depending on the loudness of the cat calls from the audience. There's just the quiet Aussie girl and Carly left up there. And after a dance-off, the Aussie girl beats Carly, who seems a bit more self conscious.

And who would blame her?

Meanwhile, Nadine and the two blokes – who are Danish or Dutch or something – leave and Dave rejoins me. We head to Surreal on Rees St. And, it's oh-so-quiet. At one stage I go out on the veranda at the front for a cigarette and there's this Aussie girl sitting there with two Kiwi guys.

Hoy, yo're the goy frum Poyg's (*Póg's* bar opposite) the otha' noight," she goes. She looks familiar. Aha.

"I wouldn't know you now that you're dry," I tell her, having seen her dance on a bar with a wet tee-shirt not an hour ago. She came third.

"You wo' givin' moy the evil oye (eye) the otha' noight," she says. But I can't remember even seeing her at Póg's. However, I've been told that I'm good at doling out the cutting looks, though it's NEVER intentional. Honest. I didn't even see this person the other night.

Though I *may* have been giving her devilish glances during the competition earlier. I'm flesh and blood, am I not?

289

DAY SEVENTY

It's Friday, and it is a miserable day in Queenstown. So, I must be an optimist or at least a masochist because I go down and book the Milford Sound tour for tomorrow. I book it through the Kiwi Discovery office on Camp St. and it sets me back $145, with a $20 discount I'm told. But I pay the extra $10 for the packed lunch. Then I go to Monty's and sip on a cappuccino as I chat with Holly. The staff here are setting up for a Pearl Jam tribute band that will start later. It's an apparent consolation for those that can't go to see the real band play live in Christchurch and Wellington over the weekend. They're showing this Pearl Jam rockumentery DVD at the bar so I decide to ignore the rain and stay for another coffee. I also have a Monteith's black beer, which is kind of similar to the genuine article – fizzy stout from a glass bottle, as is popular back in my hometown. I know, us Irish think that we actually own alcohol: all of it.

I go back to my hostel to chillax for a few hours.

I'm back at Monty's, the rain has died down and the music has started. The Pearl Jam tribute basically consists of Kane and some other local musicians. I meet David, a man in his 40s from Cornwall who's staying at my hostel and has just finished doing the three-day Milford Sound trek. He's inside, drinking with Brent – the Editor of *Great Walks* magazine who's from Sydney and lives there – along with some other guides he's met on the walk. He tells me to join them and I get chatting with Brent about the magazine. He gives me the lowdown on journalism in Australia and New Zealand, and shares some tips with me on pitching this book to publishers. A nice guy, he gives me his contact details and tells me to look him up "whin ya come ova' ta Sydney". Funny, I'm sure I told him that I'd already been there.

I head home after I've had a couple of beers – the chest infection is still lingering and I want to be fresh for Milford Sound in the morning.

DAY SEVENTY ONE

I'm on a coach and there's about fifty of us heading south to Lake Te Anu and on to Milford Sound. The landscape – down to Te Anu – is fairly predictable by New

Zealand's high standards. Mimicking a large, circular mirror, the beautiful and perfectly-still lake perfectly reflects the perfectly clear blue sky. Perfectly. Covering an area of 344 square kilometres, Lake Te Anu is the second largest in terms of surface area, while the largest is Lake Taupo, as we know. Lake Te Anu runs from north to south and is sixty five kilometres in length and its maximum depth is 417 metres and while its altitude is just over 200 metres, a considerable chunk of it clearly lies below sea level.

A while after leaving Te Anu, these large snow-capped peaks erupt suddenly into view. We're awestruck by Mirror Lake and the numerous waterfalls. All of these offer spectacular sights for tired eyes. Mostly, only the clicking of digital camera-buttons can be heard over sharp intakes of air, as light speedily filters in some of the most dramatic scenery that most of these blinking eyes have ever rested upon. Giant powdery glaciers boast unapologetically, daring us to even try to formulate fitting words and syntax in description. The entrance to Homer's Tunnel, a 1.2 kilometre gap drilled through sheer rock, is flanked by walls of ice. An alpine parrot, a Kea Bird, comes up to say hello to our bus as we wait for the lights to change. Mitre Peak, at 1,692 metres in elevation, looms large in the distance.

The tunnel seems to go on forever and the awesome fiordland beyond continues to bear down on us with its beauty. The majestic Milford Sound, we learn, is known by the Maori as Piopiotahi and was also named after Milford Haven in Wales, by the British, obviously. In fact, the Sound was 'discovered', if you will, by Captain John Grono in 1812 and named Milford Haven after his homeland before it was later renamed Milford Sound.

Before we disembark, our driver tells us to board "The Sunbed", or something sounding just like it.

I need to go for a piss, badly. So I do so – all over the coach.

Ha!

Seriously, I've never been as glad to see a queue for anything as I am now. There are lines of people inside as I rush into the bathroom at the terminal. Sweet as. However, when I come out, the terminal is almost empty – all the lines have cleared. I run through and on to the marina and there's about ten cruisers there, waiting to take tourists like me on two-hour trips around Milford Sound. Some workers are busy doing this and that so I approach one of them and show him my ticket. He tells me to "gow roight". I run down but it turns out that the Old Wally has sent me the wrong way. I run back up and mention it to another deckhand further up and luckily *The Sinbad* is right next to her.

The "Sunbed". Of course. I run on-board and grab my pre-paid lunch, which contains an apple, apple juice, sandwiches, cheese and crackers. I buy a packet of crisps also because it's actually illegal to eat sandwiches without them. Not a lot of people know that, but it is. I swear, I wouldn't lie to you. I'm sitting next to this Belfast girl that I got talking to on the bus down. She's wolfing down this huge salad – along with rice cakes dipped in humus. She doesn't talk for about twenty minutes as she scoffs. I'm thinking, *This girl likes her grub but is clearly calorie-conscious.* However, at the rate she's eating, she'll probably take in the same amount of calories as she would if she were eating fish and chips.

After lunch, we go up to the main deck where I meet Nadine.

Of course, the cameras are working overtime. Huge walls of cliff face sustaining all manner of life make up the flanks of a natural corridor for us to travel down, as we go deeper into the Fiordland National Park in the south west of this beautiful country. The Sound was understandably called "the eighth wonder of the world" by Rudyard Kipling. Scientific evidence aside, I find it hard in situations such as this, to believe in concepts such as evolution alone over God – or whatever you might choose to name your version of a possible unseen and omnipresent, life-giving force if you believe in it.

Phew, dodged that one relatively unscathed I think.

Milford Sound is flanked by sheer rockface rising to about 1,200 metres and the rainforests along the cliffs headlines the living organisms in the water below. Seals, dolphins, penguins and even whales are among the mammals sustained in the water. Milford Sound counts Elephant Head (at 1,517 metres – LARGE head, what?) and The Lion (at 1,302 metres – KING of the jungle!) among its peaks and Stirling Falls is one of the permanent waterfalls found here. However, there are hundreds of waterfalls that are subsidised by rainwater and are pouring down the cliffs. Our cruiser pulls up close to one of them and the wind blows the stream out from the rock and into our faces.

And I feel tiny compared to the majestic Milford Sound; a micron against millions of yards of rock.

On the bus back to Queenstown we're subjected to a movie starring everybody's favourite cannibal, Hannibal. I'm talking about the brilliant Welsh Actor, Anthony Hopkins, of course. However, *this* movie, *The World's Fastest Indian*, is worse than *Rocky* 956 or *JAWS* 763. It's about some old Kiwi geezer (Burt Munro): a cancer sufferer from Invercargill (also on the South Island) who gets his rocks off with a dame and then travels to the Bonneville Salt Flats in Utah to break the world land speed record on his specially made classic Indian Scout motorcycle. I know what you're thinking...does he break the record, beat the cancer, get the girl? His records in the 1950s and 1960s – for motorbikes with engines less than 1,000cc – have never been broken and that's fairly amazing when you think about it.

DAY SEVENTY TWO

It's Sunday again. How did that happen? And I want to watch Ireland take on the World Champions, South Africa, back home. However, I'll hardly make it back in time, especially seeing as my Time Machine has packed in, damn it. So, as per my last few Sunday mornings, I head on down to the Ministry of Sport. I'm outside having a cigarette on the balcony while waiting for the already-finished game of rugger to begin. As per usual in the Sunday morning sunshine, I'm expecting to see large and skulking vulturesque shadows soar across the Wakatipu rugby pitch towards The Ledge and so on. But today, handgliding has been cancelled because of the high winds that have beset Queenstown in recent days.

Inside, meanwhile, a fellow Irishman, Darragh from Co. Galway, has the place to himself. I join him and it transpires that he works for his accommodation at Base

Hostel. He apologises for basically being "death warmed up". The poor guy has lost ten kilos in bodyweight of late – out of poverty apparently – and his skin is waxen in appearance. I'm a bit worried about him and tell him so but he seems resigned to it. In fact, he's a bit chirpy about it. It turns out that he was in Oz for about eighteen months before arriving in the town of Queens, some seven months previously.

Darragh hasn't slept for four nights and is generally drinking like a fish, has a diet that would stop the heart of an athlete in its tracks and, he has no money. Correction, he will have "no money at all" after he buys yet another coke. (I buy him a coke.) He's only drinking the caffeine-laden soft drink to keep him conscious until he's seen the match in full.

I've seen this kind of thing before in my time Down Under. Darragh's mother wants him to come home to finish his degree, while Oz and New Zealand has had other plans for him, it seems. It normally goes like this: young man/woman goes for their year out with their working visa in Australia; when said visa runs out, the thought of returning home becomes too much and the person goes picking fruit or working on a farm in the middle of nowhere to give them a second year out; then, said worker goes to New Zealand for another year-long visa and often tries to convince him/herself – and anyone who'll listen really – that life in Kiwiland is much better. They will tell you that they are in Queenstown – in this instance – to save money for further travelling. However, any money earned, almost always in the tourist/hospitality industry, is likely to be spent on drink/rent/adventuring here. This, coupled with low earnings, acts as a distraction for said worker and basically prevents them from leaving the town. Hence, the worker is sucked into what I have termed, the [enter name of location here] *Queenstown Honeytrap*. Some are trapped here happily, others are pretending to be.

Ireland slays the mighty South Africa 15-10. I tell Darragh to look after himself and I bid him good luck.

This afternoon, I'm meeting Marianne in the Pig & Whistle, when she finishes work after 3pm. However, before this I head down to meet Eileen, who's working at her job in Bendon – a lingerie shop on The Mall (Ballarat St.). I'm fresh out of lacey stuff. Jokes. My camera is on the blink so Eileen has kindly lent me hers for the Milford Sound trip. She's leaving for Sydney in a couple of days time so we say our goodbyes and shortly afterwards, I'm sitting at the bar in The Pig' with Marianne. The place is heaving. The lads and lassies working in the bar are wearing white shirts while their faces are daubed in blue and white paint. The lasses have tartan bandanas in their hair and the laddies have tartan ties on. The place is jointed and there are wailing (bag) pipers marching in and out of the entrance. Little over twenty years ago I was a piper myself and I'm determined not to end up attempting to play the things for the first time in over twenty years after one-too-many libations. But it's only 4pm, the sun is shining and the beer is flowing so anything could happen.

Oh yeah, it's St. Andrew's Day. Who knew?

Surely because of my conditioning, I have a slight, underlying unease at celebrating the Scottish (and hence, British) holiday. However, the alcohol seems to cure me of this and after a couple of pints, I get Marianne to paint blue and white stripes on top of my eyebrows. After a while I head into the bathroom and look in the mirror – half expecting to look like Mel Gibson's William Wallace in the movie, *Braveheart*. Though I seem to look like Pink Floyd's tormented (well, mad really) genius, Syd Barrett, during one of his ~~creative~~ loony episodes.

Bar workers, Andy, Jane (who's actually Scottish) Una and Mark keep the pints coming into the early evening as their boss, Wol, the manager and a part-owner, is dressed as perhaps the most stereotypical Scottish person that has ever walked the face of the planet. We're talking matching tartan hat (with deranged red locks attached) and kilt with Sporran, white shirt stuffed with a pillow underneath (as if he needed to) and facepaint. He's even got woolly socks and a red flush painted onto his cheeks. And he's been on the right side of the bar, my side...since 10am. He is pissed. His charming teenage daughter is doing her first stint behind the bar and she's doing a very good job. Think of Fat Bastard in the Austin Powers movies. Imagine him drunk. No; drunker than that. *There* you are...Wol right now!

It's about 6pm or something when the buses start arriving from the Cromwell Races. The mere mention of the bastard name Cromwell, who went ethnic cleansing n Ireland in the middle of the 17th Century (1649-52), would get any real Irishman's blood boiling and this has prevented me from going to the races.

Nobody else seems bothered though.

The band has started playing and everyone – I mean EVERYONE here – is as plastered as the Sistine Chapel at this stage. Pig & Whistle worker Edwina and some of her crazy gang literally burst in the doors and up the ante. A cluster of these drunken women next to me at the bar are particularly wild and they home in on me. They are dressed well but they're acting like a rugby team on a stag night. One of these is trying to kick me to get my attention while another is trying to get me to buy her a drink. The smell of drink coming from her facial cave has probably killed a few horses at Cromwell. Darragh, who's in charge of the bar today, cuts off the kicker as her mauling gets out of control. A youth with a Mohican haircut tells me that his mate, a Rugger Bugger who's standing next to him and is surely the largest man in the Southern Hemisphere, has "gun daaa'n (gone down)" on some female in the bus on the way down from the races. Said friend confirms this to me even though I don't ask him. Bill, a broad-brimmed, hat-sporting Builder from Wellington who's a regular at the bar, has won a few bob at Cromwell and buys about ten of us these weird tequila shots. I then buy a round of Marianne's buttery Southern Comfort shots. After some more pints of Celtic Red, Monteith's Cider and shots of Sambuca and Jägermeister, I find myself standing on the stage with the band singing Pink Floyd song, *Another Brick in the Wall*.

"All in all, you're just a-nother drink in the Wol."

Huh...Wait; hang on, I know this one.

Edwina joins the band and I onstage. She starts rapping on in an apparent attempt at some free-flowing jazz nonsense. Exit stage left. Wol takes his turn now. He plays spoons. It is Una's last night working at the bar and she's pissed. Some of us are taking turns at playing songs on the acoustic guitar and singing, while Marianne and Wol are pissed and sitting on the floor. Either that or they're spilling drink and swaying to the music because they've regressed to infanthood. Waterfordians (or "Blaas" back home) Ian and Una are also here. I'm sitting on the highstool banging out some U2 number or other when I hear this loud thud and suddenly, Catherine is being handed a First Aid kit. It turns out that the ill-sounding calamitous wallop was actually Una's eye socket hitting a chair. OUCH! She has been plied with drink as a kind of farewell celebration.

Most of us, including Una, head down to Bardeaux and I end up playing some childish chasing game with her there. Then I imitate a priest and bless some English girl I get talking to by putting my hand on her head and spouting Scripture. It is 4am. And in our infinite wisdom and mindful clarity, we actually grumble because they've closed the bar (it has previously been closed at 5am). Some of us, actually, only Marianne and I really, have been drinking for twelve hours at this stage. Jane, who herself is leaving Queenstown in one week, is crying now – apparently because of Una's leaving. Meanwhile, Una is laughing. But she's not laughing at Jane. Nor is she laughing at the situation. She's just laughing.

Next thing, I'm in this Night n' Day store, New Zealand's answer to a 7-11, and I'm on my way back to my lodgings, eating a mince and onion pie. Two pies to be exact. Okay, okay – I ate ALL the pies. I somehow end up in my dorm drinking a bottle of champagne (that I'd had in my fridge) with this English stray I've just picked up. I was always charitable like that. She thinks that she's about to get sick and we're looking for the door but we can't turn on the light because some new residents have apparently moved into the nuthouse. On most nights, you arrive home tipsy and there's some random person unconscious in the room. You'd be surprised how used to all of this you get. The obligation is to remain quiet out of respect or perhaps, fear. The healthy fear of waking a Sleeping Giant out of a peaceful slumber and therefore transforming them into an angry deconstructive machine, that is.

DAY SEVENTY THREE

"Saaaa, then she's laike, 'It's a dorm' and 'I feel sick' and it's like, *Oh really?*"

The girl on the veranda outside my dorm is speaking with this heavy, annoying, urbanised, mundane American accent. She's there with her English boyfriend and she's talking to some others who I can't hear. The window is closed but my head is ight next to it. I've just been woken up by the talking, which is vying with the humping in my head, in the being heard stakes. The thought that my fellow residents want me to hear them crosses my mind.

"And dur's like, boddles uf wine banging and I'm like, 'FUCK THEEEAT'!"

Then, presumably for affect, she adds: "UN-FUCKING BOL-EEEVE-ABUL!"

I'm tempted to open the window to let them know that I'm listening but I suppose I can't blame her for being annoyed really. I would be and have often been annoyed at, an infuriating stupid o'clock alarm call. I actually put my head under the duvet and pretend to be asleep when this Harried American Girl (HAG) and her boyfriend come into the room. I'm relieved when they leave shortly afterwards. It turns out that they've been bitching to this German chap, who's travelling with his girlfriend and his sister. The sister is staying in our dorm while the couple are holed up in the double room next door. The more awake I become, the more I remember. Suddenly, I have flashing images of the drunken and oblivious English girl trying to climb into the bottom bunk opposite. Of course HAG's boyfriend was already asleep in said bed so my understanding of the HAG's annoyance deepens instantly. HAG was on the top bunk so you imagine her waking up and not being best pleased. Of course the hammered English girl had thought that the bed was empty. I remember stopping her just as she was sitting on the edge of the bed and about to get in.

It's a dramatic start to an uneventful day. But it's also kind of funny.

DAY SEVENTY FOUR

(*Puts back of hand to fevered brow*) A dreaded imbibing malaise hath overcome me.

I go to AJ Hackett's on Shotover St. and buy the images of my bungee jump so that I can upload them onto Facebook. Never said I wasn't a Big Showoff. I have a coffee and a pint of ale in Monty's and then I head down to the Pig & Whistle for some of their gorgeous chips covered in gravy with bread. Mmmmm.

That is all.

15. Heading Above

DAY SEVENTY FIVE

Today is my last day in Queenstown. I decide to treat myself so I leave Southern Laughter and book a double room at Crowne Plaza. It costs $189 (that's about ninety of your European Euro) for a night. It's expensive accommodation for New Zealand on a budget but the room is awesome, class, deadly. In the afternoon I head up to The Mall to buy my nephew, Eugene, an All-Blacks jersey. After this I step out into the rain and head around the corner to meet Marianne at Dux du Lux as agreed. I order this disgusting Monteith's lager that tastes like nettles or piss or something (I've actually never tasted either), while she's on the bourbon and Coke.

Anyway, after a few rounds we rent a DVD before heading up to hers. I order a pizza and a small bottle of Coke but they actually deliver a large bottle of Sprite. Aaah, New Zealand, yer Gas! The pizza's a large one so, at $23 including the delivery charge, it's not too unreasonable. The movie we've chosen is called *Still Waiting* and it's God-awful.

After a couple of hours, I say Goodbye and get a taxi down to Surreal for one final drink. It's Tuesday night so it's packed with bar workers, local musicians and backpackers as per usual. A couple of the musicians who run the Open Mike night here tip their glasses at me from the other side of the bar. I do likewise; though little do they know (or perhaps care) that it is a Goodbye gesture. I finish my drink and head back to my hotel. Here, I run a bath and while I'm waiting, I fill the sink with boiling water and pour in some eucalyptus before creating a kind of tent with a large bath towel. Bending over and inhaling deeply, the potency of the fumes almost chokes me, while I'm hoping the potion will clear my head and lungs, which are still a bit congested. I pour some of this bubble bath nonsense into the bath and get in. I don't normally subscribe to such girlie activities but I only have a shower at home and I decide to see what all the fuss is about because it's been a while since I've had a bath. I've had the odd shower though, now that you mention it...and a Jacuzzi at my gym of course.

After twenty minutes I pull myself out of the bath and I dry off with a towel.

I'm in bed and realising that I have to get up at 7am, which leaves me with four-and-a-half hours sleep. But alas, sleep is not forthcoming. Not for a while anyway.

DAY SEVENTY SIX

I wake up and get out without any dramas and even have time to get a cappuccino and a pie form Alpine Supermarket. The Numans coach leaves from the carpark here and the driver is efficient. What I mean is that she drives us (safely) north at a fair clip and doesn't prattle on too much. Behind me on the bus is Emily – a chatty Canadian who impresses me by telling me that she remembers me from Fergburger on Shotover St. She has been working there. Her recognising me is an idle boast on my behalf; just how many of those things did I have? I'm only flattered until she says the same thing to an Aussie couple and then an Indian guy when they get on the bus at a couple of pick up points.

When we arrive at Lake Tekapo, I stroll up to McKenzie's, which is the restaurant where I again expect to wait forty minutes for a bowl of soup. You think I'd have learned my lesson but I'm curious to see if the same thing will happen again. But there's actually a queue here now and I didn't bring my razor so I won't risk growing the beard. When I get back to the bus, Bob is talking to our former driver. Oh no, bang goes my thoughts of a lecture-free trip to Christchurch. I'm just joking really. Bob is alright; I don't foresee any mishaps. We're waiting to board and I'm telling the Australian bloke about my journey south from Christchurch three weeks ago when we're interrupted by a small commotion near the bottom step of the coach. Our eyes dart over and land on Bob, who's doubled up, grimacing and rubbing his chin profusely. The other driver is asking him if he's okay and it's obvious that he has bashed his leg on the step. Unbelievable, he hasn't even put the key in the ignition. And it's the same stories and anecdotes, all the way to Christchurch.

My new Waterford friends, Una and Catherine, are driving up here from Queenstown in Una's car. She offered me a lift but I'd already bought my ticket and wanted to get up a bit earlier (and they're not leaving until noon). I've decided to try the YHA Central Hostel on Manchester St. and it turns out that the girls, who are going on a tour north, are staying here too. It's a nice place and I prefer it to the Base Hostel I've already stayed at down the road. They don't even ask me for a deposit and don't charge me the $5 to rent a towel at reception. I'm sans towel because, as far as I know, mine could be still hanging on the balcony at Southern Laughter in Queenstown where I've left it. My heart is wrapped up inside it. Awwwww-barf!

I head out onto the streets and make my way to Mickey Finn's and sip on a couple of pints of Kilkenny Ale. Una texts to tell me that they're just leaving Lake Tekapo and might see me in Finn's later but I tell her that, alas, I'll be long gone. I'm planning on getting to bed by 10pm to get at least a few hours sleep before I leave for the airport at 3.30am. First, I indulge in a steak at some steak house.

It turns out that the girls have picked up some Mexican backpacker who smokes joint after joint in the back of the car. I text them and warn them to beware of a man fitting this description who's on the run from the Heat down south...that I've just heard it on a news bulletin. So, they don't challenge him on the joints, obviously. The suspect is thought to be a cereal killer. Apparently, he destroyed a bowl of cornflakes in the South Island this morning.

Sorry.

I'm laying (as opposed to *lying* to a backpacker about my exploits) in my double bed in the dorm after my shower when the phone goes off. The girls are down in the kitchen making some dinner. I can't sleep so I decide to go down and meet them for a cuppa. When I tell them that I'm going out for a cigarette, Una tells me that my friends are "on the bridge outside". And it's only when I'm at Reception that the penny actually drops. Outside, a man slows down and then pulls up in his car, some ten metres ahead of me to my left on Manchester St. He's wearing glasses, is looking lubious and the car seems to be full of papers and books. He's clearly a customer for the Ladies of the Night on the bridge about one hundred metres away.

Hey, I hope he doesn't think that he's going to be a client of mine.

When I'm back out at the front of the hostels with the girls, a van full of hooded young males passes and shout, "Thievin' caaants" or something like it in our direction. We're amused, and clueless as to Who or What the Hell they think we are.

It's all too much excitement for me: we say our goodbyes and I head for bed.

DAY SEVENTY SEVEN

It's 3am and I'm fumbling around – like a Big Fumbler – on the floor in the pitch dark for my mobile phone. It's still charging and I have a vague idea as to where I've left it. The bloody alarm. I'm conscious that I'll wake the others staying here.

I make it down to Reception at 3.30am on the dot and my carriage awaits me. My *carriage* is an Airport shuttle bus that I've paid $15 to take me there. It's amazing what you can do when not hungover. I've remembered to pack my toothbrush and toothpaste in my manbag. So, after a questionable Panini and a cappuccino, I head to the bathroom at Christchurch International Airport to brush my canines. However, I can't find the bloody toothbrush but then I do, exactly where I've already just looked for it. On the flight I fall into a fitful sleep and when I awake a couple of hours later, I'm in Melbourne again.

I'm extra careful not to repeat my mistake of eleven weeks ago (*i.e., forgetting to collect my bag at the carousel*). When I get outside in Victoria's morning sunshine, I'm taken aback by the humidity. It's hot also in that it's like opening an oven door. And once again I'm on the Skybus back into Southern Cross Station.

There are two middle-aged, middle class women sitting behind me. Not for the first time on this tour, I'm indulging in a bit of eavesdropping. One of them is asking the other if she's still having the affair and whether she's using contraception because she's a Catholic. Apparently she is, on both counts. Being a Catholic down here is different, I suspect. I, you know, expect that you actually get a choice growing up. And, you can have affairs.

The questioner goes on to tell her friend about her brother, "who refuzis ta grow ap". It passes the time until we reach the station.

I go to King St. Backpackers once again and pay $27 (once again) to get my head down for a few hours. I have a sixteen-hour stopover here in Melby before my flight to London Heathrow via Singapore. I'm leaving at five minutes before midnight. It's just after 9am and they don't know if they will have room at the inn until 10.30. I head down the block to Bourke Mall and order a fried breakfast for $14, and the price reminds me that I'm back in an Aussie city. Tea is $3 extra. There is room at the inn, apparently, so after a failed effort at a couple of hours sleep and a shower, I'm back on the streets. I do like Melbourne; much more so than Sydney.

So the day consists of strolling around Melbourne. I spend a couple of hours at the Immigration Museum on Flinders St. and another couple looking for an Internet cafe. I get distracted easily, soaking up everything and imagining what it would be like to live here, imagining that I *do* live here. Because, I'm considering applying for residency – one of the few options open to those who *got* skills, are over thirty-five and want to come and live here. Of all the places that I've seen, I can probably see myself living here.

Anyway, I go back to King St. to rest for another hour or so.

I'm going in to have a shower and I've got this towel, rented from Reception, wrapped around my waist.

Keys? Check. Toiletries? Check. Towel around waist? Check. Absentmindedly running from dorm and straight into Ladies showers opposite? Che- WHAT THE?

Once inside the shower room, I noticed that it was empty so I loosened my grip on the towel and suddenly, I heard a female voice.

"Sorry, this is the- "

"OH SHIT," I shouted, as I quickly wrapped the towel about me once again and ran back out.

How did I miss her? I somehow thought that the female shower room was the one directly opposite. The sound of shrill female laughter echoed around the room and is still ringing in my ears. That laughter does nothing for a Man's esteem, I can assure thee.

The sound echoes around my brain.

I get my shit together and check out and I then head down to the train station for the 8.30pm Skybus back out to the airport. I'm sipping on a pint of Heineken, the first in almost three months, at the Irish Bar there called P.J. O'Brien's. I get talking to the Irish bartender who says he's from Finglas in Dublin and has been living here with his girlfriend for eighteen months. What a waste. He'd have gotten her pregnant twice in that time if he'd stayed at home and remained miserable like the rest of us. Ha!

Outside, while smoking the last cigarette (I light a second one from the first) that I'll have for almost twelve hours, I spot the seemingly endless queue of yellow taxis vying for space at the rank. Two ambulances are making attempts to park up before its paramedics make their way into the Arrivals terminal. After spending about forty minutes in the book shop, I finally settle for Nick Hornby's latest offering, *Silent, Naked.* I used to read his stuff some years ago and it's sure to be an easy read. Perfect flight reading I hope, though the Cormac McCarthy novel I've bought in Heathrow three months earlier is currently moulding at the bottom of my bacteria infested backpack. Unread. Unread and hating me, I'm sure of it.

The heavily pregnant Qantas woman who's checking me in tells me that I won't have to pick up my bags in Singapore but I'll need to in Heathrow before embarking on the final leg to Dublin. When I show her a head full of pearly canines and ask her if extra legroom is possible without having to fork out a couple of hundred dollars, she stares thoughtfully into the screen. I can have a seat at the Emergency Exit if I take an oral pledge (not quite) to help open the door in the event of some catastrophe. The ring of confidence. Ding!

Don't worry love – at the slightest creak or turbulence, I'll be out the door myself.
Apart from agreeing to this not being the smartest move, I have a feeling that it's not

what they will be requiring of me. I'm picturing myself, like Fr. Jack, taking the last two parachutes and strapping one of them to the drinks trolley.

Of course, I'm checked for explosives again as I go through the boarding area and on to my Gate. However, I can't find my phone so I have to go back to the security point.

They must have me on some forgetful list in Melbourne because one of them is holding my phone aloft as I approach.

It's just gone midnight and we've been waiting on the tarmac for over thirty minutes for our takeoff. And I'm bored to tears already so I turn my watch to *Irish* time, if you will. It's the middle of the afternoon but it's not and it's dark. I'm playing Piggy in the Middle: to my left (at the window) is a French guy and to my right is a small, squat Aussie with blond curly hair. Everyone's knackered and the only words I will speak to either of these men will be to say "Sorry" to the very understandable French chap when I wake up to almost find my head resting on his shoulder. He'll be laughing away while the stewardess opposite us will be strapping herself in. I'll still be groggy and to be honest, clueless as to where I am, for a good few seconds. The stewardess will tell me to put a neck cushion behind my neck to "stop ya geddin' a poyn (pain) in ya nick" or rather *to stop annoying the poor French guy by dribbling on his fucking shoulder you utter asshole,* or whatever. When it all happens, I'm a bit self-conscious about it. Bloody Hell. It dawns on me suddenly: we haven't even left the tarmac yet.

And I can't even get back to sleep.

According to today's (no, yesterday's) *Herald Sun*, graduates of "Australia's only circus school are to be put through the hoops three years after training and tertiary study". The article says: "Once happy to fly around the world as a hostie [air hostess], contortionist Jess Ward, 21, decided to hang up her uniform to pursue a career as a circus performer." The graduates, just hours earlier actually, appeared in the 2009 Circus Showcase Premiere at the National Circus Centre in Green St., Prahan.

Ms Ward adds: "I thought while I still have youth, stamina and a supposedly bendy body, I might as well pursue my circus career because I can always go back to flying.'

305

I'M NOT GOING TO SAY IT. I AM. NOT. GOING. TO SAY. IT.

I can think of a few other careers that she could partake in, with those attributes.
There, I've said it; we all knew that I would.

Ha! It's plain to see that Australian-New Zealand rivalry is still alive and kicking.
n what it has to be said is a fairly smug report in the same paper, there's a yarn
eadlined, "Kiwis work the machines". It goes on to tell the reader that "Kiwis who
nigrate across the Tazman are far more likely to work in blue collar jobs than as
rofessionals". The findings were released as part of a New Zealand Government
nvestigation into raising Kiwi wages in line with those of Aussies "to stop the heavy
Tasman migration". Wellington demographer James Newell found that 2.8 per cent of
hose employed in the latest Aussie Census were New Zealand born, according to the
eport.

"They make up 4.3 per cent of machinery operators and drivers in Australia and
3.4 per cent of all labourers. They make up only 2.4 per cent of all professionals."
The story cites "another recent report" that found "Aussies live longer in bigger
nomes, with more money and leisure time".

Ouch!

The imbalance is "clearly getting" to the Kiwis, however. Well, duh, would you
blame them for their annoyance? *The New Zealand Herald* "said yesterday" that
'even their Christmas parties are better than ours". This, I doubt. The Kiwis, like the
rish, could make a party from nothing at all.

I remember reading somewhere that the Irish media tycoon, Sir Antony O'Reilly,
was earlier this year trying to offload *The New Zealand Herald*, *The Listener*
magazine and other Australasian media assets.

've sat in this seat before. Well, not this seat exactly but in a seat at this part of the
aircraft. Well, not this aircraft to be precise but you get the idea, Goddamn it. But
when it comes to eating, I forget where the tray is because it's clearly in a different
spot than in the cheap seats (haha). It's far down by my right leg – as is the screen
where I will watch some very forgetful movie. Of course the screen is stuck and it's

hard to eat because we're lodged in the seats. I imagine that I'm a Royal plonker at some formal dinner function. By this, I mean that I'm sitting upright – elbows held tightly at my sides and wrists bent in order to be able to use my PLASTIC knife and fork. The utensils and foil tray bring any such notions of upperosity crashing down let me reliably inform you. (Memo to self: change from "crashing" symbolism immediately and stop using dodgy, strangdarmy makey-uppey wordagems.)

The airlines generally place strong-ish blokes in these Exit seats to help with the doors, as I've already mentioned. However, that's not much good if we can't get out of the bloody things, now is it?

When we arrive at Singapore Changi International Airport, I'm asked to remove my Akruba. Well, they don't say Akruba – it isn't strictly an Akruba anyway – but sure it's close enough and I've gone on about all of this already. I head into Duty Free and buy three cartons of cigarettes. Six hundred Silk Cut Purple cigarettes for AU$57 But the severe-looking woman there won't let me buy a one litre bottle of Teachers scotch for my old dear because my final destination is actually Dublin and not London. Great, I'll have to get it in Heathrow now. I'm told all of this quite sternly. You'd swear I'd asked her if she had any ten-gram bags of heroin for anal concealment.

Perhaps Fr. Jack has been through recently. He really does ruin it for the rest of us Irish blokes.

At Gate 16, from where I'll depart for London, I'm told that I must go to Gate 25 i I wish to smoke a ciggie or 17. So I do. But like most of the weary travellers here, I smoke two cigarettes in succession. A friendly Fijian gent and a young lady from Melbourne include me in their conversation about travelling, smoking and education. After availing of the free Internet terminals nearby, I buy a coffee with the change from the cigarettes. I can't get over how clean and ordered the airport here is.

It's stupid o'clock in the morning and I can't even bear to *think* about the arduous thirteen-hour journey to London.

Throughout the flight I'm crashing, then waking; crashing then waking; crash- you get the picture. As I've said, crashing is probably not the best word to use in this instance. The naps last exactly thirty-minutes each, and I imagine this is how Bill Murray's frustrated character felt in the brilliant *Groundhog Day* movie. The time in between naps is broken by listening to music, eating and drinking (mainly) water and soft drinks, taking short walks around the aircraft, watching DVDs that I obviously never get to finish and directly upon waking; looking at the flight plan on my screen and trying to guess how much time has been spent sleeping. Progress is being made alright, though you wouldn't know it by looking at the plan every thirty minutes. I have a couple of those small bottles of red wine and a small can of Heineken in, like, a two-hour period but I stop when I realise that I'm having the hangover as I'm drinking the bloody things. Perhaps it's because I'm flying against time. Hmmm. Or maybe it's an intensified version of the Instant Karma that Lennon sang about.

This woman from Leeds opposite tells me that she's been on a "mission of meh-say (mercy)" in Adelaide. Her friend found out just two weeks ago that her Dearest Husband was having a sordid affair and this girl took holidays and rushed over to be there for her.

Now that's a friend. She's quite a girl.

After landing and the obligatory parking and the whole waiting-for-an Age-before-being-allowed-off thing, we're allowed onto English soil. SHIT! My little Soldiers of Death are not in The Overhead. Come to think of it, I don't remember putting them there and the last thing I remember of seeing them was when I placed them at my feet while checking my damned email and Facebook. Curses. Though of course I hope the cigarettes don't do any harm to the lucky bugger who found them. *Harm of the year go with it* (an Irish saying at such times), I tell myself in solace – even if I don't really mean it. Not just yet. Oh well, "Fake it 'til ya make it", a woman much drunker than me once instructed me. So, that's what I'll do.

Grey faces inside the Arrivals terminal warn us of even greyer skies outside, and of course the airport is far less colourful and smart than the one I've left over twenty four hours before this. So after carefully dodging; negotiating my mass through what

308

seems like about six million teenage Japanese schoolchildren and even some Europeans, I'm through customs and I'm down to collect my bag. And everybody's collecting their bags, except a group of six people and me that is. So we wait. And then we wait some more. This is followed by more waiting. An hour later and guess what we're doing...yup, we're waiting.

Strangely enough, we waited this long before asking the good folk at the luggage desk, you know, *Where the hell are our bleedin' bags?* It turns out that our bags are already on our connecting flights, even if we're not. So the woman in Melbourne got it right? Wrong, she said I'd have to collect mine at Heathrow. However, I must get to Terminal 1 in one half of an hour and the luggage bloke, a decent and well-meaning Cockney sort as they generally are, tells me that it will take about ten minutes if I run and, if the walk-on conveyors are working.

"But this is Heaf'row awfter-oll ma'e."

I'm not very reassured.

I do run, in the main, and the conveyors are working but it still takes me twenty minutes. When I get there, the gate hasn't even opened yet, thank God. I'm sweatier than a fat German banker in a Stockholm sauna competition. Suits massage egos, possibly pretending to do more business on iphones, laptops than they do, while others read newspapers, check watches. The flight is late. It's hard to describe but when I'm on the Aer Lingus aircraft and I'm listening to the cheesy yet enchanting lilting, generic Celtic tunes that they play onboard, I'm kind of glad to be heading back to Ireland. I'm sure this feeling will change, however.

15. At Home Again....naturally!

'm on the Airport bus link into the city centre. And of course it's cold, damp, dark and it's raining intermittently. There are different groups of Scottish folk on my bus and I'm trying to help them with their directions. It makes a change after being the seeker of locations for the past three months. There's a feel good vibe on the bus. It's Friday, post-work time, the passengers are either coming home or, are visiting. And, it's three weeks to Christmas. A couple in their maturing years want Smithfield; two women, who I suspect have just narrowly escaped from their husbands and kids, are looking for Aston Quay. Meanwhile, the singer in some obscure, underground punk band has to go and meet some guy under the clock on D'olier St. The latter is the old *Irish Times* building, *The Old Lady of D'olier St.* as 'she' is affectionately known in my profession.

I dispatch the weary travellers in their various directions; the locations are all in close enough proximity to each other actually. I'm going to try for a room at the Temple Bar Hotel, where I have stayed in a couple of times before and it's very near to D'olier St. So I walk the punk to the clock. It's a long way for her to come for a blind date.

The bloke working at the hotel is looking for my Laser card and asks me for some ID. I show him my press card and he's studying it. He speaks with an Arabic accent so I'm guessing that he wasn't born here.

"So, where are yew frum?" he asks me.

I'm aware that I'm looking at him with a confusion expression.

"Ireland," I reply. "Why?"

"Rilly?" he goes on. "Yew do not look Airish."

I'm thinking, *Really? You don't look like a cop in behind that desk there but let's get things moving all the same if that's okay with you.*

He charges me €120 for a single room (with breakfast) and I'm sure that's cheaper than last year because of the recession, and the prices will have come down again in

January. But I know that Dublin and Ireland in general is not trying to rip me off as such. It's just the country's quirky little way of letting me know that I'm home. Thoughtful, huh?

The room is fine and I lay off on the bed as I text my cousin, Jason, who's been living in Dublin more-or-less since he graduated as a graphic designer over sixteen years ago. He replies and it turns out that he is in The Morgan, which is one of the few cool (sort of pretentious) places on Temple Bar. It's very handy for me, as the place is just a few doors away from here. I try to get a couple of hours' sleep but it's not happening as I'm jetlagged, overtired. I have also texted a Waterford friend, Kat, who's been living here for donkey's years. After a while, I turn on the TV and *Coronation Street* is on UTV. It's Friday night and *down with that sort of thing* so I have a shower and iron a tee shirt and a pair of jeans.

The bouncer at The Morgan, eyeing up my Asics trainers and my hoodie, tells me that I can't enter dressed this way. I forgot where I was – the dress code down under is a little bit more relaxed. "No iff-ence (offence)," he goes, and there's none taken. I head in and change the hoodie for a sweatshirt, my trainers for shoes. It's actually the first time I'm wearing the shoes since I left the Small Dog.

The shoes are a pair of comfortable leather slip-on shoes by Clarks that you could literally wear with anything, with the exception being a suit of armour, maybe. Or shorts. Or tracksuit bottoms. And overalls. The shoes have been stuck in the bottom of the bag since the middle of September and are flatter than a pint of North American Beer. I hope they haven't been thinking that I'm ashamed of them. The Cormac McCarthy book and the devilish shoes are conspiring to kill me and they will do *just* that when I set them free. I just know it. The spilled organic vitamins will probably help them. I'm just not sure about the how, exactly. It doesn't bear thinking about.

Inside the bar, we're drinking with some of Jay's workmates and the barman just deadpans me coldly when I double up, with a suspected ruptured spleen. It's his fault. He's just asked me for €6.20 for a pint of Heineken. It's now that I really feel At Home. And a Céad Míle Fáilte to you too, Bucko!

My cousin's mates are going to some cheesy joint but we opt for Hogan's, a favourite old haunt of mine on South George St. at the intersection with Fade St.

It's past midnight and finally Saturday when we head up to Whelan's where we've arranged to meet Kat and her friend, Clodagh. They've been onto us to go with them to Murray's on O'Connell St. because someone they know is DJ-ing there.

Eh, NO!

They go, we stay and there are plans to maybe meet up later. We get talking to some girls from down the country somewhere and it's not long before I'm arm-wrestling this busty, curly blond-headed woman who I end up snogging. But she gets more plastered than a child's cut knee and I later see her doing the same with another bloke on the dancefloor. I imagine that I'm *The Geeky Guy* in some cheesy teen-flick US drama that looks on forlornly from the sidelines. The difference here is that I couldn't give a shit. And, oh, I'm not a teenager – more's the pity.

Jay and I are at some really dodgy *session* with Kat, Clodagh and some of the Murray shower that they've just met. Some of this lot, who I don't know from Adam himself, are necking pills (Ecstasy) as if they're vitamins in a retirement home or Smarties at a children's Birthday party. Now, I'm fond of Glasgow Celtic FC but I wouldn't wear their jersey to a club that's not at all soccer related, while sporting a haircut that couldn't possibly have been done without the help of a bowl. That's all I'm saying. And I don't own any gold. Not our scene. The girls apologise for dragging us there and we go back to Kat's for a bit. We get a taxi and stop at a filling station to get provisions. I buy this Goodfellas frozen pizza but because she doesn't have conventional oven as such, I end up grilling it through to its core in this weird, well, grill contraption that she does have.

Taxi.

It's been the longest Friday in history. I can't even calculate how long it's been since I slept in a bed. It's not too long before I'm crashed out in bed.

312

DAY SEVENTY EIGHT

I miss breakfast, even though I wake early enough – after my usual three-and-a-half hours sleep. It's amazing what the body can get used to.

The train back to Waterford costs €27 for a single journey ticket, which is fairly sobering it has to be said. I'm seated with two women, while across the aisle opposite there are four Dublin city women who are clearly on a weekend away "down de cuntry". They are loud, rough in an earthy, charming way, and are great craic.

I'm writing, well, I'm writing this and then I'm reading about Liam Clancy's death in the *Irish Examiner*. RIP Liam, Bob Dylan's old friend and favourite balladeer, I remember reading somewhere before. The former performer – with the hugely successful Irish folk outfit, The Clancy Brothers and Tommy Makim – passed away last night and the story has quite rightly secured the front page. I find myself recalling the one and only conversation I had with the man. I had been reporting on a planning story for *The Irish Times* and Liam certainly had an opinion to offer. The entertainer was bemoaning the fact that young locals of An Rinn (known as "Ring" in Waterford) a Gaeltacht or Irish-speaking area in Co. Waterford, could not buy houses there because of the inflated prices, if I remember correctly. Meanwhile, these houses were being snapped up by foreign types, mostly German folk I suspect.

The only time I speak to the girl opposite is to apologise when I accidentally move her bag with my foot.

It's dark and raining in Waterford when I disembark from the train in the early evening. No surprises there. I'm walking with my backpack on my back for the last time on this tour. I trundle across the bridge in my hometown and down the dimly-lit Quay, noticing that some new businesses have cropped up in my absence, while others have gone to the wall, or have closed up at any rate. One of the new ones is an off-licence, while another is this mid-range eatery. Now, I'm back in Jordan's Bar where I started. Well, the night before I left anyway. I chat with proprietor Andy and the barmaid Shauna, and the place is decked out for Christmas. One pint of Heineken ater, I leave to go home. In about three hours time I will be de-briefing my friend Conor, my cousin Liam who is Jay's younger brother and the designer of this book's illustrations. And, another cousin and friend of ours – the erstwhile Liam Russell.

There are pints in Geoff's Bar on John St., and then there are more in Electric Avenue – a late night music venue next door that plays host to the scarily accurate [The] Kings of Leon tribute act, The Knights of Leon. In another joint, Harvey's on The Manor, some girl comes up to me and tells me that I looked "pensive" on the train earlier and maybe I was distracted because she's a Looker and I didn't recognise her until she started teasing me for trying to steal her bag. Of course I deny all accusations.

When I step out onto the city streets and the early Sunday morning madness, it has stopped raining and the words of the old song *Sit Down* by the Manchester band, James, spring forth into my mind.

If I hadn't seen such riches, I could live with being poor.

I'm kind of singing it to myself as I'm walking home.

And with that my mind drifts to other adventures that are waiting for me. Like an impatient and expectant lover, on some distant, glistening shore.

The End

ACKNOWLEDGEMENTS

I wish to thank all of my friends at home who have extended their solid support, help and goodwill in relation to me writing this book. Of course, to all of the new friends that I made on tour who brought my travels, and therefore this book, to life, *Go raibh mile maith agat* (Thank you very much). I would like to pay a particular tribute to the Waterford contingent living Down Under, who gave of their valuable time and went out of their way to ensure that I had an enjoyable experience: to Gerry Green in Sydney who meant well, to the amazing Symes family (especially Alan and Angela) in Auckland and to Marianne Finn and the rest of the Waterford gang in Queenstown, a special word of thanks. To all of the Australians and New Zealanders (regardless of ethnic origin) that I met on my way, you may not always get on, but both of your countries and your peoples are wonderful with so much to offer the world.

I would like to say thank you to my family, especially to my mother Lily and my sister Lorraine – and to my dog, Holly, for such a good welcome home.

A special note of thanks must go to Bill Murphy from the library at DIT (Dublin Institute of Technology), Bolton St. and to all of the very helpful staff at the Waterford City Council Library Service – particularly Jane Cantwell and the Staff at the Central [Municipal] Library on Lady Lane. Thanks also to Michael Walsh and Conor Nolan. Thank you Liam Russell, who was first to read the original draft and later gave of his free time to make sure that the launches went well. Thanks also to Confectioner Catherine Hartery for the gorgeous cake and to Liam Power, thank you, Sir, for the awesome illustrations on the book's cover. Similarly, thanks to Patrick Browne for the excellent photographs. Thank you(s) to Sir Ranulph Fiennes and Tim Severin for your help. And thanks also to the following for help with the city launch: Andrew Jordan from Jordan's Bar, Donal O'Brien from The Front Lounge, Deirdre Houlihan from The Tower Hotel Group, Sinead Frisby from The Copper Hen restaurant, Brian Power from Geoff's and John de Bromhead from Downes. Thanks to the The Dungarvan Observer, The Munster Express, Waterford Today, Waterford News&Star

nd to Beat 102-103fm and WLRfm for the publicity. I would like to express my gratitude to Jan Rotte and the Committee of the Immrama Festival of Travel Writing n Lismore – for the opportunity to launch this book there. And big thanks also to the xcellent Staff at Garter Lane Arts Centre, for a second launch in Waterford city one veek later.

And finally, Thank You...The Reader.

long with various websites, the following sources were of great help to me in this vork: *Ireland, Australia and New Zealand – History, Politics and Culture* by Laurence M. Geary and Andrew J. McCarthy (Irish Academic Press, 2008); *Arguments About Aborigines* by L.R. Hiatt (Cambridge University Press, 1996); *Aboriginal Culture Today*, ed. Anna Rutherford (Dungaroo Press – *Kunapipi*, 1988); *Live&Work in New Zealand* by Susan James (Crimson Publishing, 2008); *Live&Work in Australia* by Jodie Mcmullen Seal (Crimson Publishing, 2008); content from *Lonely Planet New Zealand* by Charles Rawlings-Way, Brett Atkinson, Sarah Bennett, Peter Dragicevich, Errol Hunt (Lonely Planet Publications Pty Ltd, 2008) reproduced with permission from Lonely Planet New Zealand© 2008Lonely Planet; content from *Lonely Planet Australia* by Becca Blond, Lindsay Brown, Terry Carter & Laura Dunston, George Dunford, Simone Egger, Katja Gaskell, Rowan McKinnon, Alan Murphy, Charles Rawlings-Way, Sarah Wintle (Lonely Planet Publications Pty Ltd, 2007) reproduced with permission from Lonely Planet Australia© 2007Lonely Planet; *Māori Tribes of New Zealand* by various contributors (Crown Copyright, 2008); *Inside Australia and New Zealand* by John Gunther and completed by William Forbis (Jane Perry Gunther, 1972); *Australia & New Zealand – Economy, Society and Environment* by Guy M. Robinson, Robert J. Loughran and Paul J. Tranter (Guy M. Robinson, Robert J. Loughran and Paul J. Tranter, 2000) reproduced with permission from Hodder Education; *The Power of Now* by Eckhart Tolle (Hodder and Stoughton, 2005); *An Account Of The Voyages Undertaken By The Order Of His Majesty, For Making Discoveries In The Southern Hemisphere (Vol. III)* by Commodore Byron, Captain Wallis, Captain Carteret and Captain Cook (Nabu Press, 2010); *An Account*

316

Of The Voyages Undertaken By The Order Of His Majesty, For Making Discoveries Ir The Southern Hemisphere (Vol. IV) by John Hawkesworth, John Byron, James Cook (Nabu Press, 2010).

Thanks to all of you for your kind permissions. Efforts were made to contact all of these and other sources. If any author or publisher feels aggrieved at a possible omission or mis-representation, please don't hesitate to contact me. I would be more than willing to help clear up any matters arising.

Ciarán Murphy,
Waterford city,
May 2012.